Robert Carrier's
ENTERTAINING

Robert Carrier's
ENTERTAINING

A & W Publishers, Inc.   New York

First published in the United States of America in 1978 by
A & W Publishers, Inc.
95 Madison Avenue
New York, New York 10016

Published in 1977 by Sidgwick and Jackson Limited, England

Library of Congress Catalog Card Number: 78-58768

ISBN: 0-89479-034-X

Designed by Helen Barrow
Line drawings by Vana Haggerty
Printed in the United States of America

CONTENTS

Robert Carrier's
ENTERTAINING

Introduction: Tips on Entertaining

MANY of us approach entertaining with mixed emotions. While there is the pleasant prospect of gaiety and conviviality in the offing, there is also, for the host or hostess who wants to give a memorable luncheon or dinner party, a lot of real hard work. And yet party giving can be great fun if we learn to be realistic about our budgets—and our capabilities—and remember that the true purpose of getting friends and family together is enjoyment.

I receive many letters every day from readers of my monthly columns in *House Beautiful*, *Homes and Gardens* and *High Life*—letters from cities as far apart as Saigon and Sydney, Portland and Rome—and most of these letters deal in one way or another with the problems of party giving:

"What menus can I serve to a house party of six for a weekend in the country?"

"What wines should I choose for a cold buffet meal?"

"What is an inexpensive way of entertaining if I have no dining room?"

"What are easy dishes based on rice to feed a crowd?"

Finding the right answer to these queries began to fascinate me. And my letters, recipe suggestions, menus and party ideas became the central core of this book, *Entertaining*. Its aim is to broaden the scope of everyday entertaining beyond the traditional luncheons or dinners we are so used to. There are so many other opportunities for welcoming friends and relations to our homes—breakfast parties, brunches, wine tastings, barbecues, after theater or movie suppers, picnics, punch parties, cocktail parties, children's parties and all kinds of buffet meals.

The Basics

Good food and good conversation are the two inseparable ingredients of a good party. I think it was the famous film maker and party giver Alfred Hitchcock who said, "For truly great conversation, there should never be more than six to dinner . . . if more, the conversation tends to dissipate, ideas begin to founder."

Impromptu parties can be fun. Deciding what kind of party to give is a simple matter of finding out what you've got and what you can do with it, and not trying to do a classic dinner party in a situation that doesn't fit a classic dinner party.

To entertain apparently effortlessly, do as much "do-it-ahead" preparation as possible, either in the morning or preferably the day before.

Plan your meals to leave yourself as free as you can so that you can enjoy your guests—and perhaps even more important—so your guests can enjoy you.

Don't go in for numbers of courses. It is too difficult to manage.

If you have no help: serve the first course with the drinks.

If you specialize in small dinner parties, build your table wardrobe around one or two beautiful centerpieces or serving dishes. If buffets are your forte, start with cook-and-serve pieces you'll be proud to show off on the table.

Develop a trio of dishes that you do especially well and feel completely at ease in preparing. Then add a few new specialities each year.

Keep a record of the parties you give and the guests who attend them and what you give them to eat. A hostess friend of mine—noted for the charm and gaiety of her parties—even keeps a list of the table decorations and china used for each party.

If you are trying out a new dish that sounds fabulous: (1) try it out on the family or close friends so that you can have a taste and time rehearsal. Nothing worse than being flustered at the last minute if the flavor is not exactly as you had wanted it; (2) check that it doesn't take twice as long to cook in your oven as you had counted on.

There's No Such Thing as a Born Cook

If you have ever wondered whether you had a talent for real cooking—the ability to prepare and serve a perfect dinner—here is your opportunity to find out. *Entertaining* is designed to sweep you along dish by dish, menu by menu, to heights of culinary skill which you never before imagined possible. After a few short chapters, you too will be able to prepare delicious meals based on savory French casseroles and quiches, Italian pasta dishes, perfect omelets, fragile soufflés and a host of really super desserts.

You will learn professional tips and special dishes to stretch your budget . . . international cooking secrets . . . and what utensils to use. You will discover what wines to serve with meals, what drinks and what snacks to serve at cocktail parties. From now on, you will know how to plan a buffet party, a barbecue, a picnic; how to cook delicious Continental summer meals and how to combine hundreds of exciting dishes in everyday and party menus that you, your family and your friends will long remember.

Cooking is fun—and it is easy. I've always said: if you can read, you can cook! All you need is a little know-how and a little practice. But, a word of warning: there is no such thing as a born cook. You must learn step by step, one dish at a time. Of course, we all have some friends who cook better than others; *the truth is they have enough patience, time, curiosity and imagination to cook really well.*

Bored?

How often have you asked yourself: "What shall I cook tonight?" If you are bored with serving the same kind of basic meal week after week, take advantage of this opportunity to get out of your everyday cooking rut. Surprise your guests with quickly made Beef Stroganoff, thin strips of lean beef simmered in butter and sour cream with mushrooms and onions. Follow with a salad with a special hard-boiled egg dressing, and the day is made. It's that easy.

You will need no exotic equipment to follow this book; no hard-to-find ingredients. Of course, you will require a certain number of utensils—good solid kitchen tools—to help you on your way to being top cook in your neighborhood. So buy the best quality heavy-duty cookware you can find. Make sure it is handsome enough to go straight from oven to table. Buy just one or two pieces at a time, for good cookware is expensive. And only buy just what you need. You will be amazed at how many complete luncheons and dinners you will be able to turn out with one or two frying pans, a medium-sized saucepan and a good-sized casserole. My old friend, the late Nancy Spain, descendant of the great Mrs. Beeton, used to boast that given a sharp knife, a wooden spoon and a saucepan with a thick bottom that she could trust, she could happily cook up a storm.

"The whole secret," according to a really famous cook—Alexandre Dumaine, often called the greatest chef in France—"is enhancing the intrinsic flavor of the ingredient to be cooked. If one *just* cooks, it is not worth the trouble." Take a tip from this great chef: you don't have to be a genius to cook really well. Take it slowly as you would any other branch of learning and you can astound your friends and delight yourself. For there is something vastly satisfying about cooking.

Learn to experiment with flavors, with textures, with heat. For heat is the most important friend—or foe—that any cook can have. Just how a fish or a piece of meat is "seized" in butter or oil at its first contact with the heat is as important to its final flavor and texture as its freshness and quality. You'll find that meat tends to dry out and toughen if cooked at too high a temperature; so watch your oven and make sure your stove really does simmer at the lowest possible temperature. Many a dish has been ruined, many an otherwise delicious meal spoiled because the meat was boiled when it should only have simmered.

Don't make the mistake of trying to economize on the basic necessities of good cooking. You will need good butter and cooking oils to cook with; a few jars of dried herbs—bay leaves, thyme, rosemary and sage—as well as coarse salt and freshly ground black pepper to add a little zest and excitement to your cooking. And you should always have a few onions, some carrots and garlic on hand. You'll find it makes all the difference and means that you don't have to run out to the supermarket every time a recipe reads "take an onion" or "add a pinch of thyme."

For best results all butter and cooking oils (the most practical and most pleasant to use are olive, corn and peanut) should be of the best quality. For slow frying, I like to mix olive oil and butter in equal quantities, putting the oil in the pan first to keep the butter from browning; or I use a combination of olive oil and corn or peanut oil for lighter casseroles of chicken, rabbit or vegetables. But whatever cooking you intend to do, a supply of good olive oil is essential for salads and as a sauce for spaghetti and bean dishes in the Italian manner.

The onion family—onions, shallots, leeks and garlic—is a must for all casserole dishes and stews. Try the French cook's trick of browning a little finely chopped onion and garlic in olive oil and butter before adding meat and vegetables for a meat casserole. These lusty aromatics will greatly enhance your dish. (But a word of warning: do not let onions or garlic get too brown before adding your meat, or they will become bitter.) For a simple sauce that will add much to the savor of broiled steak, lamb chops or fish, try a little finely chopped onion—just a tablespoon or two, no more—simmered in butter with a little finely chopped parsley and a hint of garlic.

Working Girl

I often get letters from young working girls about to get married who have never before cooked anything more ambitious than a TV dinner: "Give me some simple dishes I can cook for my husband and friends that do not take too much time; that are not too expensive and that I can do without being a master chef in the kitchen." Two dishes that answer these specifications perfectly are Beef Stroganoff and Spaghetti Parmesan—dishes I often rely on at weekends when a hungry look comes into my guests' eyes and it is time to rustle up something quick and easy.

I'm a social cook, working at my best when I'm being jostled by a kitchenful of people. Beef Stroganoff is easy to serve to a lot of people at once or as a quick dinner for two or four. Spaghetti Parmesan is one of my favorite pasta dishes. The recipe here I learned when I lived in Rome. It's never failed me on weekends in the country when I've found myself in charge of the kitchen. All three of the following recipes serve four people.

❀

RED WINES
Macon Rouge
Gigondas
Chianti Ruffino Red

❀

EASY BEEF STROGANOFF

Trim fat from 1½ pounds rump steak or sirloin and cut into steaks a little over 1 inch thick. Then cut each steak across the grain into slices ¼ inch thick. Season meat generously with salt and freshly ground black pepper and then flatten each strip with a wooden steak mallet. This will tenderize the steak and make each slice bigger. If no wooden mallet is available, use a potato masher or the side of a kitchen cleaver.

Simmer 4 tablespoons finely chopped onion in 4 tablespoons butter in a thick-bottomed frying pan, stirring constantly, until it just begins to turn golden. Add sliced, seasoned beef and continue to cook for about 3 minutes longer, turning slices with the prongs of a kitchen fork until they are brown on all sides. Remove meat from frying pan and keep warm.

Add 2 tablespoons olive oil to the pan; pour in any juices from the meat; add ¼ pound thinly sliced mushrooms and simmer, stirring constantly, until they begin to turn brown. Season to taste with salt, freshly ground black pepper and a dash of cayenne.

Return meat strips to the pan and add ⅔ cup sour cream. Stir well over low heat to blend juices and make sure each strip is coated with the creamy sauce. Heat through.

Transfer to a heated serving dish; sprinkle with 2 tablespoons of chopped parsley and serve with **boiled rice** (see page 89) or **mashed potatoes** (see page 67).

SPAGHETTI PARMESAN

Bring 3 to 4 quarts well-salted water to the boil in a large saucepan. Add 1 pound spaghetti and cook for about 12 to 15 minutes, or until it is tender but still firm—*al dente*, as the Italians say, which means just firm enough to bite comfortably but not so soft that it is mushy.

Melt 4 tablespoons butter in a large saucepan. Drain spaghetti, and while it is still very hot, toss it in the butter.

Pour beaten yolks of 4 eggs and ½ cup cream over spaghetti; add salt, freshly ground black pepper and a dash of nutmeg. Stir for a minute; remove from heat and add more butter. The sauce and the eggs should not begin to solidify. Serve immediately in a large heated bowl or serving dish with freshly grated Parmesan and additional butter.

Follow either of the above two dishes with a salad of tender lettuce leaves dressed with a special dressing. The dressing has lots of character without garlic, but include it if you like a touch of the south of France in your cooking.

SALAD CARRIER

Wash the leaves of 1 or 2 heads of lettuce well in a large quantity of water. They should be left whole, never cut. Drain well and dry thoroughly.

To make dressing: combine 1 chopped hard-boiled egg with 6 to 8 tablespoons olive oil and 2 tablespoons wine vinegar, seasoned to taste with a little dry mustard, salt, freshly ground black pepper and a squeeze of lemon juice. Add a little finely chopped parsley and scallion or chives, plus 1 small clove of garlic finely chopped, if desired.

Pour dressing over lettuce just before serving and toss until each leaf is glistening.

Utensils

Most young cooks begin their culinary experiments with the minimum of equipment: a roasting pan and a broiler pan—they come with the stove—a small saucepan, an ovenproof casserole and that old standby, a frying pan. Add to this a few knives, a wooden spoon or two, a strainer and a colander, and you are in business. But for those cooks who intend to do a little more in the kitchen, I suggest the following basic cook's tools:

Basic Cook's Tools

Frying Pans

- 1 small frying pan
- 1 large frying pan
- 1 omelet pan

Saucepans and Casseroles

- 3 enameled saucepans
- 1 oval casserole
- 1 large oval casserole
- 1 round casserole
- 1 rectangular baking dish
- 1 double boiler

Cutting Tools

- 1 paring knife
- 1 cook's knife, 7 inches
- 1 cook's knife, 9 inches
- 1 bread knife
- 1 carving knife and fork
- 1 pair kitchen scissors or poultry shears

Other Basics

1 kitchen scale
1 graduated measuring cup
1 set measuring spoons
1 chopping board
1 mortar and pestle
1 chopping bowl and round-bladed chopper
1 hanging kitchen set (fish slice, ladle, slotted spoon, fork, etc.)
1 strainer
1 colander
1 salad basket
1 grater
1 peppermill
1 salt mill
1 can opener
skewers

Mixing Bowls and Mixers

1 set graduated kitchen bowls
4 to 6 wooden spoons
1 wire whisk
1 large wire whisk
1 hand beater
1 blender or food processor

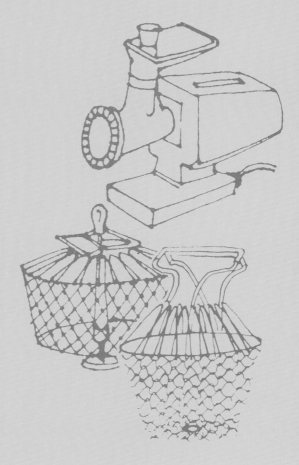

Specialized Equipment

The more advanced cook will need more specialized equipment for making pastry, cakes, pâtés and soufflés.

Tarts, Cakes and Breads

1 pastry board
1 rolling pin
1 pastry blender
1 flour sifter
1 pastry wheel
2 bread pans
2 large tart pans, with removable bottoms
6 individual tart pans with removable bottoms
1 cookie sheet
2 layer-cake pans
1 round ring mold
1 kugelhupf mold
1 pastry bag
1 candy thermometer

Pâtés and Soufflés

2 rectangular or oval pâté dishes
2 large soufflé dishes
6 individual ramekins

Tips for the Cook

How to Follow a Recipe Successfully

1 Read recipe carefully through to the end, working out the total preparation time, including hold-ups while marinating, chilling, etc.

2 Make sure you have all the necessary ingredients and utensils, and that the latter are of the correct size.

3 Remove eggs, butter, meat, etc., from refrigerator one hour before using so that they will be at room temperature by the time you start to cook.

4 Light oven if a preheated oven is required. Set refrigerator to required setting if this is called for.

5 Do any advance preparation indicated in list of ingredients. The preparation of cake pans, etc., should also be attended to before you start.

6 Measure ingredients carefully.

7 Do not be tempted to alter a recipe in midstream until you have prepared it faithfully at least once, and do not telescope or ignore directions and procedures for combining ingredients unless you are a very experienced cook.

8 Follow cooking and/or baking times and temperatures given, but test for doneness about two-thirds of the way through; be prepared to increase cooking time if it appears insufficient.

How to Measure Correctly

Accurate measurement is essential to any kind of cooking. A standard set of individual measuring spoons in plastic or metal—1 tablespoon, 1 teaspoon, ½ teaspoon and ¼ teaspoon—is ideal for small quantities. When a recipe calls for a fraction not provided for in the standard set, a dry ingredient can be measured by taking a whole spoonful, then carefully halving or quartering the amount with the tip of a knife and discarding the excess. All measurements should be level.

White Sugar

Make sure there are no lumps. Lift out a heaped spoonful and level off with a spatula or a straight knife.

Brown Sugar

Pack firmly into spoon so that when turned out the sugar will hold the shape of the spoon.

White Flour

Sift once. Dip spoon into flour, taking a heaped spoonful, and level off top with a spatula or a straight knife.

Other Flours/Fine Meals and Fine Crumbs

Stir instead of sifting. Measure like flour.

Baking Powder/Cream of Tartar/ Cornstarch/Ground Herbs and Spices

Stir to loosen if necessary. Measure like flour.

Solid Fats

Soften before measuring. Then dip spoon into fat, scoop out, and level off top.

Syrup/Molasses/Honey

Dip spoon in hot water for 30 seconds before measuring to prevent syrup sticking to sides of spoon.

Larger Quantities

For measuring larger quantities of ingredients you will also need:

A measuring cup, marked off in fluid ounces, and heatproof to withstand boiling liquids.

Kitchen Scales

Select a scale with a large enough pan to hold the quantities you are likely to be measuring.

Oven Temperatures

All the recipes in this book were tested in both gas and electric ovens which conformed to the temperatures that are given below. If in doubt about your own oven, invest in an oven thermometer, which will also allow you to make spot checks in the future. Remember, though, to light the oven at least 15 to 20 minutes before taking a reading, and be prepared for a slight variance in temperature between top and bottom of oven.

DESCRIPTION			
extremely hot	500°	moderate	350°
very hot	475°	slow	325°
hot	450°	very slow	300°
fairly hot	425°	very slow	275°
moderately hot	400°	cool	250°
moderate	375°	cool	225°

Giving a Dinner Party

"As they eat," goes an old Roman saying, "so will your guests love and remember you." This is as true today as it was over two thousand years ago. And yet how easy it is to entertain today—thanks to modern conveniences.

Now is the time to enliven meals at home with new foods, new wines and new table settings; to try out the party ideas in this section on the family, or on one or two close friends; to share with your loved one the small luxury of a superb new dish cooked just for the two of you.

Giving a dinner party for two, for four, or for more, can be wonderfully rewarding. Yet too many cooks seem to have too small a repertoire of favorite recipes. As a result, they repeat the same ones again and again.

Too many mothers allow themselves to be ruled by their children's lack of interest in trying out new dishes. How many times on my visits around the world have I met women who profess to be "real gourmets," but who restrict their daily cooking to chops, steaks and hamburgers because "that's what the children like."

Every member of the household—from father to the youngest child—should be made to devote a little time to gastronomic exploration and innovation.

It's a dull diet indeed if every day, week in and week out, we sit down to the same things, varying this regular monotony perhaps with a few seasonal delicacies—strawberries, asparagus, summer fruits—as they first appear, and then falling back into the same old weary routine of daily eating.

We can get so much pleasure and excitement from changing our daily menu; God knows, the supermarkets are full of possibilities well within our reach, both gastronomically and economically. Whether you are feeding the family or special guests, just one new dish each week will make a dramatic difference to your culinary vocabulary and give them the pleasure of voting on your latest creations.

A word of caution, though: don't go overboard with too many completely new dishes at a time. One surprise is a conversation piece, but if you have a number of them, some will be ignored—and so will you, if any of them go wrong.

LET PERFECT COFFEE BE THE PERFECT FINALE TO EVERY DINNER PARTY

"Black as night, sweet as love, hot as Hell" was the ancient Turk's recipe for coffee—the finale to every dinner party. No matter how you make it—drip, percolated, filter, espresso or infused in an earthenware jug, the golden rules for perfect coffee remain the same: use freshly roasted or vacuum-packed coffee beans; grind them just before you're ready to use them, selecting the degree of fineness suitable for your method; never let coffee boil, or it will turn cloudy and lose its flavor; and match blend and roast to the occasion, using milder coffee for the morning, strong black blends for after dinner.

❋ MENU ❋

Red Caviar Roll
Boeuf à la Ficelle
with
Potatoes in Butter
French Chocolate Pudding
SERVES 6

___

WHITE WINES
Pouilly Fuissé
Chablis
Pouilly Blanc Fumé
RED WINES
Moulin-à-Vent
Savigny-les-Beaune
Chambolle-Musigny

❋

RED CAVIAR ROLL

Roll:

    Foil, olive oil and flour for baking pan
4 tablespoons butter
8 tablespoons flour
1¼ cups hot milk
    Salt
2 teaspoons superfine sugar
    Pinch of grated nutmeg
4 eggs, separated

Filling:

1 (6-ounce) package cream cheese
1 to 2 tablespoon lemon juice
2 tablespoons sour cream
    Freshly ground black pepper
¾ cup heavy cream
3 to 4 tablespoons red caviar

Garnish:

4 to 6 tablespoons finely chopped chives
    Sour cream
    Red caviar

1 Preheat oven to 400°F. Line a 15½" × 10½" × 1" jelly roll pan with foil; brush with olive oil and dust with flour, shaking out excess.

2 **To make roll:** melt butter in a small saucepan; add 4 tablespoons of the flour and cook, stirring over a low heat to blend thoroughly. Gradually stir in hot milk and cook, stirring constantly, until sauce thickens. Bring to the boil and simmer, stirring, for 3 to 4 minutes.

3 Pour sauce into a bowl. Beat in a pinch of salt, the sugar and nutmeg.

4 Beat egg yolks lightly; pour into sauce in a thin stream, beating constantly. Cool.

5 Beat egg whites with a pinch of salt until stiff but not dry. Fold one-quarter into the lukewarm sauce.

6 Sift in 2 tablespoons of the flour, followed by a third of remaining whites. Repeat with remaining flour and egg whites.

7 Pour mixture into prepared pan; level out with a spatula.

8 Bake for 5 minutes; lower oven temperature to 300°F and continue to bake for 50 to 55 minutes, or until golden brown and springy.

9 Turn cake out on to a damp cloth lined with waxed paper. Remove foil and trim crusty edges. Roll cake loosely with cloth and waxed paper. Cool.

10 **To make filling:** Blend cream cheese, lemon juice and sour cream together. Season to taste with pepper. Whip cream until light and fluffy; fold into cheese mixture, followed by red caviar. (Remember to reserve a little sour cream and red caviar as garnish.) Correct seasoning and chill until firm.

11 Unroll baked sponge; sprinkle with chopped chives; spread with filling and roll up like a jelly roll.

12 Serve cut in slices, each portion garnished with a little sour cream and 1 teaspoon red caviar. Allow 2 thin slices per person as this is an extremely rich dish.

Red Caviar Roll

BOEUF A LA FICELLE

1½ **pounds carrots**
1½ **pounds small turnips**
 7 **cups rich beef stock**
¾ **pound button mushrooms**
 6 **slices bacon**
 6 **thick slices fillet of beef (6 ounces each)**
    Freshly ground black pepper
 6 **teaspoons brandy**

1 Peel carrots and cut them lengthwise into ¼-inch slices; then cut into thin strips, 1½ inches long. Peel turnips and cut them into strips of the same size.

2 Select a wide, deep saucepan or casserole. Pour in stock, add carrot strips, bring to the boil and simmer for 10 minutes. Then add turnips and simmer for 5 minutes longer.

3 Clean and trim mushrooms; add to pan and continue to cook gently for another 5 minutes, or until all vegetables are tender.

4 Remove vegetables from stock with a slotted spoon. Keep aside with a little of the stock.

5 Wrap a thin strip of bacon around the middle of each tournedos. Cut 6 pieces of string long enough to go round each tournedos and hang over side of pan when meat is submerged in stock. Tie one end of each string quite firmly around each tournedos to keep bacon in place.

6 **Just before serving:** bring stock to the boil and lower in tournedos side by side. Simmer for 5 minutes if you like them rare, 8 for medium, and 12 minutes for well done.

7 When tournedos are ready, remove from stock. Reheat vegetables in simmering stock. Reserve stock for another use.

Boeuf à la Ficelle

8 Remove strings and strips of bacon from tournedos and transfer steaks to a heated serving dish. Season with pepper and sprinkle with brandy. Garnish dish with vegetables; moisten with a little stock and serve immediately, accompanied by potatoes in butter and coarse salt.

POTATOES IN BUTTER

1½ **to 2 pounds potatoes**
4 **tablespoons clarified butter**
2 **tablespoons vegetable oil**
   Salt and freshly ground black pepper

1 Peel and slice potatoes paper thin. Rinse off excess starch under cold running water. Dry thoroughly.

2 Combine clarified butter with the oil, and divide half of the mixture equally between two 6-inch frying pans.

3 Arrange potato slices in pans in tight, overlapping circles, seasoning each layer generously with salt and pepper. Each cake should be ¾ inch thick.

4 Pour remaining butter and oil over the top.

5 Cook potato "cakes" over low heat for 15 minutes, or until crisp and golden brown underneath. Then turn out on to a plate; turn back into pans and cook for 10 to 15 minutes longer until cakes are golden brown all over and feel soft when pierced with a skewer.

6 Serve hot, cut in wedges.

FRENCH CHOCOLATE PUDDING

6 **slices trimmed white bread**
2 **cups heavy cream**
   Softened butter
4 **eggs**
2 **egg yolks**
½ **cup ground almonds**
   Sugar
6 **squares (ounces) unsweetened chocolate, melted**

1 Shred and soak bread in half the cream for 5 minutes.

2 In a large bowl, beat 4 tablespoons butter until fluffy. Beat in soaked bread until completely blended. Add eggs, egg yolks, almonds and 2 tablespoons sugar, beating vigorously between each addition. (Mixture may curdle when eggs are added, but this does not matter as chocolate will bind it again.)

3 Add half of the egg mixture to melted chocolate and beat well; then combine with remaining egg mixture and continue to beat vigorously until thoroughly blended.

4 Butter a tall, tapering, 4-cup mold—a metal measuring cup will do—and line base with a circle of buttered waxed paper. Pour in chocolate mixture and make a slight hollow in the center with the back of a spoon. Cover top of mold tightly with foil.

5 Place mold in a pan with water to come halfway up sides. Bring to the boil; cover pan and steam for 1½ hours, adding additional water in the pan as necessary.

6 **To serve:** whip remaining cream and sweeten lightly with sugar. Turn mold out; pipe generous swirls of cream around base. Serve immediately before cream melts from the heat of the pudding.

❊ *MENU* ❊
Chilled Vichyssoise
Lamb Korma
with
Carrot Rice
or
Rice with Peas
Petits Pots au Chocolat à l'Orange
with
Tuiles
SERVES 8

―――――

WHITE OR ROSE WINES
Sancerre
Bourgogne Aligoté
Tavel Rosé

❊

LAMB KORMA

    1 (3-pound) boneless leg of lamb
 1¼ cups yogurt
  ½ teaspoon ground cardamom
    1 teaspoon ground cumin
 1½ teaspoons ground turmeric
 1¼ cups shredded coconut
    2 tablespoons butter
 1¼ cups milk
    4 to 6 tablespoons olive oil
    2 to 3 medium onions, chopped
    2 cloves garlic, finely chopped
    1 teaspoon each ground ginger and
        dry mustard
  ½ teaspoon each freshly ground black
        pepper, cayenne pepper and cinnamon
        Generous pinch of ground cloves
    2 medium-sized tomatoes, peeled, seeded
        and diced
        Salt
    2 teaspoons lemon juice

1 Cut lamb into 1-inch cubes, trimming off excess fat.

2 In a bowl, mix yogurt with cardamom, cumin and turmeric; add lamb and toss until thoroughly coated. Cover bowl and let marinate for 1 hour.

3 Place coconut, butter and milk in a heavy saucepan and bring to the boil over moderate heat, stirring until butter has melted. Simmer for 15 minutes; then strain through a fine sieve. Put coconut and milk in separate bowls and set aside.

4 In a large, heavy casserole, heat half the oil; add lamb, together with yogurt marinade, and cook over high heat, stirring, for 5 minutes. Remove from heat.

5 Heat remaining oil in a frying pan and sauté onions and garlic until soft and golden. Remove pan from heat; add remaining spices and mix well. Cook, stirring, for 2 minutes longer to blend flavors.

6 Add onion mixture to lamb, together with tomatoes, coconut milk and a little salt, to taste. Bring to the boil slowly, stirring occasionally, and simmer, covered, for 30 minutes; then uncover pan and simmer for 30 minutes longer,

CHILLED VICHYSSOISE

    9 large leeks, white parts only
    6 tablespoons butter
    6 medium-sized potatoes
    6 cups chicken stock
        Salt and freshly ground black pepper
        Freshly grated nutmeg
 1¾ cups heavy cream
        Finely chopped chives

1 Wash leeks carefully and cut into 1-inch lengths. Melt butter in a large saucepan; add leeks and sauté gently until soft, taking great care not to let them brown.

2 Peel and slice potatoes and add to leeks, together with chicken stock. Simmer gently until vegetables are soft, adding salt, pepper and nutmeg toward the end of cooking time.

3 Blend vegetables and stock until smooth in an electric blender. Chill.

4 Just before serving, stir in cream and taste for seasoning. Serve sprinkled with finely chopped chives.

or until lamb is very tender and sauce is rich and thick.

7 Just before serving, stir in lemon juice and season with a little more salt, if necessary. If sauce seems too thin, add more coconut and simmer for 2 to 3 minutes longer.

8 Serve with **carrot rice** or **rice with peas** and the usual curry accompaniments: chutneys, pappadoms, preserved kumquats, etc.

CARROT RICE

Salt
4 tablespoons lemon juice
2 cups long-grain rice
1 cup coarsely grated raw carrot

1 Bring a large pan of water to the boil with salt and lemon juice. Dribble in rice through your fingers: stir once to dislodge any grains stuck to the bottom of the pan, and simmer for 15 to 18 minutes until the rice is just tender, with each grain separate.

2 Drain rice in a colander, then rinse well with boiling water, shaking out as much moisture as possible.

3 Fold in grated carrot gently with a fork and season to taste with a little more salt if necessary.

RICE WITH PEAS

1 Sauté 1 chopped onion and 2 cups rice in 4 tablespoons butter until rice is translucent. Add water and boil rice as usual (see page 89) with salt and lemon juice, as above. Drain in a colander.

2 Cook 1 package of frozen peas in a small saucepan with 4 tablespoons butter until tender; add drained rice and heat through. Season with salt and pepper, to taste.

PETITS POTS AU CHOCOLAT A L'ORANGE

8 squares (ounces) dark, bitter chocolate
3 oranges (2 large, 1 medium-sized)
4 tablespoons butter
Grand Marnier or cognac
4 eggs, separated

1 Break chocolate into the top of a double boiler. Finely grate the rinds of 2 large oranges; squeeze their juice and add both juice and rind to chocolate, together with butter. Heat over simmering water, stirring occasionally, until chocolate has melted. Then remove from heat; add 2 tablespoons Grand Marnier or cognac and beat until smooth.

2 In a bowl, beat egg yolks thoroughly. Strain in chocolate mixture through a fine sieve, beating constantly. Cool.

3 In another bowl, beat egg whites until stiff but not dry. Fold into chocolate mixture gently but thoroughly with a spatula.

4 Pour mixture into 8 (½ cup) ramekins or individual soufflé dishes and chill until set. (Do not use metal dishes, as chocolate may discolor.)

5 **Just before serving:** cut 4 thin slices from the center of remaining orange. Quarter each slice and place 2 quarters, point to point, on top of each dish. Add a teaspoon of Grand Marnier or cognac; swirl pot around very gently so that entire surface is moistened and serve immediately, accompanied by a dish of **tuiles.**

TUILES

MAKES ABOUT 50
5 tablespoons softened butter
5 tablespoons flour
1 tablespoon cornstarch
2 egg whites
5 tablespoons sugar
¼ cup blanched ground almonds
Vanilla and almond extracts
½ cup sliced almonds

1 Reserve 2 tablespoons *each* butter and flour for cookie sheets.

2 Preheat oven to 425°F.

Lamb Korma with Carrot Rice

3 Sift remaining flour with cornstarch three times.

4 Beat egg whites lightly with a whisk.

5 Beat remaining butter with sugar until fluffy. Add egg whites gradually, beating vigorously. Fold in flour and then ground almonds. Flavor with a few drops of vanilla and a drop of almond extract.

6 Butter 2 cookie sheets and sprinkle generously with flour. Shake off excess.

7 Drop mixture on cookie sheets by half teaspoonfuls, 2 inches apart. With a damp knife blade, spread each cookie out into a very thin disk about 1½ inches in diameter. Make sure disks are uniformly thin throughout: if slightly thicker in the center, cookies will be spongy instead of crisp. Sprinkle each disk with a few crushed almond flakes.

8 Bake for 5 minutes, or until cookies are golden, with a fine brown fringe.

9 Tuiles are shaped like Spanish roofing tiles; therefore, have ready a rolling pin or any other cold metal, glass or wooden object with a similarly curved surface on which the cookies may be shaped.

10 As soon as cookies come out of the oven, quickly remove each one with spatula and curve it around prepared shaping tool, nutty side up. Leave for 1 or 2 minutes to harden; then dislodge and transfer to a cooling rack.

❈ *MENU* ❈

Chilled Pea Soup
Roast Stuffed Shoulder of Lamb
with
Avocado Pilaf
Peaches in White Wine
SERVES 4-6

RED WINES
Macon Rouge
Beaujolais
Valpolicella

CHILLED PEA SOUP

¾ **pound shelled fresh or 1 package**
   frozen peas
1 **medium-sized potato, sliced**
1 **medium-sized onion, sliced**
1 **lettuce, quartered**
2½ **cups chicken stock**
1¼ **cups heavy cream**
   Juice of ½ lemon
   Salt and freshly ground black pepper
   Lemon slices and salted whipped cream
      for decoration

1 Place peas, potato, onion and lettuce in a large saucepan. Add half the chicken stock and bring to the boil. Cover and simmer for 15 minutes.

2 Blend contents of pan to a smooth puree in an electric blender.

3 Return puree to pan. Add remaining stock and simmer for 5 minutes.

4 Stir in cream and lemon juice and season to taste with salt and pepper. Cool soup; then correct seasoning and chill until ready to serve.

5 Serve soup in individual bowls, garnished with very thin slices of lemon which you have topped with a swirl of lightly salted whipped cream.

ROAST STUFFED SHOULDER OF LAMB

1 **(3½- to 4-pound) boned shoulder of lamb**
2 **tablespoons flour**
   Salt and freshly ground black pepper
2 **tablespoons melted butter**
2 **tablespoons olive oil**

Stuffing:

½ **onion, finely chopped**
4 **tablespoons butter**
1 **(10½-ounce) package frozen spinach**
½ **pound pork sausage meat**
1 **egg, beaten**
1 **tablespoon chopped parsley**
   Generous pinch each of rosemary and thyme
   Salt and freshly ground black pepper
   Pinch of freshly grated nutmeg

1 Have your butcher bone the shoulder of lamb but leave it unrolled. Lay meat out flat on a board, skin side down. Cut out any excess fat with a sharp knife, taking care not to pierce outer skin.

2 **To make stuffing:** sauté onion in half the butter until transparent.

3 Heat spinach gently in an uncovered pan until completely defrosted; drain thoroughly in a strainer, pressing firmly with the back of a spoon; then simmer gently in remaining butter until cooked.

4 In a large bowl, combine onion and spinach with sausage meat, egg, parsley, rosemary and thyme. Season with salt, pepper and nutmeg. Mix well.

5 Preheat oven to 325°F.

6 With a needle and thread, "sew" any holes in outer skin of lamb.

7 Spread stuffing over meat, filling all crevices so that when the lamb is rolled and sliced stuffing will produce a marbled effect.

8 If there are any loose flaps at the end of meat, bring them up over the stuffing. Then bring sides of meat together and sew securely along every seam, pushing stuffing back into meat if it tends to seep out, and making a neat, smooth roll.

Roast Stuffed Shoulder of Lamb with Avocado Pilaf

9 Dust meat with flour and season with salt and pepper.

10 Place a sheet of foil in a roasting pan and lay meat on top; bring up sides of foil slightly, but do not seal meat. Pour melted butter and olive oil over lamb.

11 Roast for 2 hours, basting occasionally with pan juices. Then raise heat to 400°F, open foil out and roast lamb for about 30 minutes longer, or until golden brown and cooked to your taste.

12 Serve on a large, heated platter, accompanied by an **avocado pilaf.**

AVOCADO PILAF

    8 tablespoons butter
    4 tablespoons finely chopped onion
    1 cup long-grain rice
    4 tablespoons dry white wine
    3 cups beef stock
       Salt
 1¼   cups sliced button mushrooms
  ½   teaspoon finely chopped garlic
    2 tomatoes, peeled, seeded and diced
  ¼   teaspoon dried oregano
       Freshly ground black pepper
    1 avocado
       Lemon juice

1 Preheat oven to 400°F.

2 Melt half the butter in a heavy casserole; add onion and sauté for 1 minute. Add rice and cook, stirring, over moderate heat for another minute.

3 Pour in wine and stock; season to taste with salt and bring to the boil. Cover tightly and transfer to oven.

4 Bake for 18 minutes, stirring rice once with a fork halfway through cooking time.

5 Sauté mushrooms in 2 tablespoons butter for 3 minutes; add garlic, tomatoes and oregano, and season to taste with salt and pepper. Simmer for 5 minutes.

6 Peel and dice avocado; brush pieces with lemon juice. Add to mushroom mixture.

7 Toss rice gently with mushrooms and avocado mixture and remaining butter. Serve hot.

PEACHES IN WHITE WINE

    2 cups sugar
 1½   cups water
    2 cloves
    3 cinnamon sticks
    2 to 3 strips of orange and lemon rind
    4 to 6 large peaches (or 8 to 12 small)
 1½   cups medium dry white wine

1 In a large, wide saucepan, dissolve sugar in 1½ cups water over very low heat; add cloves, cinnamon sticks and orange and lemon rind (pared off with vegetable peeler). Then carefully drop peaches into syrup and simmer, uncovered, for 10 minutes.

2 Add wine and continue to simmer for 10 minutes longer, taking care not to let peaches become mushy. Remove from heat.

3 Take peaches, one by one, from syrup with a slotted spoon, and holding gently with a towel so as not to burn your hand, carefully peel off skin with your fingers. Arrange peaches on a serving dish.

4 Simmer cooking juices until reduced to a light syrup. Cool syrup and spoon over peaches. Chill until ready to serve.

❀ *MENU* ❀

Eggplant Caviar
Pillows of Chicken
with
Puree Clamart
Souffléed Oranges
SERVES 6

WHITE OR ROSE WINES
Sancerre
Bourgogne Aligoté
Tavel Rosé

❀

EGGPLANT CAVIAR

4 small eggplants
2 large onions, finely chopped
2 cloves garlic, crushed
¼ teaspoon oregano
5 to 6 tablespoons chopped parsley
6 tablespoons olive oil
2 (14-ounce) cans tomatoes, drained
  and chopped
Salt and freshly ground black pepper
Generous pinch of sugar
6 small black olives, pitted and halved

1　Preheat oven to 350°F.
2　Bake eggplants for about 20 minutes.
3　In a skillet, sauté onion, garlic, oregano and 4 tablespoons of the parsley in olive oil until onions are soft and golden.
4　Add tomatoes and simmer for about 5 minutes longer until ingredients have blended into a sauce.
5　When eggplants are soft, peel off skins; drain pulp thoroughly and chop finely.
6　Stir eggplant pulp into tomato-onion mixture; season with salt, pepper and sugar and simmer for about 10 minutes longer, stirring until well blended.
7　Turn mixture into a shallow serving dish and allow to cool.
8　Serve cold, garnished with remaining parsley and olives.

PILLOWS OF CHICKEN

1½ roasting chickens, 3 to 3½ pounds each
　　Flour
　3 tablespoons olive oil
　8 tablespoons butter
　　Salt and freshly ground black pepper
1¼ cups chicken stock
　¾ pound button mushrooms
　9 tablespoons Madeira
　4 to 6 tablespoons heavy cream
　¾ pound flaky pastry
　　Lightly beaten egg yolk for glaze

1　**Prepare chicken:** with a sharp knife, cut legs off close to body, then separate drumsticks and thighs.
2　Bone both thighs; roll meat firmly into sausage shapes.
3　Take drumsticks and cut in down to bone to loosen flesh. Holding bone firmly between finger and thumb, pull flesh down and over the end in one movement, turning flesh inside out; separate flesh from bone and turn right side out again.
4　Slice down one side of breast as close to breastbone as possible; then take knife right across wing bone and through joint to sever breast from carcass. Repeat with the other 2 breasts.
5　Remove winglets and the other wing bone from each breast; cut breasts in half and roll each piece tightly into a sausage. You will now have 6 boned leg joints and 6 pieces of breast.
6　Make a rich stock with bones of carcass.
7　Dust chicken pieces with flour. In a heavy casserole, sauté chicken pieces in half the oil and 3 tablespoons butter until golden brown, seasoning generously with salt and pepper.
8　Strain chicken stock over chicken; cover and simmer for 20 minutes, or until tender. Cool.
9　Slice mushrooms thinly. Sauté in remaining oil and 3 tablespoons butter until golden. Season with salt and pepper and add 6 tablespoons of the Madeira. Cool.
10　**Make a sauce:** melt 2 tablespoons butter in a heavy saucepan; add 3 tablespoons flour and

Pillows of Chicken with Eggplant Caviar

cook, stirring, over moderate heat until a deep golden color. Remove from heat.

11 Beat in remaining 3 tablespoons Madeira and pan juices from the chicken; return to heat and stir in cream. Bring to the boil, stirring constantly to make a smooth sauce.

12 Fold in half the mushrooms and simmer for 20 minutes longer, adding a little more stock if sauce becomes too thick.

13 Preheat oven to 425°F.

14 Divide pastry into sixths. Roll each piece out and cut into a 6-inch square. Make decorative leaves out of trimmings (2 or 3 per serving).

15 Place 1 piece chicken breast and 1 piece leg on each square of pastry; cover with one-sixth of remaining mushrooms. Moisten with some of the mushroom juices; then fold pastry up over filling like an envelope and seal tightly, brushing seams with a little beaten egg yolk to seal.

16 Arrange "pillows" on a baking sheet, seam side down. Glaze with beaten egg yolk; decorate with pastry leaves and glaze these as well.

17 Bake for 20 to 25 minutes, or until "pillows" are well risen, crisp and golden.

18 Reheat sauce and serve with chicken.

PUREE CLAMART

- 2 packages frozen peas
- 6 tablespoons butter
- 6 tablespoons rich chicken stock
- ½ onion, very finely chopped
  Salt and freshly ground black pepper
- 1 to 2 baking potatoes

1 Cover peas with cold water and bring to the boil. Drain.

2 Return peas to pan with butter, chicken stock, onion and a pinch each salt and pepper. Cover and simmer until peas are tender and have absorbed most of liquid.

3 Meanwhile, peel potatoes and boil in salted water. Drain; toss over moderate heat to evaporate remaining moisture; then mash. Put about half the mashed potatoes in a large bowl.

4 Puree cooked peas, together with any remaining liquid, in a blender.

5 Gradually add blended peas to mashed potatoes in bowl, beating vigorously. If puree does not hold its shape when lifted with a spoon, beat in a little more potato. (Amount of potato depends entirely on moisture of pea puree.)

6 Add more salt or pepper, if necessary, and keep hot over a pan of simmering water until ready to serve.

SOUFFLEED ORANGES

- 6 large oranges
- 6 egg yolks
- 6 tablespoons sugar
- 6 tablespoons Grand Marnier or Marsala
- 1 cup heavy cream, whipped

To Decorate:
  Whipped cream
  Powdered cocoa or grated chocolate
- 6 lemon, camellia or other glossy leaves

1 Carefully slice off tops of oranges with a sharp knife. Scoop out all the pulp and enough of the pith to leave a firm shell. Reserve pulp and juices for another use.

2 Combine egg yolks, sugar and Grand Marnier in a bowl. Beat until smooth and creamy.

3 Fold in whipped cream to make a fairly liquid mixture.

4 Fill orange shells with cream mixture and freeze in the top of the refrigerator until firm, preferably overnight.

5 Just before serving, decorate tops with piped whipped cream; dust each orange lightly with cocoa or grated chocolate and spike with a lemon, camellia or other glossy green leaf.

6 Serve with petits fours or macaroons.

Four Dinners Based on Game

The traditional accompaniment to roast **game** birds—squab, dove, partridge and pheasant—is a crouton of bread, cut in a rectangle or heart shape, fried in clarified butter and a little olive oil. The livers of the birds, drawn from the carcass halfway through its cooking time and allowed to continue to cook in the pan juices, are pounded and spread on the crouton with a little foie gras and seasoned with a little salt and cayenne pepper.

I like to serve game accompanied by a crisp watercress salad and tart red currant jelly; or, for a more substantial meal, with a rich **red cabbage-in-the-pot.**

 MENU

Orange Vinaigrette
Roast Partridge
with
Red Cabbage-in-the-Pot
Chocolate Ice Cream Mexicaine
SERVES 4-6

RED WINES
Moulin-à-Vent
St. Emilion
Pommard

ORANGE VINAIGRETTE

4 to 6 ripe oranges

Olive and Herb Vinaigrette Sauce:

6 tablespoons olive oil
2 tablespoons wine vinegar
12 black olives, finely chopped
½ onion, finely chopped
2 to 3 tablespoons chopped fresh mint
1 tablespoon chopped fresh parsley
Salt and freshly ground black pepper
Cayenne pepper

1 Peel oranges, removing all pith, and slice crosswise.

2 To make sauce: combine olive oil, vinegar, olives, onion and herbs in a mixing bowl. Season to taste with salt, pepper and cayenne. Mix well.

3 Toss orange slices in vinaigrette sauce.

ROAST PARTRIDGE

    4 to 6 tablespoons softened butter
      Juice of 1 lemon
      Salt and freshly ground black pepper
    4 to 6 young partridge (1 pound each)
    4 to 6 slices bacon
    4 to 6 croutons of bread big enough to serve
        as base for partridge
      Clarified butter
    1 tablespoon olive oil
      Cayenne pepper
      Watercress
      Red currant jelly

1 Combine softened butter and lemon juice in a mixing bowl, seasoning with salt and pepper, to taste.

2 Fill birds with this mixture. Tie a thin slice of bacon over the breast of each bird and roast in a 425°F oven for 20 to 25 minutes (25 to 30 minutes if you prefer your birds less rare). When birds are half cooked remove livers; mash them slightly and place in pan to cook with partridge until birds are tender.

3 Just before serving: fry croutons in a little clarified butter and olive oil until golden. Spread with mashed livers and crusty bits from pan and season with salt and cayenne.

4 To serve: remove bacon and string; place one bird on each crouton and arrange on a heated serving dish. Garnish with watercress and serve with red currant jelly.

Note: Doves or pigeons may be substituted for partridge.

RED CABBAGE-IN-THE-POT

    1 red cabbage (about 2 pounds)
    4 tablespoons butter
    2 to 3 onions, sliced
    1 pound cooking apples, peeled, cored
        and quartered
    2 cloves garlic, finely chopped
    ¼ teaspoon each of ground nutmeg, allspice,
        cinnamon, thyme and caraway seeds
      Salt and freshly ground black pepper
    1 teaspoon grated orange rind
    2 strips orange peel
    2 tablespoons brown sugar
   1¼ cups red wine
    2 tablespoons wine vinegar

1 Wash and shred cabbage, removing central core, ribs and outer leaves. Cook in butter in a covered saucepan for 5 minutes.

2 Place cabbage, onion and apples in a deep ovenproof casserole in layers until casserole is full. Season each layer with garlic, spices and salt and pepper, to taste, grated orange rind and orange peel. Sprinkle brown sugar over the top and add wine, wine vinegar and a little hot water.

3 Cover and simmer in a 375°F oven until tender, adding a little more wine if necessary.

CHOCOLATE ICE CREAM MEXICAINE

    4 to 6 scoops chocolate ice cream
   12 tablespoons Tia Maria liqueur
      Whipped cream, unsweetened
      Slivered toasted almonds

1 Place one scoop ice cream in each bowl.

2 Spoon over Tia Maria and garnish with whipped cream and slivered almonds.

❀ *MENU* ❀

Sorrel Soup
Pheasant with Green Apples
with
Sautéed Mushrooms à la Bordelaise
Fresh Grape Tart
SERVES 4

RED WINES
Médoc
St. Emilion
Pomerol

❀

SORREL SOUP

- 1 onion, finely chopped
- 3 tablespoons butter
- 1 large potato, sliced
- 3 tablespoons flour
  Salt and white pepper
- 5 cups chicken broth
- 3 to 4 packed cups of sorrel leaves, washed and stems removed
- 2 egg yolks
- ⅔ cup heavy cream
  Lemon juice
  Few drops Tabasco

1 Simmer onion gently in butter until transparent. Add potato, sprinkle in flour, salt and white pepper, to taste, and continue cooking over a low heat, stirring constantly, for 3 minutes more.

2 Remove saucepan from the heat and beat in the boiling chicken stock. Add sorrel leaves and simmer for 5 minutes more; then puree in a blender.

3 Blend egg yolks and cream in a small bowl. Pour in a little of the hot soup, beating vigorously. Gradually beat in remainder of soup. Correct seasoning with salt, white pepper, lemon juice and Tabasco to taste. Cool. Chill.

PHEASANT WITH GREEN APPLES

- ¼ pound Canadian bacon, diced
- ½ large onion, finely chopped
- 1 clove garlic, finely chopped
- 2 tablespoons butter
- 2 tablespoons olive oil
- 1 pheasant
- 4 tart green apples, peeled, cored and thickly sliced
- 4 tablespoons Cointreau
- 1¼ cups heavy cream
  Salt and freshly ground black pepper

1 Sauté bacon and onion and garlic in butter and olive oil in an ovenproof casserole until golden. Remove and reserve.

2 Brown pheasant on all sides in the fat remaining in the pan. Remove and keep warm.

3 Sauté apples in remaining fat until they start to turn golden. Add Cointreau. Remove apples from casserole and skim fat from remaining juices.

4 Return pheasant to casserole; surround with apple slices, bacon, onion and garlic; simmer, covered, for 10 minutes.

5 Stir in cream, add salt and pepper, to taste; cover casserole and cook in a 275°F oven until pheasant is tender.

6 When ready to serve, remove pheasant and bacon bits to a clean casserole and keep warm; puree sauce and apples. Correct seasoning; reheat sauce; pour over pheasant and serve immediately.

SAUTEED MUSHROOMS A LA BORDELAISE

- 8 to 12 large flat mushrooms
- 2 tablespoons olive oil
- 2 tablespoons butter
  Salt and freshly ground black pepper
- 2 tablespoons chopped parsley
- 1 to 2 cloves garlic, finely chopped

1 Wash mushrooms and trim stalks. Combine oil and butter in a large frying pan; add mushrooms and sauté on both sides until tender, adding a little more oil or butter, if necessary. Season with salt and pepper and keep warm.

2 Just before serving, sprinkle with parsley and garlic.

FRESH GRAPE TART
Fingertip Pastry:

- 2 **cups sifted flour**
  Pinch of salt
- 2 **tablespoons confectioners' sugar**
- 5 **ounces softened butter**
- 1 **egg yolk**
- 4 **tablespoons cold water**

Fresh Grape Tart

Filling:

- ½ **pound green grapes**
- ½ **pound black grapes**

Apricot Glaze:

- 4 **to 6 tablespoons water**
- 1 **cup apricot jam**
  Kirsch

Decoration (optional):

- 1 **egg white**
- 1 **small bunch black grapes**
  Superfine sugar

1 **To make pastry:** Sift flour, salt and sugar into a mixing bowl. Rub in butter with the tips of the fingers until mixture resembles fine bread crumbs. Do this very gently and lightly, or mixture will become greasy and heavy. Beat egg yolk and add water; sprinkle over dough and work in lightly with fingers. Shape moist dough lightly into a flattened round; wrap in plastic and refrigerate for at least 1 hour.

2 If chilled dough is too firm for handling, let stand at room temperature until it softens slightly. Then turn it out on to a floured board and roll out as required. Line tart pan and prick with a fork. Bake "blind" (see page 125) in a preheated 450°F oven for 15 minutes; lower heat to 350°F and bake for 30 minutes longer. If crust becomes too brown at edges, cover with a little crumpled foil.

3 Peel, halve and seed green grapes; halve and seed black grapes, leaving one small bunch black grapes for decoration. Arrange grapes attractively in baked tart shell.

4 **To make apricot glaze:** add water to apricot jam and heat, stirring constantly, until liquid. Add kirsch to taste. Brush over grapes and leave to set.

5 Finally, lightly beat the egg white. Dip bunch of black grapes into egg white, holding it by the stalk. Drain slightly and then roll gently in sugar. Set aside to dry and then place in center of flan.

❀ *MENU* ❀

Grilled Pepper Salad
Rabbit with Mustard
with
Buttered Spinach
with Rosemary
Old-Fashioned Fruit Pie
SERVES 6

WHITE WINES
Lachryma Christi
Chianti Ruffino White

RED WINES
Barolo
Valpolicella

❀

Rabbit with Mustard

GRILLED PEPPER SALAD

  3 green peppers
  3 red peppers
12 anchovy fillets
  3 cloves garlic, finely chopped
  3 tablespoons finely chopped parsley
  6 tablespoons olive oil
  2 tablespoons lemon juice
     Freshly ground black pepper and salt
     Lemon juice, finely chopped parsley and
     garlic (optional)

1 Place peppers side by side in a pan and broil steadily under moderate heat until their skins blister and blacken all over and peppers become rather limp. Keep turning them so that every part is exposed to the heat.

2 Plunge peppers into a large bowl of cold water. Leave them for 2 minutes; then drain and peel. Skins will slip off quite easily if peppers have been correctly and evenly broiled. Slice peppers in half; cut out pith and rinse out seeds under cold running water. Pat each piece of pepper dry and cut it in four across the width.

3 Cut anchovies into ¼-inch lengths and combine in a deep serving dish with peppers, garlic and parsley. Toss lightly until well mixed.

4 Heat olive oil with lemon juice in a small pan. When it is very hot, pour over the peppers and mix lightly. Set aside until cold—the dressing helps to develop and blend flavors together as it cools in a way that a simple cold dressing could never do. Serve chilled.

Note: This dish is so highly seasoned that you are unlikely to need salt; but taste and judge for yourself before adding pepper, additional lemon juice, if desired, and an additional sprinkling of parsley and garlic.

RABBIT WITH MUSTARD

  1 (3- to 3½-pound) rabbit, enough to
     make 12 serving pieces
  2 tablespoons flour
     Salt and freshly ground black pepper
  2 tablespoons olive oil
  2 tablespoons butter

¼ **pound Canadian bacon diced and blanched**
4 **shallots, chopped**
Bouquet garni
⅔ **cup dry white wine**
⅔ **cup chicken stock**
1 **teaspoon Dijon mustard**
1 **teaspoon English mustard**
1¼ **cups heavy cream**

1   Cut rabbit into 12 serving pieces; roll pieces in seasoned flour, and sauté until golden in olive oil and butter with salt pork.

2   Add shallots and bouquet garni; moisten with wine and stock, cover and cook gently until rabbit is tender.

3   Drain rabbit pieces; place them in a heated bowl and keep warm. Skim fat from sauce; whisk Dijon mustard and English mustard thoroughly with cream and add to sauce in pan. Correct seasoning, adding a little more mustard, salt or pepper if desired. Add rabbit pieces; heat through thoroughly and serve in casserole.

BUTTERED SPINACH WITH ROSEMARY

4 **tablespoons butter**
2 **packages frozen leaf spinach**
1 **to 2 teaspoons crushed dried rosemary**
Salt and freshly ground black pepper

1   Melt butter in a heavy pan; add frozen spinach and thaw over very low heat, stirring occasionally.

2   When spinach has thawed completely, sprinkle with rosemary and season to taste with salt and pepper. Cover pan and simmer gently, stirring or shaking pan occasionally, for 5 minutes longer, or until spinach is tender and fragrant with rosemary.

3   Transfer to a heated serving dish and serve hot.

Note: If using ground rosemary, cut the amount by about half as it is much more concentrated in flavor.

OLD-FASHIONED FRUIT PIE

4 **firm pears**
4 **tart apples**
Juice of 1 lemon
Pastry for a two-crust pie
4 **tablespoons dark brown sugar**
1 **tablespoon flour**
⅛ **teaspoon freshly grated nutmeg**
⅛ **teaspoon ground cinnamon**
Grated rind of ½ orange
2 **tablespoons chopped raisins**
1 **to 2 tablespoons orange juice**
1 **to 2 tablespoons butter**
Heavy cream, to serve

1   Peel and core pears and apples; slice thickly. Soak in water with lemon juice to prevent discoloration.

2   Line a deep 9-inch pie dish with pastry, using your own favorite recipe.

3   Combine brown sugar, flour, nutmeg and cinnamon, and rub a little of this mixture into pastry lining. Add orange rind to remaining sugar mixture. Cover bottom of the pastry shell with sliced apples and pears and sprinkle with a few chopped raisins and some of the sugar mixture to taste. Repeat layers until pie shell is generously filled.

4   Sprinkle with orange juice and dot with butter; fit top crust over pears, pressing the edges together or fluting them. Cut slits in crust to release steam and bake in a 400°F oven for 35 to 40 minutes, or until tender. Serve warm, with cream.

❀ *MENU* ❀

Italian Pumpkin Soup
Partridge with Lentils
Tossed Green Salad
Italian Cheeses
and
Fresh Fruit
SERVES 4-6

RED WINES
Brouilly
Mercurey
Sterling Cabernet

❀

ITALIAN PUMPKIN SOUP

  1 **pound pumpkin**
  2 **to 3 potatoes**
  1 **onion**
  4 **tablespoons butter**
 ¼ **pound fresh green or broad beans**
  1 **pint milk**
   Salt and cayenne pepper
  1 **leek, cut into fine strips**
2½ **cups hot chicken stock**
 ⅔ **cup heavy cream**
  1 **cup cooked rice**
  2 **tablespoons chopped parsley**

1 Peel and dice pumpkin and potatoes. Chop onion and simmer in half the butter until golden; add diced pumpkin and potatoes, beans and milk. Bring to the boil and simmer for 45 minutes, stirring from time to time to prevent scorching.

2 Strain through a fine sieve or puree in blender in batches; pour into a clean saucepan; add salt and cayenne, to taste.

3 Sauté leeks in remaining butter until soft; add to soup with stock and bring to the boil.

4 Just before serving, stir in cream, rice and parsley.

PARTRIDGE WITH LENTILS

  2 **to 3 partridges**
   Salt and freshly ground black pepper
  2 **to 3 tablespoons butter**
  2 **tablespoons olive oil**
 ¼ **pound fat salt pork, diced**
  1 **large onion, sliced**
  2 **to 3 carrots, sliced**
 ½ **cup dry white wine**
 ½ **cup chicken stock**

Lentils:

1½ **cups lentils, presoaked**
  1 **onion, stuck with 2 cloves**
  2 **cloves garlic**
  1 **sprig fresh thyme**
  2 **sprigs fresh parsley**
   Salt and freshly ground black pepper

1 Clean and prepare partridges; sprinkle cavities with a little salt and pepper and sauté birds in an ovenproof casserole in butter and olive oil with salt pork, onion and carrots.

2 When birds are golden, add wine and cook until wine is reduced by half. Add chicken stock and season to taste with salt and pepper; cover casserole and cook over low heat until partridges are tender, about 45 minutes.

3 **To prepare lentils:** soak overnight; drain and cover with water, adding onion, garlic, thyme, parsley, salt and pepper, to taste. Bring to the boil, reduce heat and simmer until tender but not too soft. When cooked, drain and remove onion, garlic and herbs.

4 **To serve:** place partridges on a hot serving dish and surround with cooked lentils. Skim fat from pan juices; strain juices and pour over birds.

TOSSED GREEN SALAD

(For recipe, see **green salad and variations**, page 146.)

ITALIAN CHEESES AND FRUIT

(For **cheese**, see pages 146–147.)

Partridge with Lentils

Supper Parties

A famous hostess once said to me: "Togetherness is caviar and a cheese omelet coupled with the right people."

A wonderfully simple way to entertain, I thought, caviar not withstanding, and late-night suppers immediately became my favorite trouble-free party plan.

What could be easier and more pleasing after an evening at the movies or the theater, or, more simply, after an evening spent at home with friends playing cards or watching the late-night TV? Less important than a formal sit-down dinner, you can center your late-night supper around a dish as simple as Italian pasta tossed in egg yolks, cream and freshly grated Parmesan (page 64), spaghetti Bolognese (page 178) or a chilled platter of thin slices of rare roast beef and prosciutto served with a delicious potato horseradish salad (page 42).

High on the honors list in today's circles is the informal buffet supper after a cocktail party. Emphasis is on a long table piled with a lavish spread of food. Cold glazed ham or roast turkey, Italian vitello tonnato (see below) and a crisp salad are suggestions for the bill of fare.

Wine can be served from the cask, or in magnums for festive effect.

Parties-with-a-theme are becoming an intrinsic part of the supper-party picture: for example, a French Bistro Party; gay red-checked tablecloths, café-sized tables, guttering candles and hearty French food.

Try a jellied consommé, or filets d'harengs à l'huile, smoked herring fillets soaked for 12 hours or more in olive oil with a bay leaf and several slices of onion and carrot. Follow with a French country speciality like boeuf en daube (page 132) served with plain boiled potatoes, and finish off with individual chocolate puddings (see page 48) or a glazed fruit flan (see page 122). Serve French bread and red wine throughout the meal.

Or try the following hot-weather menu for a supper party with an international flavor: the veal recipe below from Italy, a fresh-tasting rice salad from Hong Kong, followed by Camembert and a chilled red fruit bowl from France.

A bright easy idea for informal entertaining is the Dip-In Supper Party, glamorous, fun and guaranteed to bring out the best and the worst in everyone. Easy-to-produce "dip-ins" range from Swiss fondue (see page 168) to Italian Bagna Cauda (see page 162), to Fondue Bourguignonne (see page 170).

MENU
Vitello Tonnato
with
Oriental Rice Salad
Soused Camembert
Red Fruit Bowl
with Raspberry Puree
SERVES 6

WHITE AND ROSE WINES
Lachryma Christi
Soave
Tavel Rosé

VITELLO TONNATO

    1   (2½- to 3-pound) boned leg of veal
    6   anchovy fillets
        Bay leaves
    1   large onion, sliced
    2   carrots, sliced
    2   celery stalks, sliced
    2   sprigs parsley
    2   cloves
        Salt and freshly ground black pepper
  1¼   cups dry white wine (optional)
        Lemon slices and capers for garnish

Tuna Fish Sauce:

    1   (7 ounce) can tuna fish
    6   anchovy fillets
    1   teaspoon capers
    2   tablespoons lemon juice
        Freshly ground black pepper
   ⅔   cup homemade mayonnaise (see page 141)
        Olive oil (optional)

1 Start this dish the day before you intend to serve it. Have your butcher bone and tie a piece of leg of veal.

2 Cut anchovies into small pieces; push these into holes pierced in surface of meat. Place several bay leaves along top of veal.

3 Place meat in an ovenproof casserole with onion, carrots, celery, parsley and cloves. Season to taste with salt and pepper. Pour in wine and add just enough water to cover meat (or use water only).

4 Bring to the boil. Skim; lower heat so that liquid barely simmers; cover casserole and simmer gently for 1½ to 2 hours.

5 When veal is tender, remove string and return to stock. Set aside until cold.

6 **To make tuna fish sauce:** combine tuna fish, anchovies, capers, lemon juice and pepper in the container of a blender. Gradually add mayonnaise and blend until sauce is smooth. Add a little strained veal stock if sauce seems too thick.

7 Drain cold veal thoroughly and place in a bowl. Cover with sauce and refrigerate overnight.

8 One hour before serving, remove veal from sauce; scrape excess sauce into bowl. Cut veal into thin slices and arrange them in a row, slightly overlapping, on a meat platter. Cover veal slices with remaining sauce, thinned down with a little more stock or olive oil if necessary, and refrigerate until ready to serve.

9 Serve garnished with lemon slices and capers.

ORIENTAL RICE SALAD

  1½   cups long-grain rice
        Salt
        Lemon juice
    1   cup cooked green peas
    ½   green pepper, seeded, cored and finely diced
    ½   red pepper, seeded, cored and finely diced
    6   tablespoons finely chopped parsley
    6   tablespoons finely chopped scallions

Dressing:

    2   tablespoons lemon juice
    ½   clove garlic, crushed
    6   tablespoons olive oil
        Salt and freshly ground black pepper

1 Boil rice in plenty of salted water until tender but still very firm. (Add a little lemon

juice to keep it white.) Drain thoroughly and allow to cool.

2 In a serving bowl, toss rice with peas, green and red peppers, parsley and scallions.

3 **To make dressing:** mix lemon juice with garlic. Beat in olive oil with a fork and season generously with salt and pepper.

4 Pour dressing over rice mixture; toss thoroughly and taste for seasoning, adding more salt, pepper, oil or lemon juice, if necessary. Chill covered until ready to serve.

SOUSED CAMEMBERT

(For the recipe see page 183.)

RED FRUIT BOWL WITH RASPBERRY PUREE

> 1½ **pounds ripe cherries**
> 2 **pints ripe strawberries**
> 1 **pint red currants**
> 2 **pints ripe raspberries**
> **Cognac**
> **Lemon juice**
> **Confectioners' sugar, sifted**

Raspberry Puree:

> 2 **pints ripe raspberries**
> 2 **to 3 tablespoons lemon juice**
> 2 **to 3 tablespoons confectioners' sugar**

1 Pit cherries; hull strawberries; strip red currants from their stalks.

2 In a glass bowl, combine prepared fruit with raspberries. Flavor to taste with cognac, lemon juice and sugar, tossing fruit gently to avoid crushing it; chill for at least 30 minutes before serving.

3 **To make raspberry puree:** wash raspberries and puree in an electric blender, then strain. Flavor to taste with lemon juice and sugar. Chill.

4 Serve fruit accompanied by chilled raspberry puree.

Vitello Tonnato with Oriental Rice Salad

❀ MENU ❀

Sherried Mushroom Tartlets
Cold Roast Beef
with Parma Ham
Potato Horseradish Salad
Walnut Roll
SERVES 8

WHITE AND ROSE WINES
Soave
Lachryma Christi
Chianti Ruffino White

❀

SHERRIED MUSHROOM TARTLETS

16 prebaked small pastry shells

Sherried Mushrooms:

> 6 **tablespoons butter**
> 2 **tablespoons flour**
> 1¼ **cups chicken stock**
> 4 **tablespoons milk**
> 6 **tablespoons heavy cream**
> 1 **pound button mushrooms, sliced**
> ½ **cup finely chopped shallots**
> **Salt and freshly ground black pepper**
> 4 **tablespoons dry sherry**

1 Use individual pans with removable bases to shape pastry shells. They should be left in their pans until just before serving.

2 **To make sherried mushrooms:** in a heavy pan, make a roux with 2 tablespoons each butter and flour, stirring over a low heat for 2 to 3 minutes, taking care it does not burn. Then gradually stir in chicken stock, followed by milk and cream; bring to the boil and simmer for 15 minutes, stirring occasionally.

3 Sauté mushrooms and shallots in remaining 4 tablespoons butter until soft, 3 to 5 minutes; season to taste with salt and pepper.

4 Fold into sauce; add sherry and correct seasoning if necessary. Keep hot.

5 Reheat pastry shells in their pans for about 5 minutes in a 350°F oven. Remove from pans and arrange on a dish. Fill with hot mushrooms and sauce and serve at once.

COLD ROAST BEEF WITH PROSCIUTTO

1 to 2 cloves garlic
1 (2½-pound) rib roast
20 thin slices prosciutto, about 10 ounces
1 strip fat salt pork
3 to 4 tablespoons oil
   Salt and freshly ground black pepper
12 gherkins for garnish

1 Preheat oven to 450°F.

2 Peel and sliver garlic. Make deep slits all over beef with the point of a sharp knife and push in slivers as deeply as possible.

3 Wrap roast in 4 slices prosciutto and then in salt pork; tie securely with string. Brush with oil; place in roasting pan and roast until done to your taste, 45 to 50 minutes for rare beef.

4 Remove meat from oven and let cool. When completely cold, remove larding strip and ham and cut beef into 16 slices. Season each slice with a sprinkling of salt and pepper.

5 Arrange beef slices on a long serving platter, alternating them with thin slices of prosciutto.

6 Slice gherkins very thinly lengthwise without cutting right through to the ends, and fan them out attractively. Use them to decorate platter of beef and prosciutto.

POTATO HORSERADISH SALAD

12 medium-sized potatoes
   Salt
2 cups homemade mayonnaise (see page 141)
2 to 4 tablespoons grated horseradish
2 to 4 tablespoons finely chopped parsley
   Freshly ground black pepper

1 Scrub potatoes clean and boil them in their skins in salted water until cooked but not mushy. Drain; cool slightly and peel off skins. Cool and slice or dice potatoes into a serving bowl.

2 Combine mayonnaise with horseradish, to taste, and parsley, and fold into potatoes carefully to avoid breaking slices; season to taste with salt and pepper and chill until ready to serve.

Cold Roast Beef with Prosciutto

Walnut Roll

WALNUT ROLL

   2 tablespoons flour
      Pinch of salt
  ½ teaspoon baking powder
  ½ cup coarsely chopped walnuts
  6 eggs, separated
  ½ cup sugar
      Sifted confectioners' sugar, to decorate

Filling:

 1¾ cups heavy cream
  ½ cup sugar

1 Select a jelly roll pan 15½″ × 10½″ × 1″. Brush lightly with oil and line with waxed paper; oil paper lightly as well.

2 Preheat oven to 350°F.

3 Sift flour, salt and baking powder into a bowl.

4 Grind walnuts coarsely—they must not be ground too finely or they will release too much oil and make the cake heavy.

5 Beat egg yolks with sugar over hot water until mixture leaves a ribbon on the surface when beaters are lifted. Remove bowl from heat and continue to beat mixture until cold.

6 Fold in ground walnuts with a spoon.

7 Beat egg whites until stiff but not dry. Fold into the walnut mixture gently but thoroughly.

8 Fold in sifted flour mixture.

9 Pour batter into prepared pan and spread it out with a spatula. Bake for 20 to 25 minutes, or until springy to the touch.

10 While cake is in the oven, prepare a surface for rolling it: put a damp cloth on the surface, cover with a sheet of waxed paper and sprinkle with 1 teaspoon superfine sugar.

11 Turn cake out on to sugared paper and carefully peel off waxed paper.

12 Replace with a new piece of waxed paper and carefully roll cake up together with papers and cloth, starting at one of the longer sides. Set aside to cool.

13 When roll is cool, whip cream until it forms soft peaks and sweeten to taste with superfine sugar.

14 Carefully unroll cake and remove top paper. Spread cake evenly with whipped cream and roll it up again, this time without the cloth and paper underneath.

15 Place on a long, flat serving dish, seam side down, and dust liberally with sifted confectioners' sugar.

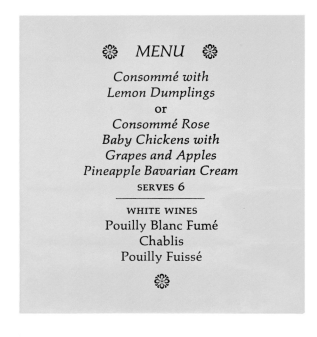

❀ *MENU* ❀

Consommé with
Lemon Dumplings
or
Consommé Rose
Baby Chickens with
Grapes and Apples
Pineapple Bavarian Cream
SERVES 6

WHITE WINES
Pouilly Blanc Fumé
Chablis
Pouilly Fuissé

❀

CONSOMME WITH LEMON DUMPLINGS

- 2 **carrots, thinly sliced**
- 2 to 3 **celery stalks, thinly sliced**
- 3 to 4 **leaves of leek, finely diced**
- 5 **cups clear hot consommé**
- 3 to 4 **tablespoons Madeira**
  Finely chopped parsley

Lemon Dumplings:

- ¾ **cup coarse stale bread crumbs**
- ¼ **teaspoon grated lemon rind**
  Generous pinch of thyme
- 1 **tablespoon finely chopped chives**
- 2 **tablespoons butter, softened**
- 1 **egg yolk**
  Pinch of freshly grated nutmeg
  Salt and freshly ground black pepper
  Finely chopped parsley

1   To make dumplings: combine ingredients to form a smooth dough, adding nutmeg, salt and pepper, to taste. Roll into 30 small balls.

2   Poach in lightly salted water for 30 to 40 minutes; drain well.

3   To finish consommé: simmer vegetables in a little consommé until tender, 8 to 10 min-

utes; combine with remaining consommé and flavor to taste with Madeira.

4   Serve hot, garnished with lemon dumplings and sprinkled with parsley.

CONSOMME ROSE

- 1 **pound ripe red tomatoes**
- 2 **celery stalks**
- 2 **carrots**
- 5 **cups rich chicken stock**
  Salt and freshly ground black pepper

To Garnish:

- ½ **pound firm tomatoes**
- 1 **4-ounce can red pimentos**
- 2 **tablespoons finely chopped parsley or chives**

1   Chop tomatoes, celery and carrots coarsely. Place them in a large saucepan with chicken stock; bring to the boil and simmer for 30 minutes.

2   To make garnish: peel and seed tomatoes, and cut them into small dice. Drain pimentos and dice them also.

3   To finish consommé: strain stock through a cheesecloth-lined sieve. Add diced tomato and pimento garnish; season to taste with salt and pepper and bring just to boiling point again.

4   Remove from heat: sprinkle with parsley or chives and serve immediately.

BABY CHICKENS WITH GRAPES AND APPLES

- 6 **(1-pound) chickens**
- 2 to 3 **(8-ounce) packages cream cheese**
  Salt and freshly ground black pepper
- 3 **tablespoons olive oil**
- 8 **tablespoons butter**
- 3 **pounds tart green apples, peeled, cored and diced**
- 2 **pounds black grapes, halved and seeded**
- 6 **tablespoons brandy**

1   Preheat oven to 450°F.

2   Wipe chickens clean and dry them thoroughly inside and out.

Consommé Rose

Baby Chickens with Grapes and Apples

3   In a large bowl, beat the cheese with a fork until smooth, adding a generous amount of salt and pepper. Stuff body cavity of each bird with the cheese. Then truss them.

4   Heat oil with 4 tablespoons of the butter in a large, heavy frying pan. Sauté birds one or two at a time over a steady, moderate heat, turning them over so that they brown evenly. When birds are all browned, transfer to a roasting pan, large enough to hold them comfortably side by side.

5   Pour over fat remaining in pan and roast them, uncovered, for 25 minutes—10 minutes on each side and a final 5 minutes on their backs—basting with pan juices each time you turn them. Check to see if they are cooked by pushing a skewer through the thickest part of the leg: the juices should run clear. If not, return birds to the oven for a few minutes longer.

6   **To make fruit garnish:** toss diced apples in the remaining 4 tablespoons butter until golden but not disintegrating. Remove from heat, add grapes and mix carefully.

7   Remove chickens from oven. Spoon over apples and grapes, and pour a tablespoon of brandy over each bird. Cover the pan securely with a large sheet of foil and return to the oven for a further 10 minutes to develop flavors.

8   **To serve:** with a large, sharp knife slice each chicken in half down the middle. Re-form birds and arrange them side by side on a long, heated serving platter. Surround with fruits; pour cooking juices over fruits and serve immediately.

Note: The only accompaniment needed is a large bowl of crisp salad tossed with a light, lemony **vinaigrette dressing** (see page 146).

PINEAPPLE BAVARIAN CREAM

    1   envelope gelatin
    ⅔   cup pineapple juice
    6   egg yolks
    ¾   cup granulated sugar
    1   tablespoon cornstarch
    2   cups milk
    5   egg whites
        Generous pinch of salt
    1   tablespoon sugar

    3   tablespoons lemon juice
    ½   cup heavy cream, chilled
    2   to 3 slices pineapple, fresh or canned, shredded

To Decorate:

Pineapple rings, halved maraschino cherries and angelica

1   Sprinkle gelatin over pineapple juice and set aside to soften.

2   In a large bowl, beat egg yolks with granulated sugar until fluffy and lemon colored; add cornstarch and continue to beat until smoothly blended.

3   Scald milk; add to egg yolk mixture in a thin stream, beating vigorously with a whisk. Then pour into the top of a double boiler and cook over hot water, stirring constantly. As soon as custard coats back of spoon, plunge base of pan into cold water to stop cooking process.

4   Add gelatin and pineapple juice mixture to hot custard, stirring until completely dissolved. Pour custard into a large bowl.

5   Beat egg whites with salt until soft peaks form. Add superfine sugar and continue to beat to a stiff meringue. Fold gently but thoroughly into warm custard mixture and flavor to taste with lemon juice (flavor should be rather sharp). Allow mixture to cool, drawing a large metal spoon through it occasionally to prevent it from separating.

6   When custard mixture is on the point of setting, whip chilled cream (by hand for maximum volume) until it almost holds its shape. Fold into custard, together with shredded pineapple.

7   Rinse an 8-cup loaf pan (or mold) with cold water, shaking out all excess. Fill with pineapple cream mixture; cover with waxed paper and chill in refrigerator until firmly set, preferably overnight.

8   **To serve:** plunge mold into very hot water for 1 second only and turn out on to a flat serving dish. Decorate with halved pineapple rings, maraschino cherries and angelica sprigs and return to refrigerator until ready to serve.

MENU ❁

*Oeufs en Cocotte
Broiled Salmon
Steaks with Snail
Butter
Fresh Cucumber Salad
Chocolate Towers*
SERVES 6

WHITE WINES
Pouilly Blanc Fumé
Riesling d'Alsace
Pouilly Fuissé

❁

OEUFS EN COCOTTE

(AND VARIATIONS)

This dish makes a wonderfully light, elegant appetizer to serve when time is short.

1 Preheat oven to 375°F.
2 Butter 6 ovenproof ramekins (about ⅔-cup capacity) and arrange them side by side in a wide, deep pan.
3 Carefully break 1 or 2 eggs into each ramekin. Season lightly with salt and a turn of the pepper mill, and swirl a little hot heavy cream over the top.
4 Pour hot water into pan to come half-way up sides of ramekins; cover lightly with a sheet of foil and bring back to a simmer. Bake for 12 minutes, or until whites are just beginning to set but yolks are still runny.
5 Serve eggs immediately, as they tend to continue cooking from heat of dishes.

Oeufs en Cocotte with Bacon:

As above, but add to each buttered ramekin a mixture of 1 tablespoon each crisp-fried crumbled bacon and finely chopped parsley before breaking in eggs. Pour a tablespoon of heavy cream over each ramekin just before serving.

Oeufs en Cocotte with Ham

Butter 6 ramekins as above.

1 Combine 12 tablespoons finely chopped ham with 6 tablespoons each finely chopped parsley and fresh bread crumbs.
2 Use three-quarters of the ham-parsley-bread crumb mixture to coat individual ramekins generously.
3 Break 1 or 2 eggs into each ramekin; cover with remaining ham and bread crumb mixture and bake as above.

BROILED SALMON STEAKS WITH SNAIL BUTTER

6 salmon steaks, 1 inch thick
2 to 3 tablespoons olive oil
Salt and freshly ground black pepper

Snail Butter:

6 tablespoons butter
1 to 2 cloves garlic, crushed
½ tablespoon very finely chopped shallot
1 tablespoon very finely chopped parsley
Salt and freshly ground black pepper

1 **To make snail butter:** work butter with a wooden spoon until slightly softened; add garlic, to taste, and beat until thoroughly blended; then beat in shallot and parsley and season to taste with salt and pepper.
2 Shape butter into six small balls and chill on a dish until firm again. (Cover dish tightly with foil or plastic to avoid a strong garlic odor permeating other dishes in refrigerator.)
3 **To cook salmon:** Preheat broiler for about 20 minutes before cooking salmon.
4 Brush both sides of each steak with olive oil and sprinkle with salt and pepper; arrange steaks side by side on a rack in a broiler pan.
5 When ready to cook steaks, reduce oven temperature to 375°F and broil steaks for 16 to 20 minutes, turning them once. Steaks are ready when fish flakes easily when tested with a fork.
6 Transfer salmon steaks to a heated dish. Top each one with a generous pat of the chilled snail butter and serve immediately.

FRENCH CUCUMBER SALAD
(For the recipe, see page 71.)

CHOCOLATE TOWERS
Cake:

        Butter
    3   eggs
    ¾   cup sugar
    ½   cup flour, sifted

Chocolate Filling:

    3   squares (ounces) unsweetened chocolate,
            grated
        Finely grated rind of 1 orange
    ⅔   cup milk
    1   egg, separated
    ¼   cup sugar
    1   teaspoon unflavored gelatin
    ⅔   cup heavy cream

Crème Anglaise:

    1   pint milk
    ¼   teaspoon vanilla
    2   teaspoons cornstarch
    ¼   cup sugar
    6   egg yolks

1   Grease a jelly roll pan (12 × 8 inches) and line with buttered waxed paper. Preheat oven to 350°F.

2   **To make cake:** beat eggs and sugar over hot water until mixture leaves a ribbon on the surface. Remove from heat and fold in flour.

3   Put cake mixture into pan and level off with a spatula.

4   Bake for 15 to 20 minutes, or until cake is golden and springy.

5   Turn out on to a wire rack; peel off waxed paper. Cool.

6   **To make chocolate filling:** combine chocolate with orange rind and milk; bring to the boil, stirring constantly. Remove from heat. Beat egg yolk with half the superfine sugar; then gradually beat in hot chocolate milk. Dissolve gelatin in 1 tablespoon cold water in a cup. Set aside for 10 minutes. Place cup in a bowl of hot water and stir until gelatin has completely dissolved. Blend thoroughly with chocolate mixture. Whip cream lightly; fold into chocolate mixture. Beat egg white until stiff; add remaining sugar and continue to beat until stiff and glossy. Fold into chocolate mixture. Set aside while you prepare molds.

7   Line 6 turret molds with cake as follows: cut a circle to fit the bottom of each mold; then cut a strip to fit completely round inside of each mold, trimming ends so that there is no overlap.

8   Fill cake-lined molds with chocolate mixture and chill until firmly set.

9   **To make crème anglaise:** bring milk to the boil with vanilla. Mix cornstarch with superfine sugar; add to egg yolks and beat until smooth. Pour in milk gradually, beating constantly with a whisk; then transfer mixture to the top of a double boiler and cook over hot water, stirring constantly, until sauce coats back of spoon. Do not let sauce boil or egg yolks will curdle. Pour into bowl; cool and chill.

10   **When ready to serve:** turn chocolate towers out on to a wire rack over a flat dish. Coat each tower completely with crème anglaise and transfer to individual dishes.

11   Serve remaining sauce in a separate bowl.

Meals Built Around Four Family Favorites

Vary the menus with exciting appetizers and desserts to complement these four family favorites: roast leg of lamb, roast chicken, steak and kidney pie and the "no-roast" roast beef, to give yourself sixteen different menus.

MARINATED MUSHROOMS

2 pounds small button mushrooms
  Juice of ½ lemon
  Salt
⅔ cup wine vinegar
⅔ cup olive oil
4 cloves garlic, crushed
1 sprig thyme
2 sprigs parsley
1 bay leaf
4 to 6 peppercorns
12 coriander seeds

1 Trim stems and wash mushrooms thoroughly. Drain and place in a saucepan with cold water, lemon juice and salt to taste. Bring gently to the boil; lower heat and simmer for 10 minutes. Drain and place blanched mushrooms in a shallow earthenware dish.

2 Combine the remaining ingredients in an enameled saucepan; bring to the boil, lower heat and simmer for 20 minutes. Pour mixture over mushrooms and marinate covered in the refrigerator for 24 hours.

❀ *MENU* ❀

Marinated Mushrooms
or
Avocado Soup
Roast Leg of
Lamb with Garlic,
Lemon and Parsley Dressing
Old English Trifle
or
Elizabeth Moxon's Lemon Posset
SERVES 4

RED WINES
Pomerol
Beaujolais
Châteauneuf-du-Pape

❀

Marinated Mushrooms

AVOCADO SOUP

>   2 ripe avocados
>   1 teaspoon curry powder
>   Salt and freshly ground black pepper
>   ½ cup heavy cream
>   2½ cups stock
>   2 teaspoons lemon juice
>   Cayenne pepper
>   Finely chopped parsley

1 Peel avocados thinly and halve each one lengthwise; remove pits and dice flesh, reserving a little of the darker green flesh for garnish. Blend diced avocado in an electric blender together with the curry powder, salt, pepper and cream.

2 Combine stock and lemon juice. Bring gently to the boil; add a little to the avocado and cream mixture, and then blend all together with the remaining stock and reheat gently.

3 Correct seasoning, adding a little cayenne and more lemon juice, if desired. Serve in individual dishes, garnished with chunks of dark green avocado and parsley.

ROAST LEG OF LAMB WITH GARLIC, LEMON AND PARSLEY DRESSING

>   1 (3½- to 4-pound) leg of lamb
>   1 tablespoon butter
>   4 to 5 potatoes, peeled and sliced
>   Salt and freshly ground black pepper
>   1¼ cups rich chicken stock

Garlic, Lemon and Parsley Dressing:

>   6 cloves garlic, finely chopped
>   6 tablespoons finely chopped parsley
>   6 tablespoons fresh bread crumbs
>   6 tablespoons softened butter
>   Juice of 1 lemon
>   Salt and freshly ground black pepper

1 Have your butcher trim and tie a leg of lamb. Butter a shallow ovenproof casserole or gratin dish just large enough to hold leg of lamb comfortably.

2 Arrange potatoes in the bottom of the dish in overlapping rows. Salt and pepper them generously.

3 Place lamb on the potatoes and pour in

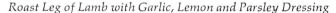

Roast Leg of Lamb with Garlic, Lemon and Parsley Dressing

chicken stock. Season generously with salt and pepper.

4 Roast lamb in a preheated 400°F oven for 25 minutes per pound, or until lamb is pink and tender. If you prefer lamb well done, increase time to 30 minutes per pound.

5 **To make dressing:** make a smooth paste of the garlic, parsley, bread crumbs, butter and lemon juice and season to taste with salt and pepper.

6 One hour before lamb is due to come out of the oven, remove it; allow to cool for 15 minutes, spread it with dressing and return it to the oven for an hour.

OLD ENGLISH TRIFLE

    1 **can peeled whole apricots**
    1 **jelly roll**
  ½ **cup sweet Marsala**
    2 **tablespoons cornstarch**
    2 **tablespoons sugar**
1¼ **cups hot milk**
    3 **egg yolks**
    1 **cup crumbled macaroons**

Topping:

2½ **cups heavy cream**
  ½ **teaspoon vanilla**
     Sugar
     Fresh strawberries or crystallized fruits,
       to garnish

1 Drain syrup from a can of peeled whole apricots. Remove pits and puree apricots in an electric blender. Cut jelly roll into slices. Arrange slices in the bottom of a large glass serving bowl, reserving 4 to 6 for decoration. Pour Marsala over slices and spread apricot puree over them.

2 **To prepare custard:** mix cornstarch and sugar to a smooth paste with a little milk; combine with remaining hot milk in the top of a double boiler and bring to the boil. Cook over water, stirring continuously, until the mixture thickens. Remove from heat and beat in egg yolks one by one. When well blended, simmer gently over water, stirring constantly, for 10

minutes. Stir in crumbled macaroons and leave to soak until soft; then beat well to dissolve them. Cool custard. Arrange reserved jelly roll slices around dish and fill dish with custard. Chill for 2 hours.

3 Just before serving, beat heavy cream with vanilla and sugar to taste until thick. Then, either cover custard with whipped cream and decorate with fresh strawberries or crystallized fruits, or pipe whipped cream over custard, serving remainder separately, and decorate with strawberries or fruits.

ELIZABETH MOXON'S LEMON POSSET

2½ **cups heavy cream**
     Grated rind and juice of 2 lemons
  ½ **cup dry white wine**
     Confectioners' sugar
    3 **egg whites**
     Freshly grated orange peel

Add the lemon rind to cream and beat until stiff. Stir in lemon juice and wine. Add sugar to taste. Beat egg whites until they form peaks, then fold into whipped cream mixture. Serve garnished with a little freshly grated orange rind.

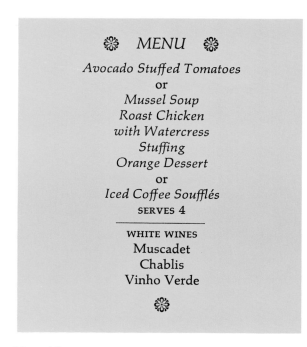

Mussel Soup

AVOCADO STUFFED TOMATOES

   8 to 12 ripe tomatoes

Guacamole Filling:

   2 ripe avocados
      Juice of 1 lemon
   1 to 2 tablespoons onion juice
   1 clove garlic, mashed
      Salt and freshly ground black pepper
      Chili powder to taste
   4 tablespoons finely chopped celery or
         green pepper
   1 tablespoon finely chopped fresh coriander
         or parsley for garnish

   1 Plunge tomatoes into boiling water, one at a time, and holding each tomato in a clean towel, peel off the skin with a sharp knife. Slice off top and carefully scoop out all pulp and seeds. Cover tomatoes loosely with aluminum foil and chill until ready to use.
   2 To make guacamole filling: peel and mash avocados lightly with a wooden spoon. Add lemon juice and seasonings. Fold in celery and chill.
   3 Just before serving, fill each tomato with guacamole mixture; sprinkle with coriander.

MUSSEL SOUP

   1 large onion, finely chopped
   1 clove garlic, finely chopped
   1¼ cups dry white wine
   2½ cups water
   1½ to 2 quarts mussels, cooked in 2½ cups
         water
      Salt and freshly ground black pepper
      Dry mustard
   4 tablespoons butter
   4 tablespoons flour
      Coarsely chopped parsley
      Heart-shaped croutons
      Turmeric (optional)

   1 Cook the onion and garlic in white wine, water and strained mussel liquor until vegetables are soft. Season to taste with salt, pepper and mustard.

2   Make a roux with the butter and flour, and thicken soup. Add the mussels in their shells and reheat soup.

3   Serve sprinkled with parsley and accompanied by croutons. Add a little turmeric, if desired.

ROAST CHICKEN WITH WATERCRESS STUFFING

    1 (3½- to 4-pound) roasting chicken
    3 to 4 strips bacon
       Butter for basting
       Flour
       Watercress for garnish

Stuffing:

      6 tablespoons finely chopped onion
      6 tablespoons finely chopped celery
      6 tablespoons butter
      1 bunch watercress, finely chopped
         Salt and freshly ground black pepper
    1½ cups dry bread crumbs

1   **To make stuffing:** sauté onion and celery in half the butter until soft. Add watercress and season to taste with salt and pepper. Cook until all liquids evaporate.

2   Melt remaining butter; stir in bread crumbs and add to watercress mixture.

3   Stuff chicken with this mixture; place 3 or 4 strips bacon over the breast. Cover the bird with foil and roast in a 325°F oven, removing foil from time to time to baste chicken with butter. Cook chicken for 1 to 1½ hours, according to size. Test it by piercing the flesh of the leg with a skewer or sharp pointed knife. When juices seem clear, it is cooked. But don't be worried if the meat near the bone of the thigh is still a little pink; your chicken will only be more moist if this is so.

4   A few minutes before the end of cooking time, remove the paper and bacon; sprinkle the breast lightly with flour; baste well and brown quickly.

5   **To serve:** put chicken on a hot serving dish and garnish with watercress.

ORANGE DESSERT

    3 tablespoons sugar
    1 tablespoon cornstarch
    6 tablespoons water
   ⅔ cup orange juice
   ½ teaspoon finely sliced orange rind
    2 tablespoons Cointreau
    2 tablespoons cognac
       Pinch of salt
    2 to 3 tablespoons butter
    6 navel oranges
       Sprigs of mint

1   Combine sugar, cornstarch, water and orange juice in the top of a double boiler. Cook over low heat, stirring constantly, until thickened. Remove from heat and stir in orange rind, Cointreau, cognac, salt and butter. Cool.

Orange Dessert

2   To prepare oranges: cut through the rind of each orange vertically from the stem almost to the bud end, forming 8 segments, and curl each segment of peel inward under the fruit at the base of each orange.

3   Loosen orange segments just enough so that they can be eaten easily with a knife and fork. Trim away any excess membrane and glaze oranges lightly with sauce. Chill. Just before serving, spoon a little more sauce over orange sections and decorate with sprigs of mint.

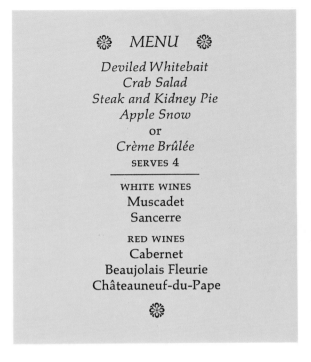

❀ *MENU* ❀

Deviled Whitebait
Crab Salad
Steak and Kidney Pie
Apple Snow
or
Crème Brûlée
SERVES 4

WHITE WINES
Muscadet
Sancerre

RED WINES
Cabernet
Beaujolais Fleurie
Châteauneuf-du-Pape

❀

ICED COFFEE SOUFFLES

    4   **eggs**
    ½   **cup sugar**
    2   **tablespoons instant coffee**
    2   **squares (ounces) unsweetened chocolate**
    2   **tablespoons water**
    2   **tablespoons rum**
  1¼   **cups heavy cream**
        Grated chocolate

1   Separate eggs and beat yolks with sugar and instant coffee until mixture is thick and creamy. Melt chocolate with water in a small saucepan; add rum and stir into egg and coffee mixture.

2   Whip cream and fold into soufflé mixture. Beat egg whites and fold into mixture. Fold in 2 tablespoons grated chocolate; pour into individual soufflé dishes or custard cups and freeze for 4 hours. Decorate with a little grated chocolate.

DEVILED WHITEBAIT

  1½   **pounds whitebait**
        Ice cubes
        Salt and freshly ground black pepper
        Flour
        Lard, for frying
        Cayenne pepper
        Lemon wedges

1   Put whitebait to firm in a shallow bowl with ice cubes and a little water. Just before frying, spread fish on a clean dish towel to dry. Place on paper liberally dusted with well-seasoned flour and dredge with more flour; place in a wire basket, a portion at a time, and shake off surplus flour. Then plunge the basket into very hot lard and fry quickly for 3 to 5 minutes, shaking basket continually to keep fish apart while cooking.

2   Lift basket from fat and shake it well before transferring fish to paper towels to drain. Place whitebait on a serving dish in a warm oven while remainder are fried. Season with freshly ground black pepper and cayenne and serve with lemon wedges.

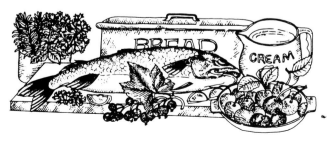

CRAB SALAD

> 1¼ cups homemade mayonnaise (see page 141)
> 2 tablespoons ketchup
>   Tabasco or Worcestershire sauce
> 3 tablespoons olive oil
> 1 tablespoon wine vinegar
> 2 tablespoons finely grated onion
> 2 tablespoons finely chopped parsley
> 6 tablespoons heavy cream, whipped
>   Salt, freshly ground black pepper and
>   cayenne pepper
> 1 to 2 tablespoons chopped olives
> 2 cups cooked crabmeat, flaked
> 4 to 6 tomatoes
>   Lettuce and sliced hard-boiled eggs for
>   garnish

1 Blend together mayonnaise, tomato ketchup, Tabasco sauce, olive oil, vinegar, onion, parsley and whipped cream. Season to taste with salt, pepper and a dash of cayenne. Stir in olives and chill for 1 or 2 hours before serving. This sauce is delicious for all seafood cocktails.

2 Add crabmeat.

3 Slice tomatoes in half; place on salad plates; pile crab salad on tomatoes and garnish with lettuce and hard-boiled eggs.

STEAK AND KIDNEY PIE

> 1½ to 2 pounds beef—chuck, rump, or round
> 1 veal, or small beef kidney
> 4 tablespoons flour
>   Salt and freshly ground black pepper
> 1 cup freshly grated beef suet
> 2½ cups sifted flour
> 1 teaspoon baking powder
>   Butter
> 4 tablespoons finely chopped shallots
>   or onion
> ¾ cup rich beef stock
> 2 to 4 tablespoons port (optional)

1 Cut steak and kidney into rather small pieces. Combine 2 tablespoons flour, ½ teaspoon *each* salt and pepper and coat meat cubes thoroughly with the seasoned flour.

2 Combine suet with sifted flour, adding baking powder and pepper and salt to taste, to make a fairly soft suet crust.

3 Grease a mixing bowl with butter, line it with two-thirds of the pastry and put in the seasoned meat and shallots. Combine stock, and port (if desired), and fill the basin nearly to the top with this mixture, adding a little water if necessary. Roll out the remaining pastry to form the pastry lid, making sure that the edges are well sealed to keep in the steam. Cover the whole pie with a floured cloth and simmer or steam on a rack over boiling water for 3 to 4 hours, replenishing the water as necessary. The crust should be rather damp.

APPLE SNOW

> 1½ pounds tart, green apples
> ¾ cup sugar
>   Lemon juice
> 2 egg whites
>   Whipped cream
>   Toasted slivered almonds

1 Core apples, cut in thick slices and put with very little water in a covered saucepan. Cook until soft; blend in a blender and measure off 1¼ cups puree. Add sugar and lemon juice, to taste. Cool.

2 Beat egg whites until stiff, fold in apple mixture and beat until stiff and fluffy.

3 Pile into tall glasses and decorate with whipped cream and toasted almond slivers.

CREME BRULEE

> 4 tablespoons sugar
> 1 teaspoon cornstarch, dissolved in
>   3 tablespoons water
> 1¼ cups light cream
>   Grated rind of 1 lemon
> ½ to 1 teaspoon vanilla
>   Light brown sugar

1 Add 4 tablespoons sugar and dissolved cornstarch to cream in the top of a double boiler and bring mixture to the boil, stirring constantly.

Steak and Kidney Pie

Then gradually pour the cream over the egg yolks, stirring until well blended. Return egg and cream mixture to the top of the double boiler; add lemon rind to taste and cook over simmering water, stirring, until mixture thickens to a custard-like consistency. When thick enough, flavor with vanilla and pour into an ovenproof soufflé dish or individual soufflé dishes to set. Chill.

2   When thoroughly set, cover with a thick layer of light brown sugar and place under a preheated broiler until the sugar caramelizes. Cool. Chill briefly before serving.

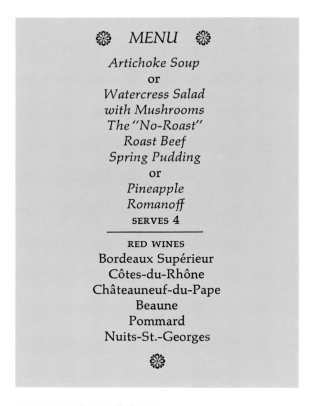

ARTICHOKE SOUP

 1½ pounds Jerusalem artichokes
 4 cups rich chicken stock
 3 large potatoes, peeled and quartered
 1 large onion, quartered
  Salt and freshly ground black pepper
  Freshly grated nutmeg
 1 egg yolk
 1¼ cups light cream

Garnish:

  Lemon slices
  Heavy cream
  Cayenne pepper

1 Put artichokes in a saucepan of cold water and bring gradually to the boil. Drain; cool under running water and then peel.

2 Simmer artichokes in chicken stock with potatoes and onion until all vegetables are soft, 15 to 20 minutes.

3 Puree with stock in an electric blender; season to taste with salt, pepper and nutmeg.

4 Beat egg yolk into cream; add to soup and heat, stirring constantly, until soup is heated through. Do not allow it to come to the boil, or the egg will curdle.

5 Decorate with slices of lemon, topped with a swirl of cream sprinkled with cayenne.

WATERCRESS SALAD WITH MUSHROOMS

 1 bunch watercress
 1 head lettuce
 8 to 12 walnuts
 ¼ to ½ pound mushrooms
  Vinaigrette dressing (see below)
 2 tablespoons finely chopped parsley
 2 tablespoons finely chopped chives

1 Wash and trim the watercress. Wash and dry the lettuce leaves. Shell and halve the walnuts. Wash mushrooms, trim stem ends and slice mushrooms thinly.

2 Make a vinaigrette sauce with 2 tablespoons wine vinegar, 6 to 8 tablespoons olive oil, coarse salt and pepper.

3 Toss walnut halves and sliced mushrooms in the vinaigrette sauce.

4 Line a salad bowl with lettuce leaves. Arrange the prepared watercress in the center. Scatter nuts and sliced mushrooms over, together with vinaigrette sauce. Garnish with herbs. Toss at the table in front of guests.

THE "NO-ROAST" ROAST BEEF

Lovers of perfectly rare beef, pink and juicy from end to end, with just the outer surface richly crusted, should try the following method when next cooking a roast weighing 5 pounds or more. I have attempted to adapt it to smaller pieces of beef, but must admit defeat, which is sad, as the method is otherwise foolproof.

 1 (6-to-9 pound) rib roast of beef
  Salt and freshly ground black pepper
 4 tablespoons butter
 1 teaspoon rosemary
 6 to 8 tablespoons red wine, stock or water

1 Ask your butcher to trim off rib bones close to the meat.

2 Set the oven temperature at 500°F and give the oven at least 20 minutes to heat up before proceeding.

3 Rub roast all over with salt and pepper; spread it with butter and sprinkle with rosemary. Place on a rack in a roasting pan.

4 Put meat into the oven. Roast for 5 minutes per pound; then, without opening the oven door, switch off the heat and leave for a further 2 hours. *Do not, under any circumstances, open the oven door during this time.*

5 When the 2 hours are up, open the door and, without removing the pan from the oven, touch the beef with your finger. If it feels hot, go ahead and serve it. However, as some ovens do not retain their heat as well as others (electricity is often rather better than gas in this instance), you may find the beef on the lukewarm side. If so, close the door, relight the oven, still at 500°F, and give it a further 10 minutes or so. This will raise the temperature of the beef without affecting its rareness.

6 To serve roast beef: when the roast is done to your liking, season it with additional salt and pepper. Transfer it to a heated platter, large enough to allow the carver to operate comfortably, and let it stand for 15 to 20 minutes at the front of the turned-off oven with the door open. This will allow the cooking to stop and the juices to subside, making it easier to carve neatly.

7 In the meantime, pour off most of the fat in the roasting pan and use the juices and sediment that remain, reinforced with a little red wine, stock or water, and the juices that poured from the roast as it "set," to make your gravy. Make sure your gravy boat and plates are very hot, too.

SPRING PUDDING

> **2 pounds spring rhubarb**
> **1½ to 2 cups sugar**
> **3 tablespoons lemon juice**
> **Butter**
> **Thin slices of white bread**
> **Whipped cream**

1 Wash and trim young rhubarb stalks; cut them into 1-inch lengths. Combine rhubarb, sugar, lemon juice and 3 tablespoons butter in a thick-bottomed saucepan. Bring gently to the boil, stirring constantly; lower heat and simmer, stirring all the while, for about 5 minutes, or until rhubarb becomes soft but still keeps its shape. Don't let stalks disintegrate entirely; they must remain slightly firm to be at their best. (Rhubarb varies enormously in flavor when cooked; so add a little more sugar if too tart, a little more lemon juice if too sweet.)

2 Lightly butter a soufflé dish; trim crusts from bread; cut each slice in half lengthwise and line sides of soufflé dish. Then cut enough thin triangles of bread to cover bottom of dish, and trim off bread slices at rim of dish.

3 Fill dish with rhubarb mixture, reserving a little of the juice. Cut additional bread triangles to cover the top of the pudding. Chill in refrigerator overnight.

4 Just before serving, turn pudding out on a serving dish. Pour over reserved rhubarb juice. Serve with whipped cream.

PINEAPPLE ROMANOFF

> **1 large pineapple**
> **6 tablespoons confectioners' sugar**
> **3 tablespoons Cointreau**
> **3 tablespoons rum**
> **1¼ cups heavy cream**
> **3 tablespoons kirsch**
> **Grated rind of 1 orange**

1 Slice top off pineapple. Scoop out flesh to within 1 inch of the bottom, being careful not to damage shell. Dice flesh and toss segments in a bowl with 2 tablespoons of the confectioners' sugar. Pour over them a mixture of Cointreau and rum; chill in the refrigerator.

2 One hour before serving: whip cream; add remaining 4 tablespoons confectioners' sugar and flavor with kirsch. Spoon whipped cream into marinated pineapple pieces, tossing until every piece is coated with creamy liqueur mixture. Spoon into pineapple shell—or into individual dishes—and sprinkle with grated orange rind. Keep cold until time to serve.

One-Dish Meals for Easy Entertaining

If you are a beginning cook—the kind who complains, "I can't even boil water without burning it"—or if you are one of those who stick to steaks and chops because you can't be bothered with all those "fussy little bits"—I say, *cook it in a casserole*. For with a casserole your very first recipe will turn out as if you had been cooking—flawlessly and effortlessly—for years. Casseroles can open the door for you to a whole school of cooking that has produced some of the greatest dishes of the world. Each country has its native one-dish meals, usually brought to the table in the classic earthenware or iron pots in which they have been cooked. These basic, slow-cooked dishes are simple to prepare, improve with keeping and reheating and are much more time-saving, economical and delicious than the so-called shortcut foods that so many cooks rely on today.

The great thing about casserole cooking is that there is no last minute fuss; no worry about plates getting cold while you cope with the carving. If you are giving a dinner party, guests can be late; if it's just you and the family, you can linger over that last drink while your casserole simmers gently in the lowest of ovens.

Most cooks, I think, tend to make things too difficult. They get nervous and tend to over-decorate and be too ambitious with what they want to do. Casserole cookery can be relied on to make even the least desirable cuts of meat taste delicious. Just brown the meat in a little butter or olive oil; season it with herbs—marjoram, rosemary, thyme or tarragon—add a touch of onion or garlic, and then let it simmer in the oven for an hour or two in a sauce made rich with stock, a little wine or a little cream. And even these additives need not be too expensive. A good light stock for a casserole can be made with a cube or a can of bouillon. Perfectly good wines for cooking are still reasonably cheap (especially when you consider that most casserole recipes use no more than a few fluid ounces), and cream is well within the budget for most of us. You'll find that most casseroles seem to go further, too.

I make no bones about it. I far prefer to serve economical cuts of meat for earthy stews and casseroles where long, slow cooking brings out the utmost in flavor and tenderness. French lamb stew, my favorite combination of low-budget meats and vegetables, simmered in a little light stock flavored with tomatoes, makes for delicious eating. A plump chicken, cooked in a little light stock with vegetables—onions, turnips and mushrooms—and then coated with a sauce made rich with egg yolks and cream, makes a Sunday spectacular your friends will rave about.

So be adventurous in trying out new cuts of beef or lamb. You will find the long, slow cooking cuts are good bargains. They are moist and well flavored, they cut well, and they will not turn stringy if simmered in a very slow oven (275°F to 300°F) for beef and veal or a slow oven (325°F) for lamb and pork. Or, if you prefer, you can cook them slowly in a casserole on top of the stove. But either way, make sure that the liquid in which they are cooked barely bubbles.

On lecture tours throughout the world I always tell the cooks in my audience that the liquid in a casserole must never boil or even bubble merrily. It should just go "plop, plop . . . plop" at one side of the casserole if the meat is to be tender and moist. Too quick cooking in liquid tends to make meat stringy and tough. So use this gentle bubbling of the steam escaping from the bottom of the casserole as your guide. You will be able to see at a glance: if the liquid is bubbling all over the casserole your heat is too high.

It is always difficult for me to give exact measurements for a casserole, but as a general rule 2 pounds of meat makes an adequate stew for four persons. But then, if you trim the pieces of meat of skin, bones and surplus fat (leaving some fat with the meat, of course, for succulence and flavor) you should allow an extra ½ pound meat; and if, like me, you are apt to favor ample helpings, it is best to add another ½ pound. So let us say 2½ to 3 pounds meat when boned for a comfortable meal for four persons, allowing

just that little bit extra for larger helpings, or for an unexpected guest. You'll find you can't really have too much of a good thing.

Most casserole dishes are better if allowed to cool, so that the fats may be skimmed off the top, and then brought slowly to the correct temperature before serving. In this way the main dish for your dinner can be prepared in the morning or even the night before, and thus free you for the other pains and pleasures of entertaining.

If you desire, other seasonings may be added while your casserole is reheating. It is really a dash of this or that seasoning that turns an ordinary dish into something special. Here are three delicious casserole dishes, all of which need little more than a salad to turn them into a meal to be proud of. Each one of them could be the basis for a fine little dinner to invite friends to, or a weekend "special" for you and the family to enjoy. All three recipes serve four people.

OSSO BUCCO

The joy of this traditional Italian dish is that the bone with its marrow filling gives substance and flavor. Don't forget to supply a small teaspoon for each guest to extract the deliciously flavored marrow.

   4 **pieces knuckle of veal, with the bone**
      Flour
      Salt and freshly ground black pepper
      Olive oil
   3 **cloves garlic, finely chopped**
   ½ **onion, finely chopped**
   ⅔ **cup chicken stock**
   ⅔ **cup dry white wine**
   4 **to 6 tablespoons tomato paste**
   4 **anchovy fillets, finely chopped**
   4 **tablespoons finely chopped parsley**
      Grated rind of 1 lemon

   1   Choose a knuckle of veal with plenty of meat and have your butcher saw it through the bone into 4 pieces about 2 inches thick and

4 to 6 inches in diameter. Dust pieces with flour and season generously. Simmer in olive oil in a thick-bottomed casserole on top of the stove until lightly browned on each side.

   2   Add 1 clove of the garlic and the onion; pour chicken stock, white wine and tomato paste over the meat. Cover the casserole and continue to simmer over low heat for 1½ hours, adding a little water if sauce gets too dry.

   3   Then add anchovies and remaining garlic. Blend thoroughly, heat through and serve sprinkled with parsley and lemon rind. In Italy this highly flavored dish is always served with **saffron rice.**

Osso Bucco with Easy Saffron Rice

EASY SAFFRON RICE

   ½ teaspoon ground saffron
   6 tablespoons dry white wine
   4 cups chicken stock
   2 cups rice
      Salt and freshly ground black pepper

1 Dissolve saffron in wine; add it to hot chicken stock and combine in a large saucepan with rice and salt and pepper to taste.

2 Cover pan and simmer until all the liquid is absorbed and the rice is tender, about 30 minutes.

BEEF IN BEER

  2½ pounds round, rump or chuck steak,
       1 inch thick
   2 tablespoons olive oil
      Salt and freshly ground black pepper
   2 tablespoons butter
   2 large onions (or 4 medium-sized),
       thinly sliced
   2 tablespoons flour
   1 bottle beer
      Light beef stock (made with a cube)

1 Cut the beef into cubes about 1½ inches square. Season cubes generously with salt and pepper and then brown on all sides in the heated oil. Transfer meat to an ovenproof casserole.

2 Add butter to the frying pan and gently sauté onions until they are soft and just beginning to turn color. Sprinkle onions with flour; stir well and then add mixture to meat in casserole.

3 Add beer and just enough light beef stock (or water, if no stock is available) to cover the meat. Cover the casserole and simmer over a very low heat—or in a very slow oven (275°F) for about 2 hours, or until beef is tender. Check occasionally to make sure that the liquid in the casserole is just simmering, not bubbling. In this way you will ensure that your beef is meltingly tender.

4 Correct seasoning and serve with **mashed potatoes** (see page 67) or **boiled noodles** or **boiled rice** (see page 89).

❊

RED WINES
Beaujolais
Châteauneuf-du-Pape

❊

SUNDAY CHICKEN TARRAGON

1 (3½- to 4-pound) roasting chicken
   Olive oil
   Salt and freshly ground black pepper
1 tablespoon dried tarragon
4 carrots, peeled and halved
4 medium-sized onions
4 mushrooms
4 3-inch pieces celery
4 sprigs fresh parsley
   Light chicken stock (made with a cube)

Sauce:

3 tablespoons butter
2 tablespoons flour
1¼ cups chicken broth
½ cup dry white wine
1 tablespoon dried tarragon
½ cup cream
2 egg yolks

1 Wash a plump, tender roasting chicken, and pat dry. Rub with a little olive oil inside and out, then dust chicken with salt, pepper and tarragon.

2 Place the chicken in a large ovenproof casserole with carrots, onions, mushrooms, celery and parsley. Add chicken stock to almost cover; then cover casserole and cook gently on top of the stove or in a 325°F oven until chicken is tender, removing cover of casserole and skimming froth from time to time. A bird of this size—if simmered at a very low heat to keep it moist and tender—will take from 1 to 1½ hours to cook. Test for tenderness at end of first hour by sticking thigh of bird with the prongs of a fork. When chicken is tender, remove the casserole from the heat and allow chicken to steep in its own liquids while you make the accompanying sauce.

3 **To make sauce:** melt butter in a thick-bottomed saucepan or in the top of a double boiler. Add flour and cook, stirring, over medium heat until flour and butter are bubbling and well blended. Then remove pan from heat. Strain hot chicken broth into a measuring cup and pour it, stirring continuously, into the butter and flour mixture. Return the saucepan to low heat—or, if using a double boiler, place top part over boiling water—and cook, stirring, until sauce begins to thicken. Add wine and tarragon and allow sauce to simmer gently until you are ready to use it.

4 Remove chicken and vegetables from the casserole and cut the bird into serving pieces, removing skin from each part, if desired, to make a more presentable dish.

5 Strain remaining broth into a bowl and put in the refrigerator to use on another day.

6 Wash casserole and return chicken pieces to it. Return carrots, onions and mushrooms to casserole. Put casserole in the lowest of ovens to keep warm.

7 Combine cream and egg yolks in a bowl and you are ready to complete the dish.

8 **To complete dish:** pour a little of the hot sauce into the egg yolk and cream mixture and mix well. Remove remaining sauce from heat and slowly add the egg yolk and cream mixture to it, stirring constantly. Then return pan to the lowest of heats (or over hot but not boiling water) and let sauce simmer gently until it thickens. Check seasoning. Do not let the sauce boil or it will curdle.

9 Spoon hot creamy sauce over chicken and vegetables and serve immediately from the casserole.

WHITE WINES
Muscadet
Sancerre
Chablis
Pouilly Blanc Fumé

Elegant Entertaining —Inexpensively

Three Simple Menus Based on Ground Beef

Good cooks the world over rely on ground beef because it is as easy to cook as it is to eat; because it is economical to buy and a little can be made to go a long way; and because it gives free rein to their inventiveness, for it can be stretched, shaped, seasoned and sauced in a variety of ways. For the best results, of course, it pays to grind the meat yourself, or ask your butcher to do it especially for you. In this way you know exactly what you are getting. Ground beef must not have too much fat, for instance; 2 ounces fat to 1 pound beef is about right.

I have enjoyed super hamburgers and meat loaves in America, pâtés and mousses in France and meatballs in almost every country of the world. Whether the origin of the dish is Moroccan or Egyptian, French or Scandinavian, Greek or Italian, it all comes down to the same basic recipe: *take a pound of ground beef.*

 MENU
Fettuccine al Burro e Formaggio
Italian Stuffed Peppers
Green Salad with Italian Dressing
Cassata alla Siciliana
SERVES 4-6

WHITE WINES
Soave
Verdicchio
Lachryma Christi

FETTUCCINE AL BURRO E FORMAGGIO

1 pound thin noodles
Salt
Freshly grated Parmesan cheese for garnish

Sauce:

8 tablespoons butter
4 to 6 tablespoons heavy cream
1 cup freshly grated Parmesan cheese

1 Cook the noodles in boiling salted water for 5 to 8 minutes until just tender, or a little longer if you like your pasta more thoroughly cooked, stirring it with a fork from time to time to separate the strands.

2 Meanwhile, prepare the sauce: beat the butter until light, then gradually beat in the cream, followed by the cheese.

3 When cooked, drain the noodles and turn immediately into the Parmesan mixture. Toss to coat the strands thoroughly with the sauce. Sprinkle with additional Parmesan and serve immediately.

ITALIAN STUFFED PEPPERS

> 4 to 6 green peppers
> Olive oil
> Butter
> Salt and freshly ground black pepper
> 1 large onion, finely chopped
> 1 pound ground round or chuck
> Freshly grated nutmeg
> 2 tablespoons grated Parmesan cheese
> 12 black olives, pitted and chopped
> 3 tablespoons seedless raisins
> 2 tablespoons chopped chives
> 2 tablespoons chopped parsley
> 1¼ cups chicken stock
> Strips of canned pimento

1 Remove the tops of the peppers and scoop out pith and seeds. Place peppers in boiling water to cover; add 2 tablespoons olive oil and set aside for 5 minutes. Drain well and dry.

2 Place a small pat of butter in the bottom of each pepper and season well. Sauté onion in 4 tablespoons olive oil until onion is soft. Add beef and continue to cook, stirring constantly, until meat just begins to brown. Drain off excess fat, if necessary. Add salt, pepper, nutmeg, Parmesan cheese, black olives, raisins, chives and parsley and mix well.

3 Stuff peppers with this mixture and place in a flat ovenproof dish. Pour chicken stock over peppers and bake in a preheated 375°F oven for 30 to 40 minutes, or until done, basting them frequently. Just before serving garnish each pepper with thin strips of pimento. Serve hot as a main course, cold as an appetizer.

Italian Stuffed Peppers

GREEN SALAD WITH ITALIAN DRESSING

> 1 to 2 heads lettuce

Italian Dressing:

> 1 tablespoon lemon juice
> 1 to 2 tablespoons wine vinegar
> ¼ teaspoon dry mustard
> Pinch of dried oregano
> Coarse salt and freshly ground black pepper
> 6 to 8 tablespoons olive oil

1 Wash lettuce leaves in a large quantity of water. They should be left whole, never cut.

Drain well and dry thoroughly so that there is no water left on them to dilute the dressing.

2 To make dressing: combine lemon juice, vinegar, mustard and oregano, and season to taste with salt and pepper. Add olive oil and beat with a fork until the mixture is well blended.

CASSATA ALLA SICILIANA

    1 pint vanilla ice cream
  ½ pint strawberry or raspberry ice cream
      Chopped crystallized fruits
      Chopped nuts
  ½ pint pistachio ice cream
      Crystallized fruits for decoration

1 Spoon vanilla ice cream evenly around the inside of a 2-pint bombe mold and place a smaller mold or bowl in the center to hold the ice cream in position. Freeze.

2 Carefully remove the inner mold. Spoon the strawberry ice cream inside the vanilla layer and, as before, place a still smaller mold or bowl in the center. Freeze.

3 Carefully remove the center mold. Stir the crystallized fruits and nuts into the pistachio ice cream. Remove the center mold and fill with the pistachio ice cream. Freeze once more.

4 To serve: unmold and decorate with crystallized fruits.

Cassata alla Siciliana

 MENU
Moroccan Meatballs
with
Mashed Potatoes
and
Sautéed Zucchini and Tomatoes
Moroccan Orange Salad
SERVES 4-6

WHITE WINES
Gewürztraminer
Alsatian
Vinho Verde

MOROCCAN MEATBALLS

    1 pound ground beef or lamb
    4 tablespoons butter
  ½ large onion, finely chopped
    6 mint leaves, finely chopped
    6 sprigs parsley, finely chopped
  ¼ teaspoon dried marjoram
  ¼ teaspoon ground cumin
  ¼ teaspoon cayenne pepper
  ¼ teaspoon paprika
  ¼ teaspoon cinnamon
      Salt and freshly ground black pepper
      Butter

Sauce:

    4 to 5 tomatoes, peeled, seeded and coarsely chopped
  ½ large onion, finely chopped
    2 tablespoons finely chopped parsley
    1 clove garlic, finely chopped
    4 tablespoons olive oil
    1 cup water
      Paprika
      Cayenne pepper
      Salt

1 Combine meat and butter with onion, mint leaves and parsley. Mix well and add marjoram, cumin, cayenne, paprika and cinnamon, together with salt and pepper to taste.

2 Form into little balls the size of a marble and poach gently in water for 10 minutes. Then sauté gently in butter until lightly browned.

3 **To make sauce:** combine tomatoes with onion, parsley, garlic, olive oil, water. Add paprika, cayenne and salt, to taste (the sauce, too, should be very spicy), in a saucepan and simmer for 1 hour, uncovered.

4 Finally, simmer meatballs in sauce for at least 10 minutes before serving. Serve in sauce or on a bed of **boiled rice** (see page 89) or **mashed potatoes** (see next recipe) with sauce passed separately.

MASHED POTATOES

> **2 pounds potatoes**
> **Salt**
> **1 cup hot milk**
> **4 tablespoons butter, melted**
> **4 tablespoons heavy cream**
> **Freshly ground black pepper**
> **Freshly grated nutmeg**

1 Peel potatoes and if they are very large, cut them up into roughly even-sized pieces.

2 Boil potatoes in salted water until they feel soft when pierced with a fork but are not mushy. (Overcooked potatoes will produce a soggy puree, not a fluffy one as you might expect.)

3 As soon as potatoes are cooked, drain them thoroughly and toss in the dry pan over moderate heat until remaining moisture has completely evaporated.

4 Mash potatoes to a smooth puree and return them to the pan.

5 Gradually beat in hot milk with a wooden spoon or whisk. (If potatoes are particularly dry, you may need to use more milk.) Then add melted butter and cream and continue to beat vigorously until potatoes are light and fluffy.

6 Season to taste with salt, pepper and a grating of fresh nutmeg, and beat over a moderate heat until potatoes are thoroughly hot again. Take great care not to let them boil, or they may discolor. Serve immediately.

Note: Although ideally mashed potatoes should be served as soon as prepared, you can keep them hot for up to half an hour by putting them in a buttered mixing bowl over hot water, covered with well-buttered waxed paper. Just before serving, beat again to restore texture.

SAUTEED ZUCCHINI AND TOMATOES

> **12 zucchini**
> **Salt**
> **6 tablespoons flour**
> **6 tablespoons freshly grated Parmesan cheese**
> **Freshly ground black pepper**
> **4 tablespoons olive oil**
> **4 tablespoons butter**
> **1 large onion, coarsely chopped**
> **6 tomatoes, peeled, seeded and chopped**
> **4 coriander seeds, crushed**

1 Slice zucchini thickly and cook in boiling salted water until just tender, about 5 minutes. Drain thoroughly, then dry slices with paper towels.

2 Combine flour with Parmesan cheese, salt and pepper to taste. Toss zucchini slices in this mixture until lightly coated.

3 Heat oil in a heavy skillet and sauté zucchini over a moderate heat until golden brown on all sides. Remove from skillet with a slotted spoon; drain thoroughly on paper towel. Pile in center of a serving dish and keep hot.

4 Melt butter in skillet and sauté onion until soft and transparent. Add tomatoes and coriander seeds and simmer for 2 to 3 minutes longer.

5 Surround zucchini with sautéed onion and tomato mixture. Serve hot.

MOROCCAN ORANGE SALAD

> **4 to 6 ripe oranges**
> **6 to 8 dates, chopped**
> **6 to 8 blanched almonds, slivered**
> **Lemon juice and confectioners' sugar**
> **Ground cinnamon**

1 Peel oranges, removing all pith, and slice crosswise. Place in a salad bowl with dates and almonds and flavor to taste with lemon juice and sugar.

2 Chill. Just before serving, sprinkle lightly with cinnamon.

❀ *MENU* ❀

Meat Loaf
with
Baked Stuffed Potatoes
and
Tomatoes Provençale
Fruits in Marsala
or
Strawberries with Marsala and Pernod
SERVES 4

RED WINES
Mâcon Rouge
Beaujolais
Valpolicella

❀

BAKED STUFFED POTATOES

 6 **medium-sized cold baked potatoes**
 4 **tablespoons light cream**
 4 **tablespoons softened butter**
 4 **to 6 tablespoons freshly grated**
    Parmesan cheese
    Salt and freshly ground black pepper

1 Preheat oven to 375°F.
2 Cut a thin slice from each potato and with a spoon scoop out the potato into a bowl, leaving a firm shell.
3 Mash potato smoothly with cream, butter and Parmesan and season with salt and pepper.
4 Pile the mashed potato back into shells and place potatoes on a wire rack.
5 Bake for 25 to 30 minutes, or until potatoes are heated through.

MEAT LOAF

 2 **pounds ground lean beef or 1½ pounds**
    ground beef and ½ pound ground pork
    or sausage
 1 **large onion, finely chopped**
 2 **teaspoons salt**
    Freshly ground black pepper
 ½ **teaspoon dried rosemary, marjoram or sage**
 2 **eggs, well beaten**
 4 **slices white bread**
 ½ **cup milk or light beef or chicken stock**
    Butter
 2 **slices bacon**

1 In a large mixing bowl combine beef with onion, salt, pepper, rosemary and eggs.
2 Trim crusts from bread and shred into milk or stock. Add bread and liquid to the meat mixture and blend thoroughly.
3 Pack mixture into a lightly buttered loaf pan 9 × 5 × 2½ inches mounding it slightly on top (or, if you prefer, shape it into a long, thin loaf on a baking sheet); top with bacon slices and bake in a 350°F oven for 1¼ hours. Serve hot—or cold as a picnic loaf.

TOMATOES PROVENÇALE

 4 **firm tomatoes**
    Butter
    French mustard
    Salt and freshly ground black pepper
 ½ **to ¾ cup soft white bread crumbs**
 2 **tablespoons finely chopped parsley**
 2 **to 3 teaspoons olive oil**

1 Grease a wide, shallow baking dish lightly with butter.
2 Slice tomatoes in half horizontally and arrange them side by side in the dish, cut sides up. Spread lightly with mustard and season with salt and black pepper.
3 Toss bread crumbs with parsley and sprinkle over tomatoes. Trickle a little olive oil over each tomato.
4 Bake on shelf below meat loaf (350°F) for 20 minutes, or until bread crumbs are brown.

Italian Fruits in Marsala

FRUITS IN MARSALA

   1 cup sugar
 ¾ cup water
   Juice of 1 lemon
 ⅔ cup Marsala
   4 to 6 small peaches
   1 small pineapple
   1 half pint strawberries

1   Dissolve the sugar in water and lemon juice, and boil to form a heavy syrup. Allow to cool. Stir in Marsala and leave until cold.

2   Blanch the peaches by plunging quickly into boiling water, then remove the skins. Immerse in the syrup.

3   Peel the pineapple and cut into thick slices. Add to the peaches. Wash the strawberries, but do not remove the stems and leaves. Stir into the syrup.

4   Chill thoroughly before serving.

STRAWBERRIES WITH MARSALA AND PERNOD

 1½ pints of ripe strawberries
   Juice of 1 lemon
   6 tablespoons Marsala
   3 tablespoons Pernod
   Sugar

Wash and hull strawberries, discarding any berries that are not perfect. Slice strawberries in half and sprinkle with lemon juice, Marsala and Pernod. Toss well and add sugar, to taste. Chill until ready to serve.

Making the Most of Lamb

 MENU

Taramasalata
Lamb Hash Parmentier
Tossed Green Salad
Cheeses and Fruit
SERVES 4-6

WHITE WINES
Retsina
Muscadet
Sancerre

Meat is expensive today. With increasing inflation around the world, it is most important that we get the most out of every cut of meat. A leg of lamb—lean, with a small amount of bone—may be roasted as it is; boned by your butcher and then stuffed; poached in stock and served with caper sauce; or braised or casseroled in any number of ways. If a whole leg is too large for a small family, ask your butcher to cut it into two pieces; one to roast, the other to braise or stew. Or cook the whole roast and then use the leftovers for one or two delicious meals based on tender, succulent lamb.

Choosing Lamb

High-quality lamb is firm and fine textured, varying in color from dark pink to light red. It has a smooth covering of clear pinkish-white brittle fat over most of the exterior. Over this is a thin paperlike covering called the "fell." It is not necessary to remove this fell from the leg before roasting. In fact if you leave it on the leg it will hold its shape better, be juicier and cook faster.

COOKING LAMB

Lamb should never be overcooked. It is at its succulent best—moist and richly flavored—when it is just a little pink on the inside. So do not roast it until it is a dull grayish-brown in color, with the meat falling off the bones, the flesh dry and stringy. Instead treat lamb gently, as the French do, roasting it until the juices run pink when it is cut. For maximum juiciness and minimum shrinkage, I like to sear it in a hot oven for 15 minutes and then cook it at a relatively low temperature (325°F) for 15 to 20 minutes per pound.

TARAMASALATA

 1 **(6-ounce) jar smoked cod's roe**
 6 **slices white bread**
 ¼ **large onion, grated**
 1 **to 2 cloves garlic, mashed**
 8 **tablespoons olive oil**
 6 **tablespoons heavy cream**
  Juice of 1 lemon
 1 **teaspoon gelatin dissolved in 1 tablespoon water**
 1 **tablespoon finely chopped parsley**
  Black olives
  Hot toast

1 Place roe in a mortar. Trim crusts from bread; soak bread in water; squeeze lightly and add to roe. Pound mixture to a smooth paste. Stir in onion and garlic. Then add olive oil, cream and lemon juice alternately in small amounts, stirring well, until the mixture is smooth and uniform.

2 Transfer to a blender and blend until smooth.

3 Beat in dissolved gelatin.

4 Pipe mixture into individual soufflé dishes or ramekins, sprinkle with parsley and garnish with black olives.

5 Serve with hot toast. I also like to stuff 2-inch lengths of crisp celery with this mixture as a light appetizer.

LAMB HASH PARMENTIER

    6 medium-sized potatoes
    4 tablespoons butter
    1 egg, well beaten
       Salt and freshly ground black pepper
       Butter
       Olive oil
    1 onion, finely chopped
    1 pound cooked lamb, diced
 1¼ cups rich tomato sauce (or thickened
       tomato-flavored lamb gravy)
    3 to 4 tablespoons freshly grated
       Parmesan cheese

1 Peel and boil potatoes. Mash 4 of them with butter and egg; season to taste with salt and pepper and force through a pastry bag to make a border around a shallow ovenproof dish.

2 Dice remaining 2 potatoes and fry in equal quantities of butter and olive oil until golden. Drain and reserve.

3 Sauté onion in 2 tablespoons olive oil until transparent. Add lamb to onion in pan and continue to cook until both begin to turn golden. Season generously with salt and pepper. Stir in fried potatoes; pour in tomato sauce and simmer gently for 10 to 15 minutes, stirring from time to time. Correct seasoning.

4 Spoon hash into center of potato border; sprinkle with Parmesan cheese and bake in a 450° oven for 10 to 12 minutes, or until golden brown.

TOSSED GREEN SALAD

(For recipe, see **green salad and variations, page 146.**)

CHEESES AND FRUIT

(For **cheeses,** see pages 146–147.)

French Cucumber Salad

 MENU

French Cucumber Salad
Lamb in the French Manner
with
Pommes au Beurre
Fresh Strawberries with Raspberry Puree
SERVES 4-6

RED WINES
Pomerol
Beaujolais
Fleurie

FRENCH CUCUMBER SALAD

    1 large cucumber, or 2 small ones
    1 tablespoon salt
       French dressing (see below)
    2 tablespoons finely chopped fresh parsley
    1 tablespoon finely chopped fresh tarragon
       Salted whipped cream

1 Peel and slice cucumber thinly; sprinkle with salt and place under a weighted plate in a glass bowl for at least 1 hour. Wash well; drain.

2 Make a French dressing with 3 tablespoons olive oil, 1 tablespoon wine vinegar, salt and freshly ground black pepper, to taste.

3 Place drained cucumber slices in a serving bowl; add dressing and toss. Chill in refrigerator for at least 30 minutes.

4 Just before serving, sprinkle with parsley and tarragon, and garnish with whipped cream to which you have added salt to taste.

LAMB IN THE FRENCH MANNER

   1 to 2 cloves garlic
   1 (3½- to 4-pound) leg of lamb
   1 teaspoon crushed rosemary leaves
   Juice of ½ lemon
   4 tablespoons softened butter
   Salt and freshly ground black pepper

1 Cut garlic cloves into slivers. Make small slits in lamb and insert slivers.

2 Combine rosemary with lemon juice, butter, salt and pepper, to taste.

3 Spread lamb with this mixture and place on a rack in a roasting pan. Roast meat, uncovered, in a preheated 450°F oven for 20 minutes; reduce oven temperature to 325°F and continue to roast for 20 minutes per pound, or until done to your taste.

4 When lamb is cooked, transfer to a heated serving platter and let it stand for 15 minutes before carving.

POMMES AU BEURRE

   2 pounds potatoes
   Oil for deep-frying
   Salt and freshly ground black pepper
   Butter
   Oil
   Finely chopped fresh parsley

1 Peel the potatoes and cut them into small balls with a melon scoop or a vegetable cutter. Soak the potato balls in ice water for 1 hour, then dry them well with paper towels.

2 In a large frying pan or deep-fryer, heat

Pommes au Beurre

the oil to 370°F. Cook potato balls until golden; then remove, drain and season generously with salt and pepper.

3 Just before serving, sauté potato balls in equal parts of butter and oil until brown and cooked through.

4 Drain; sprinkle with parsley and serve immediately.

FRESH STRAWBERRIES WITH RASPBERRY PUREE

   2 pints fresh strawberries
   2 pints fresh raspberries
   Lemon juice
   Confectioners' sugar

1 Wash and hull strawberries; chill.

2 Put raspberries in electric blender with 2 tablespoons *each* lemon juice and sugar and blend until smooth, adding more sugar or lemon juice as desired. Strain into a bowl and chill.

3 **To serve:** pile strawberries into a glass serving bowl and spoon over raspberry puree, covering each berry with the puree. Serve immediately.

Leg of Lamb and Accompanying Spices

Italian Cauliflower Appetizer

ITALIAN CAULIFLOWER APPETIZER

  1 **cauliflower**
    Salt
  6 **anchovy fillets, finely chopped**
12 **black olives, pitted and finely chopped**
  3 **tablespoons finely chopped parsley**
  1 **clove garlic, finely chopped**
  1 **tablespoon finely chopped capers**
  6 **tablespoons olive oil**
  2 **tablespoons wine vinegar**
    Freshly ground black pepper

Garnish (optional):

Anchovy fillets
Halved tomatoes

1 Remove green leaves from cauliflower, trim stem and cut off any bruised spots. Break or cut into flowerets and poach in lightly salted water for about 5 minutes. Drain and place in a bowl of cold, salted water for 1 hour. Drain well.

2 Combine anchovies, olives, parsley, garlic and capers with oil and vinegar in a large mixing bowl; add cauliflower and season with salt and pepper to taste. Allow cauliflower to marinate for at least 2 hours in this dressing.

3 **To serve:** arrange marinated cauliflower and dressing in a salad dish; garnish, if desired, with anchovy strips and tomatoes.

ITALIAN SAUTE OF LAMB

4 **to 6 large, firm tomatoes**
4 **tablespoons olive oil**
1 **pound cooked lamb, cut into strips**
  Salt and freshly ground black pepper
2 **cloves garlic, finely chopped**
6 **scallions, thinly sliced**
6 **tablespoons finely chopped parsley**
  Grated rind of ½ lemon

1 Drop tomatoes into boiling water for about 30 seconds. Peel them at once and cut into quarters. Remove seeds from each quarter; cut remaining outer shell and membranes of each tomato quarter into thin strips.

2 Heat olive oil in the bottom of a large thick-bottomed frying pan; add lamb strips and cook over a high heat until well browned on all sides. Season generously with salt and pepper and 1 clove of the garlic. Add tomato strips and continue to cook, stirring constantly, for about 3 minutes, or until the tomato strips are barely cooked through.

3 Add the scallions and parsley. Toss well over heat; then sprinkle with lemon rind and remaining garlic; cover pan and allow to heat through for 3 minutes before serving. Serve with **boiled rice** (see page 89) and **zucchini à la Grecque.**

ZUCCHINI A LA GRECQUE

- 8 **small zucchini**
  Salt
- 4 **tablespoons butter**
- 1 **medium-sized onion, chopped**
- 1 **clove garlic, finely chopped**
- 4 **ripe tomatoes, peeled, seeded and chopped**
  Freshly ground black pepper

1 Score zucchini lengthwise with the tines of a fork or the end of a pointed teaspoon. Poach them lightly in ⅔ cup salted water and 2 tablespoons of the butter for 6 to 8 minutes, depending on size of zucchini. Keep warm in cooking liquid.

2 Sauté onion and garlic in remaining 2 tablespoons butter until transparent. Add tomatoes and cook until soft but not mushy. Season generously with salt and pepper.

3 Remove zucchini from cooking liquid; drain and arrange in a heated oblong gratin dish. Pour over tomato and onion mixture and serve immediately.

BAKED VANILLA CUSTARD

- 4 **egg yolks**
- 2 **egg whites**
  Sugar
  Pinch of salt
- ½ **teaspoon vanilla**
- 2½ **cups milk**
  Butter

1 Beat the egg yolks and whites in a bowl with 2 tablespoons superfine sugar, salt and vanilla.

2 Heat the milk without allowing it to boil and pour it slowly into the eggs, stirring constantly. Strain the mixture into a well-buttered soufflé dish.

3 Place the dish in a baking pan with a little cold water around it and cook in a 375°F oven for about 1 hour, or until the custard sets and the top is golden brown. (The water in the pan will prevent the custard from becoming too hot and curdling.)

4 Sprinkle with a little sugar before serving.

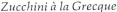

Zucchini à la Grecque

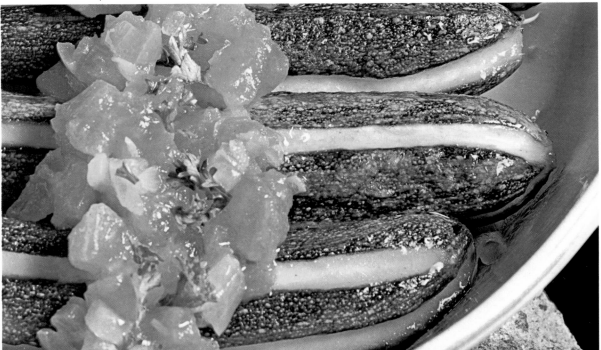

It's All a Skewer

Onions à la Grecque

Skewered meats are famous the world over. Whether they are called kebabs (as they are in Turkey and the Middle East), brochettes (in France and North Africa) or satés (the Far East and Polynesia), these tender morsels of meat, fish or poultry—first marinated, then threaded on metal or bamboo skewers and grilled—add up to the same thing: a delicious meal-on-a-stick.

If you have never tried making kebabs or brochettes in your own kitchen, now is the time to start. You will find they are wonderfully easy to make, for most of the preparation is done in advance, and the actual cooking time is a matter of minutes only. And cutting up the meat, fish or poultry into small squares makes a little go a long way.

The secret of all skewer cookery lies in the marinade. One of the simplest I know—and equally good for beef, lamb, pork, chicken, fish or shellfish—is the following: combine 4 tablespoons each olive oil and lemon juice with 2 tablespoons finely chopped parsley, 2 crumbled bay leaves, a little finely chopped onion or garlic, salt and freshly ground black pepper to taste.

MOROCCAN SPICE MARINADE

White part of 1 leek, chopped
½ **large onion, chopped**
1 **teaspoon sea salt**
½ **teaspoon each of ground cumin and ginger, and coarse-ground black pepper**
4 **tablespoons olive oil**
Cayenne pepper and paprika

Pound leek, onion and salt in a mortar; add to meat and sprinkle with cumin, ginger and black pepper. Add olive oil and cayenne and paprika, to taste. Mix well.

TURKISH MARINADE

White part of 1 leek, chopped
½ **onion, chopped**
6 **tablespoons chopped parsley**
6 **tablespoons olive oil**
Salt and freshly ground black pepper

Combine leek, onion, parsley and olive oil. Add generous amounts of salt and pepper. Mix well.

Marinate meat in one of the above marinades for at least 2 hours, or overnight. Then thread the cubed meat on long metal skewers (the flat-edged variety are the best) alternately with the vegetables of your choice.

Do not push the pieces of meat and vegetables too closely together or the meat will not cook all the way through. To broil, place skewers about 3 or 4 inches from the heat and cook—turning skewers occasionally—until the meat is medium brown, basting with the marinade juices from time to time. I like lamb and beef cooked until they are well browned on the outside, but still moist and pink on the inside. Try broiling a test skewer—with just a vegetable or two on it—to see how long you should cook kebabs so that they are done to your liking.

The choice of kebab variations is practically limitless: arrange meats, poultry or fish on skewers alternately with your choice of small white onions, either raw or poached, strips of green pepper, cubes of poached potato, mushroom caps, sliced eggplant, thin wedges of apple or tomato (wrapped in bacon to keep them from falling off the skewer) or whole cherry tomatoes.

MENU

Onions à la Grecque
Turkish Lamb Kebabs
with
Saffron Rice Salad
Raspberry Bavarois
SERVES 4

RED WINES
Médoc
Beaujolais
Mâcon

ONIONS A LA GRECQUE

- 2 **pounds small onions**
- 2½ **cups water**
- ½ **to 1 cup dry white wine**
- ½ **cup sugar**
- 1 **cup raisins**
- 4 **tablespoons tomato paste**
- 4 **tablespoons olive oil**
- 2 **to 4 tablespoons wine vinegar**
  Salt and freshly ground black pepper
  Cayenne pepper
  Coarsely chopped parsley

1   Peel onions. Combine in a saucepan with water, wine, sugar, raisins, tomato paste and olive oil. Add vinegar, salt, pepper and cayenne, to taste. Simmer for about 15 minutes, or until onions are tender but still quite firm.

2   Serve cold, garnished with parsley.

TURKISH LAMB KEBABS

- 2 **pounds lamb, cut from the leg**
- 4 **tiny green peppers, caps and seeds removed (or 4 squares cut from 1 green pepper)**
- 4 **small tomatoes**
- 4 **mushroom caps**
- 2 **small zucchini, thickly sliced**

Marinade:

- 6 **tablespoons olive oil**
- 4 **tablespoons sherry**
- 1 **to 2 cloves garlic, finely chopped**

- ¼ **large onion, finely chopped**
- 2 **tablespoons finely chopped parsley**
- 1 **teaspoon oregano**
  Salt and freshly ground black pepper

1   Combine marinade ingredients in a mixing bowl. Cut meat into 1-inch squares and place in marinade mixture, making sure each piece of meat is completely covered. Cover bowl with plastic wrap and refrigerate for 12 to 24 hours. Turn meat several times during marinating period.

2   When ready to cook, place meat on 4 large skewers, alternating with green peppers, tomatoes and mushroom caps.

3   Brush meat and vegetables with marinade and cook over charcoal or under the broiler until done, turning skewers frequently and basting several times during cooking. Serve with **saffron rice salad**.

SAFFRON RICE SALAD

- ½ **teaspoon ground saffron**
- ¼ **teaspoon ground cumin**
- 6 **tablespoons dry white wine**
- 2½ **cups hot chicken stock**
- 1½ **cups Italian rice for risotto**
- ½ **green pepper, seeded and cut into squares**
- ½ **red pepper, seeded and cut into squares**
- ½ **onion, coarsely chopped**
  Salt and freshly ground black pepper

Dressing:

- 6 **to 8 tablespoons olive oil**
- 2 **to 3 tablespoons wine vinegar**
- 2 **tablespoons finely chopped parsley**
  Salt and freshly ground black pepper

1   Dissolve saffron and cumin in white wine and chicken stock. Combine in a large saucepan with rice, pepper squares, onion, salt and pepper, to taste. Cover pan and simmer until all the liquid is absorbed and the rice is tender. Add more liquid if necessary. Drain well.

2   Combine olive oil and wine vinegar; add finely chopped parsley and salt and freshly ground black pepper to taste. Add to rice salad;

toss and allow to cool. Add more oil or vinegar, if necessary.

RASPBERRY BAVAROIS

  1 **package frozen raspberries**
  6 **tablespoons sugar**
  3 **egg yolks**
1¼ **cups milk**
  ½ **envelope gelatin**
    Juice of 1 lemon
1¼ **cups heavy cream**
    Oil for mold

1 Place raspberries in a strainer over a bowl and sprinkle with 2 tablespoons sugar. Set aside until completely defrosted.

2 Beat remaining sugar with egg yolks until light and fluffy.

3 Scald milk. Add egg and sugar mixture gradually, beating constantly.

4 Transfer mixture to the top of a double boiler and stir over simmering water until sauce thickens enough to coat the back of a wooden spoon. Take care not to let it boil or egg yolks will curdle. Remove from heat and cool slightly.

5 Meanwhile, soften gelatin for 5 minutes in 4 tablespoons of the syrup from the raspberries; then stir over hot water until liquid is clear and gelatin completely dissolved.

6 Cool gelatin mixture slightly. Blend with cooling custard.

7 Puree two-thirds of the raspberries, reserving the best ones, in a blender. Combine puree with custard; then fold in whole fruit, taking care not to crush them. Add lemon juice to taste.

8 Whip half the cream lightly. Fold into raspberry custard.

9 Brush a 4-cup decorative mold with about 1 tablespoon oil. Pour in the raspberry cream and chill until firm.

10 When ready to serve: whip remaining cream stiffly.

11 Dip mold for 1 or 2 seconds only into very hot water. Turn bavarois out on to a serving dish and pipe whipped cream in a decorative pattern over top and sides. Serve very cold.

Turkish Lamb Kebabs

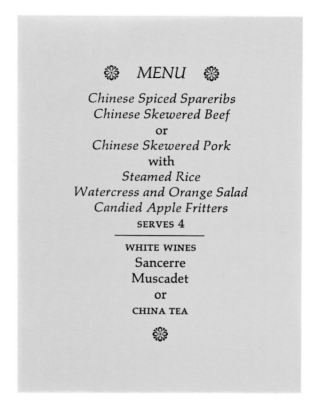

❀ *MENU* ❀

Chinese Spiced Spareribs
Chinese Skewered Beef
or
Chinese Skewered Pork
with
Steamed Rice
Watercress and Orange Salad
Candied Apple Fritters
SERVES 4

WHITE WINES
Sancerre
Muscadet
or
CHINA TEA

❀

CHINESE SPICED SPARERIBS

  4 **tablespoons dry sherry**
  4 **tablespoons soy sauce**
  1 **tablespoon sugar**
  2 **cloves garlic, finely chopped**
  ¼ **teaspoon each cinnamon, grated nutmeg
     and ground cloves**
    Salt
  2 **pounds spareribs**
    Hot mustard

1 Combine the sherry, soy sauce, sugar, garlic and spices. Add a little salt, if desired. Marinate the spareribs in this mixture for at least 2 hours.

2 When ready to cook, place the spareribs on a rack in a roasting pan and cook in a preheated 325°F oven for 1 hour, basting frequently with the marinade juices.

3 Cut into separate "ribs" and serve with hot mustard.

CHINESE SKEWERED BEEF

    1 to 1¼ pounds tender rump or sirloin steak
      Freshly ground black pepper
    1 tablespoon soy sauce
    1 tablespoon oyster sauce
    1 to 2 tablespoons fermented black beans
    1 tablespoon sugar
    1 tablespoon olive oil
    2 tablespoons dry white wine

    1 Cut beef into 1-inch cubes, removing fat and gristle. Put in a large bowl. Sprinkle with pepper.

    2 Combine soy sauce, oyster sauce, black beans (all available from Chinese supermarkets) and add sugar, olive oil and wine. Pour marinade over meat and toss well. Set aside to marinate for 2 hours.

    3 Preheat broiler at highest heat for 20 minutes before cooking.

    4 Divide marinated meat among 6 skewers. Assemble brochettes.

    5 Broil 6 to 8 minutes for rare beef, turning skewers frequently to ensure even cooking; 8 to 10 minutes for medium rare; and 10 to 15 minutes for well done. Serve immediately.

CHINESE SKEWERED PORK

    2 pounds lean pork
    1 teaspoon dry mustard
    ½ teaspoon ground ginger
    1 onion, finely chopped
    1 clove garlic, finely chopped
    4 tablespoons lemon juice
      Salt and freshly ground black pepper
    1 to 2 tablespoons honey

    1 **Advance preparation:** cut pork into 1-inch squares. Put these into a large mixing bowl and sprinkle with mustard, ginger, onion, garlic, lemon juice, salt and pepper, to taste.

    2 Add honey and toss well to coat meat thoroughly. Marinate for at least 2 hours, turning occasionally, so that meat is well flavored.

    3 **When ready to broil:** arrange pork on metal skewers and broil 3 to 4 inches from heat until done. To test pork: cut a piece open with

Chinese Spiced Spareribs

the point of a sharp knife. Pork is done only when there is no trace of pinkness in cut piece of meat.

    4 Serve with **steamed rice** and a **watercress and orange salad.**

STEAMED RICE

    4 tablespoons lemon juice
      Salt
    1½ cups long-grain rice

    1 Fill a large pan two-thirds full of water. Add lemon juice and a small handful of salt and bring to the boil.

    2 When water is bubbling briskly, pour in rice. Stir to dislodge any grains that have attached themselves to the bottom. Boil, uncovered, for 10 to 12 minutes. Rice should be cooked, but still very firm.

    3 Drain rice thoroughly in a colander.

    4 Cut a large square of double-thick cheesecloth. Heap rice in the center and wrap up in a loose bundle.

5 Place bundle in a steamer over boiling water. Cover tightly and steam for 20 to 25 minutes, or until rice grains are fluffy, tender and quite separate.

WATERCRESS AND ORANGE SALAD

    4 bunches watercress
    2 oranges

Dressing:

    6 to 8 tablespoons olive oil
    2 tablespoons wine vinegar
    1 teaspoon Dijon mustard
      Salt and freshly ground black pepper
    1 to 2 tablespoons finely chopped scallions
        or chives

1 Prepare watercress and chill in a damp towel. Peel oranges, cut into thin segments and chill.

2 Combine olive oil, vinegar and mustard. Season to taste with salt and pepper. Add scallions and mix well.

3 Just before serving, place watercress in a salad bowl, arrange orange segments on top and pour over dressing.

CANDIED APPLE FRITTERS

    ¾ cup sifted flour
      Pinch of salt
    1 small egg, well beaten
    1 cup water
      Peanut oil for deep-frying
    4 dessert apples, peeled, cored and cut
        into eighths
    6 tablespoons sugar
    3 tablespoons water
      Sesame seeds
      Butter

1 To make batter: sift the flour and salt into a mixing bowl. Gradually blend in the egg and the 1 cup water. Beat together until smooth. Set batter aside in a cool place for at least ½ hour.

2 When ready to cook the fritters, heat the peanut oil to 375°F. Dip the apple wedges into the batter and deep-fry in hot oil until golden. Drain and keep hot.

3 To make caramel: very slowly melt the sugar in 3 tablespoons water in a thick-bottomed pan. Boil until a pale golden color.

4 Remove from the heat. Quickly dip each apple fritter into hot caramel, sprinkle with sesame seeds and serve on a hot buttered dish.

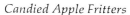

Candied Apple Fritters

Kidneys That Are the Cat's Whiskers

My cat Somi—a pale Siamese with lilac gray points—is a super talker. From a low, contented growl of greeting at breakfast time to a high-frequency shriek as he shoots up the curtains in an occasional spurt of jungle abandon, he's a never-failing source of wonder to me.

However, it's not entirely to please Somi that we have kidneys, cooked in one way or another, quite often at our house. I particularly like halved lambs kidneys grilled on a skewer—each half-kidney topped just before serving with a savory pat of "snail" butter, which is butter mashed with lemon juice, finely chopped parsley and a hint of garlic.

First take the kidneys. Remove skin and excess fat and then cut out the hard core with a pair of pointed kitchen scissors. Soak kidneys for at least 15 minutes in cold salted water before cooking—changing water at least once during this time. Since they are rather perishable, kidneys should be purchased fresh when needed and carefully refrigerated, loosely covered to permit circulation of air, until ready to cook. French cooks serve kidneys, except pork, juicily pink within. So if you want to get the best from these kidney recipes, don't overcook. Kidneys tend to toughen if they are cooked too long.

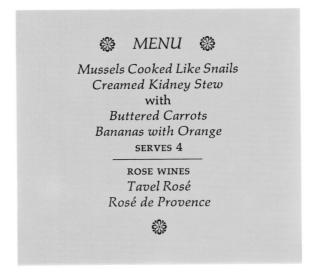

❀ MENU ❀

Mussels Cooked Like Snails
Creamed Kidney Stew
with
Buttered Carrots
Bananas with Orange
SERVES 4

ROSE WINES
Tavel Rosé
Rosé de Provence

❀

MUSSELS COOKED LIKE SNAILS

    48 mussels
     2 tablespoons chopped shallots
     2 sprigs thyme
     2 sprigs parsley
     1 bay leaf
        Salt
    ⅔ cup dry white wine

Beurre d'Escargots:

    ½ pound butter
     3 cloves garlic, finely chopped
    ¾ cup finely chopped parsley
    ¼ cup finely chopped chives

1 Choose fine fat mussels, scrape beard and wash them. Place in a saucepan together with shallots, thyme, parsley and bay leaf.

2 Season lightly with salt and moisten with wine. Steam for 4 to 5 minutes, or until the shells are well opened. Remove one-half shell from each.

3 **To make beurre d'escargots:** mash butter, garlic, parsley and chives. If chives are not available, add more parsley. Chill butter again before using.

4 Butter mussels copiously with beurre d'escargots; place them in their half-shells in 4 individual ovenproof dishes and bake in a 400°F oven for 2 to 3 minutes.

Mussels Cooked Like Snails

CREAMED KIDNEY STEW

- **2 veal kidneys**
- **4 lamb kidneys**
- **Butter**
- **2 tablespoons olive oil**
- **Salt and freshly ground black pepper**
- **1 (10-ounce) can cream of chicken soup**
- **12 cooked pearl onions**
- **4 small cooked carrots, sliced**
- **1 cup sliced button mushrooms**

1 Trim fat and skin from kidneys, remove cores and cut kidneys into lengthwise slices.

2 Melt 2 tablespoons *each* butter and olive oil in a pan; add kidneys and brown for 3 minutes on each side. Season with salt and pepper. Pour off fat and drain kidneys.

3 Return kidneys to pan; add chicken soup, onions, carrots and mushrooms, which you have sautéed in a little butter until tender.

4 Season with salt and pepper and simmer for 4 to 6 minutes. Serve with **buttered carrots** (see page 196).

BANANAS WITH ORANGE

- **4 large or 8 small bananas**
- **Juice of ½ to 1 lemon**
- **2 tablespoons butter**
- **Juice and finely grated rind of 1 orange**
- **¼ cup sugar**

1 Peel bananas. Brush with lemon juice to avoid discoloration; then set aside to absorb lemon flavor for a few minutes.

2 Melt butter in a large, heavy frying pan into which bananas will fit side by side; add orange juice, rind and sugar. Stir over low heat until sugar has dissolved.

3 Arrange bananas side by side in the pan and brown them gently all over, taking care not to burn sauce or overcook bananas. Serve immediately.

❀ *MENU* ❀

Greek Egg and Lemon Soup
Lamb Kidneys Italian-Style
with
Pommes Parisiennes
Raspberry Fool
SERVES 4-6

RED WINES
Moulin-à-Vent
Beaujolais Villages
Chianti Ruffino Red

❀

GREEK EGG AND LEMON SOUP

- **6 cups chicken stock (see page 139)**
- **1 chicken piece (leg or breast)**
- **3 eggs**
- **2 tablespoons lemon juice**
- **6 to 8 tablespoons cooked long-grained rice**
- **Salt and freshly ground black pepper**
- **2 to 3 tablespoons finely chopped parsley**

1 Bring chicken stock to the boil in a saucepan and poach chicken piece for 15 to 20 minutes.

2 Remove chicken from stock and set aside until cool enough to handle. Strain stock through a fine strainer into a clean pan and return to heat; keep hot but not boiling.

3 Skin and bone chicken piece, cutting meat into very thin slivers.

4 In a bowl, beat eggs lightly with lemon juice. Add a ladleful of hot stock to the egg mixture, beating vigorously with a whisk.

5 Now bring remaining stock to the boil. Remove from heat; add rice and slivered chicken and stir in egg mixture. Season to taste with salt and pepper and return to very low heat for 3 to 4 minutes stirring constantly, until soup is hot and creamy. Do not allow it to boil again or eggs will curdle.

6 Stir in parsley and serve immediately.

LAMB KIDNEYS ITALIAN-STYLE

    1 package frozen peas
    1 cup sliced button mushrooms
 1¼ cups tomato sauce
       Salt and freshly ground black pepper
    8 lamb kidneys
    2 tablespoons olive oil
    2 tablespoons butter
  ½ large onion, finely chopped
    3 slices cooked ham, finely chopped
       Lemon juice

1 Simmer peas and mushrooms in tomato sauce. Season with salt and pepper.

2 Remove fat and skin from kidneys; cut out hard cores and then cut kidneys into ¼-inch slices. Sauté kidney slices in olive oil and butter with onion and ham.

3 When kidneys are tender (3 to 5 minutes), add a little lemon juice and combine in a serving dish with peas and mushrooms in tomato sauce.

POMMES PARISIENNES

    2 pounds large potatoes
    3 tablespoons butter
    1 tablespoon olive oil
       Salt and freshly ground black pepper
       Finely chopped parsley for garnish

1 Peel, wash and dry potatoes.

2 Holding a potato firmly in one hand, press the bowl of a 1-inch Parisienne cutter (the same gadget you use to make melon balls) into the flesh, open side down. Twist gently from side to side until you can scoop out a neat ball of potato. Scoop as many balls as you can out of each potato—the trimmings can be used in a vichyssoise (leek and potato soup), see page 21, or boiled and mashed.

3 Dry potato balls thoroughly.

4 Select a large, heavy frying pan that will hold all the potato balls in one layer. Melt butter and oil in it and, when foaming subsides, add potato balls. Sauté over moderate heat, shaking pan frequently so that potato balls brown evenly, for 15 minutes, or until they are crisp and golden on the outside and feel soft when pierced with the point of a knife. Season to taste with salt and pepper.

5 Drain potato balls thoroughly and serve sprinkled with parsley.

RASPBERRY FOOL

 1½ pounds raspberries
    2 to 3 tablespoons lemon juice
       Sugar
  ⅔ cup heavy cream, whipped

Custard:

  ⅔ cup milk
  ½ teaspoon cornstarch
       Sugar
    2 egg yolks, well beaten
       Vanilla extract

1 Wash fresh raspberries and rub through a fine sieve (or puree in an electric blender, then rub through a sieve). Flavor to taste with lemon juice and sugar.

2 **To make custard:** combine milk with cornstarch and sugar to taste in the top of a double boiler. Bring to the boil. Pour a little of the hot liquid into well-beaten egg yolks, mix well, then return the egg yolk mixture to the milk and cornstarch and cook over hot, but *not* boiling water, stirring constantly with a wooden spoon, until custard is thick and smooth. Do not let the mixture boil. Flavor to taste with vanilla extract, strain and cool.

3 Mix custard and whipped cream (reserving a little cream for garnish) with the raspberry puree and serve in a glass bowl or in individual glasses. Garnish with whipped cream.

What's French for Rissoles?

Everyday cooking is laced with splendiferous French terms—fricassé, marinade, daube—which have entered easily into the English language. A case in point is croquettes—the most glamorous way of serving leftovers ever invented!

Croquettes—from the French word *croquer*, meaning "to crunch" or "to crackle under the teeth"—are delicate little morsels (generally shaped into diminutive sausages, rounds or squares) deep-fried in hot fat or oil until they are wonderfully crisp on the outside and meltingly creamy on the inside.

Croquettes are absolutely delicious when properly made. You'll find this great speciality of French cooking makes even the most ordinary leftovers interesting. Make your croquettes of flaked, cooked or canned fish, chopped hard-boiled eggs, ground cooked meats or finely chopped cooked vegetables, held together by a thick white sauce, coated with egg and bread crumbs and then deep-fried to a crisp gold.

Basic rule for easy croquette making:

Use 1 cup thick white sauce to bind 1 pound ground or minced solid food. Always drain moisture from solid food before combining with sauce.

THICK WHITE SAUCE:

- **2 tablespoons butter**
- **4 tablespoons flour**
- **1 cup milk**
- **1 teaspoon finely chopped onion**
- **1 teaspoon finely chopped parsley**
  Salt and freshly ground pepper
- **1 teaspoon lemon juice**

1 Melt butter in a saucepan. (I like to use the top of a double boiler for making sauces so that I can stir them over gently bubbling water without danger of scorching.) Add flour and mix well. Then add milk, onion, parsley, salt and pepper and cook until sauce is thick, stirring constantly. Stir in lemon juice.

2 To shape croquettes: spread croquette mixture—the white sauce combined with the minced solid food of your choice—about 1 inch thick in a buttered baking pan. Chill until ready to use. Then cut mixture into squares, dust with a little flour and form into the shape desired—squares, oblongs, sausages, balls, or even perfectly shaped apples and pears.

3 To coat croquettes with egg and bread crumbs: dip each croquette, formed as above, into 1 egg beaten with 2 to 3 tablespoons of water and then roll in fine dry bread crumbs to make a crisp crust when croquettes are deep-fried. You'll find that it is often wise to dip each croquette into the egg and bread crumb mixture one more time to make sure that the filling cannot ooze out during the cooking.

4 To fry croquettes: croquettes are usually fried in deep cooking fat or oil (375°F on frying thermometer) for 1 to 5 minutes, or until they are evenly browned all over. Drain croquettes on paper towels, keeping them warm in a slow oven (325°F) until serving.

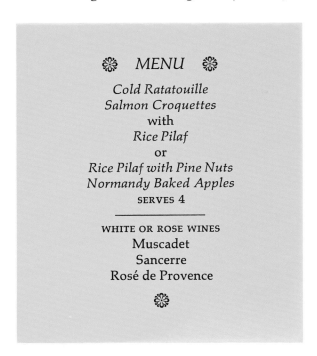

❀ *MENU* ❀

Cold Ratatouille
Salmon Croquettes
with
Rice Pilaf
or
Rice Pilaf with Pine Nuts
Normandy Baked Apples
SERVES 4

———————

WHITE OR ROSE WINES
Muscadet
Sancerre
Rosé de Provence

❀

COLD RATATOUILLE

8 tablespoons olive oil
2 onions, sliced
2 green peppers, diced
2 medium-sized eggplants, diced
2 small zucchini, cut in slices
4 to 6 ripe tomatoes, peeled, seeded and chopped
  Salt and freshly ground black pepper
1 tablespoon chopped parsley
  Pinch of marjoram or oregano
  Pinch of basil
1 large clove garlic, crushed

1   Heat olive oil in an ovenproof casserole; add onion and sauté until transparent. Add green peppers and eggplants and, 5 minutes later, zucchini and tomatoes. The vegetables should not be fried but stewed in the oil, so simmer gently in a covered pan for 30 minutes.

2   Add salt and pepper to taste, parsley, marjoram, basil and garlic; then cook, uncov-

Cold Ratatouille

ered, for about 10 to 15 minutes, or until rata- touille is well mixed and has the appearance of a ragout of vegetables—which it is.

3   Serve cold as a delicious beginning to a summer meal.

SALMON CROQUETTES

  2½ **(7-ounce) cans salmon, flaked**
      Thick white sauce (see page 85)
    4 **tablespoons freshly grated Parmesan cheese**
      Salt and freshly ground black pepper
      Finely chopped onion
      Lemon juice
      Fine dry bread crumbs
    1 **egg, lightly beaten**
      Fat for deep-frying

1   Add salmon to sauce together with Par- mesan cheese. Taste mixture, adding salt and pepper, onion and lemon juice to taste.

2   Spread mixture about 1 inch thick in a buttered baking pan. Chill.

3   Shape into 8 croquettes; roll in bread crumbs, dip into egg, lightly beaten with 2 to 3 tablespoons water, roll again in bread crumbs and chill until ready to fry.

4   Fry in deep fat (375°F on frying ther- mometer) until golden.

RICE PILAF

  1½ **cups long-grain rice**
   ½ **large onion, finely chopped**
    4 **tablespoons butter**
    2 **cups rich stock**
      Thyme
      Salt and freshly ground black pepper

1   Wash rice; drain and dry with paper towels.

2   Sauté onion in 4 tablespoons butter until a light golden color.

3   Add rice and continue to cook, stirring constantly, until it begins to take on color.

4   Pour in hot stock and season with 1 pinch thyme, salt and pepper.

5   Cover saucepan and place in a 350°F oven for 15 to 20 minutes, or until the rice is

tender, adding a little more stock, if necessary. Serve with additional butter.

RICE PILAF WITH PINE NUTS

Toss 2 ounces pine nuts in butter until crisp and golden. Just before serving, scatter over **rice pilaf** (see recipe above).

NORMANDY BAKED APPLES

  1 **pound frozen flaky pastry**
  6 **large tart eating apples**
  3 **tablespoons sugar**
    Ground cloves
  3 **to 4 tablespoons butter**
  1 **egg, beaten, for glaze**

1   Defrost flaky pastry. Preheat oven to 450°F.

2   Peel apples; core them carefully from the stem end without going quite to the bottom. Roll pastry out into a sheet about ⅛ inch thick and cut out 6 6-inch squares.

3   Moisten apples slightly and place each one in the center of a pastry square. Sprinkle each apple with a little sugar and a generous pinch of cloves. Put a generous ½ tablespoon butter into each cavity.

4   Bring pastry squares up around apples to enclose them completely; seal tightly, moist- ening seams with a drop of water if necessary and trimming off any excess pastry. Roll out pastry trimmings and cut out "leaves" to deco- rate tops of apples. (Alternatively, you can make a slightly more elaborate and very pretty decoration as follows: roll out remaining pastry thinly and cut out circles to fit tops of apples like little caps; press down lightly but firmly, then make "leaves" from remaining scraps of pastry and arrange on top so that the tips of the leaves overlap the edges of the caps.)

5   Brush apples with beaten egg. Place them on a cookie sheet and bake for 10 minutes at 450°F; then lower oven temperature to 425°F and continue to bake for 20 minutes longer, or until pastry is puffed and a rich golden color.

6   Delicious hot, sprinkled with a little more superfine sugar. Serve with cream.

❀ *MENU* ❀

Chicken Croquettes
with
Glazed Zucchini
and
Boiled Rice
Port and Apples
SERVES 4

WHITE OR ROSE WINES
Sancerre
Chablis
Tavel Rosé

❀

GLAZED ZUCCHINI

12 **small zucchini**
4 **tablespoons butter**
   Salt and freshly ground black pepper
   Sugar
6 **tablespoons light stock**

1 Cut unpeeled zucchini into quarters lengthwise; slice each quarter into 2-inch pieces and blanch in boiling water to cover for about 3 minutes. Drain.

2 Combine zucchini in a shallow saucepan with butter and salt, pepper and sugar to taste. Add light stock and simmer gently, covered, until liquid has almost disappeared and zucchini are glazed and tender.

CHICKEN CROQUETTES

   Thick white sauce (see page 85)
4 **cups diced cooked chicken**
   Dash of Tabasco or Worcestershire sauce
   Salt and freshly ground black pepper
1 **tablespoon finely chopped onion**
   Lemon juice
   Fine dry bread crumbs
1 **egg, lightly beaten**
   Fat for deep-frying

1 Combine sauce with chicken and Tabasco. Taste mixture, adding salt, pepper, onion and lemon juice as desired.

2 Spread mixture about 1 inch thick on a greased cookie sheet. Chill; then cut into 8 portions.

3 Shape each portion into a round or oblong-shaped patty and roll in bread crumbs. Dip croquettes into a lightly beaten egg mixed with 2 to 3 tablespoons water; roll again in bread crumbs and chill until ready to fry.

4 Fry croquettes in deep fat (375°F on frying thermometer) for about 5 minutes, or until golden brown. Serve immediately with **glazed zucchini** (see below) and **boiled rice** (see page 89).

PORT AND APPLES

1½ **pounds small tart apples, peeled and cored**
1 **cup sugar**
1 **inch cinnamon stick**
1 **inch whole ginger**
   Rind of 1 lemon
1 **cup port**
   Red food coloring (optional)
   Whipped cream (optional)

1 Combine sugar, 2½ cups water, cinnamon and ginger in a saucepan with the thinly peeled rind of 1 lemon, and boil for 10 minutes. Strain and cool. Pour this syrup over the apples in a bowl; cover with a plate and marinate overnight.

2 The following day, transfer apples and syrup to an enamelled saucepan and simmer until tender.

3 Remove apples with a slotted spoon and arrange in a shallow serving bowl. Add port to syrup and strain it over apples. A few drops of red food coloring may be added to syrup if desired, and apples may be decorated with a little whipped cream.

Four Meals Based on Rice

Rice is one of the easiest things to cook really well. And yet it is rare to come across rice cooked to perfection—each grain separate and fluffy, just tender, not mushy.

If you would like to make perfect rice—every time—follow the simple rules for basic boiled rice and basic risotto, below, before you go on to the special summer rice dishes. And remember, the best rice for main course dishes is long-grain rice. Keep the smaller grains for desserts only.

BASIC BOILED RICE

There are countless ways of cooking plain boiled rice. Some cooks prefer to steam it; others insist that unless a little butter or oil is added to the cooking liquid, the grains won't be separate. I like to boil it in a large, heavy saucepan capable of holding a generous quantity of water. The secret of getting separate grains of white, fluffy rice is very simple indeed; just salt the water, add a little lemon juice to keep the rice white, and when the water is boiling well, dribble the grains into the liquid through your fingers, stirring all the while. Then simply allow rice to cook, uncovered, for 14 to 18 minutes. During the last 2 or 3 minutes of cooking time watch the rice carefully, for the only real test is the *taste test.* I always pick out a grain or two with a fork and test them. When the rice is just right, with the granular core tender, but not mushy, drain it in a large colander and keep warm over boiling water until ready to serve. Serve the rice as it is to accompany curries or Chinese dishes; or add butter and a little freshly grated Parmesan if the rice is served with broiled or roasted meat or fish.

BASIC RISOTTO

One of the most delicious ways to cook rice is the risotto. Wash 1 cup long-grain or Italian rice in cold water. Drain thoroughly. Add 3 to 4 tablespoons butter, salt and freshly ground black pepper, to taste, and 4 cups chicken or beef stock, flavored with a little dry white wine. Bring to the boil, stirring; reduce heat; cover tightly and simmer gently for 14 to 18 minutes; uncover, toss lightly with a fork, add a little extra butter and some grated Parmesan and serve. The rice should have absorbed all the liquid and the grains should be moist but separate.

VARIATIONS

If a good stock is used, and you have sautéed the rice with a little finely chopped onion before adding the liquid, it will take on extra strength and flavor. Try adding to it 1 to 2 cups diced, cooked chicken or lamb that has been heated in a little stock with half an onion, finely chopped and sautéed until golden in 2 tablespoons of butter or oil. Adding a teaspoon or two of curry powder, ½ teaspoon of ground saffron, chopped nuts, diced raw apple, or raisins will also do much to change the taste and quality of your summer rice dish. This with a salad, followed by a dessert or cheese and fruit, will make a delicious and satisfying meal.

❀ *MENU* ❀

Salade de Moules
Lamb Fried Rice
with
Herbed, Buttered
Carrots
Apple Pie with
Orange Juice
SERVES 4

WHITE WINES
Muscadet
Sancerre
Chablis

❀

SALADE DE MOULES

    2 **quarts mussels**
    2 **tablespoons finely chopped shallots**
    2 **sprigs parsley**
  ¼ **teaspoon thyme**
    1 **bay leaf**
      Salt and freshly ground black pepper
    4 **to 6 tablespoons dry white wine**
    2 **tablespoons wine vinegar**
      Olive oil
    2 **tablespoons coarsely chopped parsley**

1 Scrub mussels thoroughly under cold running water and remove "beards." Discard any that are cracked or still open at the end of this operation.

2 Place mussels in a large, heavy pan with a tight-fitting lid. Add shallots, parsley sprigs, thyme and bay leaf; season very lightly with salt and pepper and moisten with wine.

3 Cover pan tightly. Place over a high heat and cook for 5 to 7 minutes, or until mussels have opened. Discard any that remain closed—they, too, are suspect.

4 Remove pan from heat. As soon as mussels can be handled, scoop them out of their shells into a bowl. You may, if you wish, pull off their dark little outer frills, but this is not necessary. Cover and keep warm.

5 Taste mussel liquor. If it is not too salty, boil it for a few minutes to reduce it and intensify the flavor. Pour a little mussel liquor through a strainer lined with a double thickness of cheesecloth or paper towels. If very salty, add a little more wine.

6 Combine 2 tablespoons *each* mussel liquor and vinegar in a small bowl. Beat in enough olive oil to make a good dressing. Stir in half the chopped parsley and season to taste with salt and pepper.

7 Pour dressing over warm mussels; toss lightly to coat them evenly and allow to cool. Then chill until ready to serve.

8 Just before serving, arrange mussels in a shallow serving dish and garnish with remaining parsley. Serve very cold.

LAMB FRIED RICE

If you have only a little cooked lamb left over—about ½ pound, say—this is an excellent recipe for making a little meat go a long way.

    2 **eggs**
    1 **tablespoon butter**
      Salt and freshly ground black pepper
    4 **tablespoons oil**
    1 **onion, finely chopped**
  ½ **pound cooked lamb, diced**
    3 **cups cold cooked rice**
    6 **mushrooms, diced**
    2 **teaspoons soy sauce or lemon juice**
      Finely chopped parsley

1 Make a thin omelet of eggs cooked in butter; season with salt and pepper; remove from pan and cut into strips.

2 Heat oil in a large frying pan and when it is hot, add onion and sauté until transparent. Add lamb and continue to cook until meat and onion are golden. Season with salt and pepper. Add rice and mushrooms and fry gently, stirring from time to time, for 5 minutes.

3 Just before serving, stir in soy sauce (or lemon juice) and 2 teaspoons water; add salt and pepper to taste. Top with egg strips; sprinkle with a little parsley and serve immediately with **herbed buttered carrots.**

HERBED BUTTERED CARROTS

- **1 pound baby carrots**
- **2 tablespoons butter**
- **2 tablespoons chicken stock or water**
- **1 clove garlic, finely chopped**
- **1 medium-sized onion, finely chopped**
- **1 tablespoon finely chopped parsley**
  Salt and freshly ground black pepper
- **½ teaspoon rosemary**
- **4 tablespoons cream**

1 Wash carrots and cut diagonally into thin slices.

2 Melt butter in saucepan, and add chicken stock, carrots, garlic, onion and parsley. Season to taste with salt, pepper and rosemary.

3 Cover and cook over a low heat for 10 to 15 minutes, or until carrots are just tender.

4 Just before serving, stir in cream and season to taste.

APPLE PIE WITH ORANGE JUICE

- **1½ pounds cooking apples**
  Juice of ½ lemon
  Pastry for a two-crust pie
- **¼ cup sugar**
- **¼ cup dark brown sugar**
- **1 tablespoon flour**
- **⅛ teaspoon grated nutmeg**
- **¼ teaspoon ground cinnamon**
  Grated rind of ½ orange
  Grated rind of ½ lemon
- **6 tablespoons chopped raisins**
- **1 to 2 tablespoons orange juice**
- **1 to 2 tablespoons butter**
  Heavy cream or cheddar cheese

1 Peel and core apples and slice thickly. Soak them in water to which you have added lemon juice to preserve their color. Line a deep 9-inch pie dish with pastry, using your own favorite recipe.

2 Combine sugars, flour, nutmeg and cinnamon, and rub a little of this mixture into pastry shell. Add grated rinds to remaining sugar mixture. Cover bottom of pastry shell with sliced apples and sprinkle with a few raisins and some of the sugar mixture. Repeat layers until pie shell is filled.

3 Sprinkle with orange juice; dot with butter and fit top crust over apples, pressing the edges together or fluting them. Decorate pastry; cut slits in top crust to release steam and bake in a 400°F oven for 35 to 40 minutes, or until fruit is tender and pastry is golden brown. Serve warm, with cream or cheddar cheese.

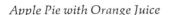

Apple Pie with Orange Juice

MENU

*Fresh Spinach
Soup
Italian Breaded
Lamb Chops
with
Harem Pilaf
Oranges with Cream*
SERVES 4

RED WINES
Brouilly
Morgon
Côte-Rôtie

FRESH SPINACH SOUP

  2 **pounds fresh spinach leaves**
  4 **tablespoons butter**
    Salt and freshly ground black pepper
  1 **cup heavy cream**
1½ **cups chicken stock**

1   Wash the spinach leaves, changing water several times; drain thoroughly.
2   Put spinach in a thick-bottomed saucepan with butter and simmer gently, stirring constantly, until soft and tender.
3   Puree in an electric blender. Season to taste with salt and pepper.
4   Combine with cream and chicken stock, add spinach and heat through. Serve immediately.

ITALIAN BREADED LAMB CHOPS

  8 **small lamb chops**
    Salt and freshly ground black pepper
    Flour
    Beaten egg
½ **cup bread crumbs**
½ **cup grated Parmesan cheese**
    Oil for deep-frying
    Lemon wedges
    Parsley

1   Season chops to taste with salt and pepper and sprinkle with flour. Dip into beaten egg and then into a mixture of bread crumbs and Parmesan to coat thoroughly. Deep-fry until golden and tender. Drain on absorbent paper.
2   Serve garnished with lemon wedges and parsley. Decorate bones with paper frills.

HAREM PILAF

4 to 6 firm tomatoes
1½ cups sliced button mushrooms
½ onion, finely chopped
   Butter
1 cup rice
4 tablespoons dry white wine or cider

4 cups chicken stock
   Salt and freshly ground black pepper
1 clove garlic, finely chopped
2 tablespoons finely chopped parsley
¼ teaspoon dried oregano
1 avocado, peeled and diced
¼ pound raw chicken livers, diced

1 Drop tomatoes into boiling water for about 1 minute. Peel them at once, then seed and dice.

2 Sauté onion in 4 tablespoons butter in a medium-sized ovenproof casserole until golden; add rice and cook, stirring, for another 1 or 2 minutes. Then pour wine and chicken stock over rice. Season with salt and pepper, to taste. Bring to the boil; cover casserole and put it in a 350°F oven for 14 to 16 minutes. After about 10 minutes of cooking time, stir once with a fork.

3 Sauté mushrooms in 2 tablespoons butter for 3 minutes. Add garlic, parsley, oregano, tomatoes and season to taste with salt and pepper. Simmer for 2 to 3 minutes longer. Scatter with avocado and keep warm.

4 In another pan sauté the chicken livers in a little butter, then stir into the finished rice mixture with a fork.

5 Form rice into a ring and fill the center with avocado and mushroom mixture.

ORANGES WITH CREAM

3 large oranges
1 cup fresh orange juice
   Sugar
1 to 1½ cups heavy cream, whipped

1 Grate the rind of 1 orange and add to orange juice. Peel all the oranges and with a sharp knife cut off all the pith. Slice horizontally.

2 Place orange slices in overlapping rows in a shallow rectangular dish. Sprinkle with orange juice and sugar to taste.

3 Whip cream; sweeten to taste and spoon over orange slices. Chill until ready to serve.

Three Rice Dishes:
Spanish Pork and Rice Casserole (left),
Harem Pilaf (top), and Kedgeree (right)

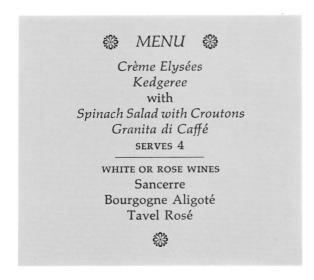

❀ *MENU* ❀

Crème Elysées
Kedgeree
with
Spinach Salad with Croutons
Granita di Caffé
SERVES 4

WHITE OR ROSE WINES
Sancerre
Bourgogne Aligoté
Tavel Rosé

❀

CREME ELYSEES

   1 package frozen peas
   5 cups chicken consommé
   4 tablespoons butter
  ½ large cucumber, peeled and seeded
   2 egg yolks
  ¾ cup heavy cream
     Salt and freshly ground black pepper

1 Defrost peas and simmer in 2 table-spoons *each* of chicken consommé and butter until cooked through. Drain and puree in an electric blender.

2 Cut cucumber into matchstick-sized slivers and sauté in remaining butter until tender.

3 Beat eggs; add cream and puree of peas.

4 Heat consommé; stir in puree mixture and cook over gentle heat, stirring constantly, until liquid is smooth and thick. Do not let soup come to the boil or it will curdle.

5 Just before serving, stir in cucumber sticks and season with salt and pepper, to taste.

KEDGEREE

   1 cup rice
     Salt
  ½ pound cooked smoked haddock
   2 hard-boiled eggs
   8 tablespoons butter
   1 ¼-inch slice cooked ham, diced

   2 level tablespoons tomato ketchup
   4 level tablespoons watercress leaves, coarsely chopped
     Freshly ground black pepper

1 Cook rice in boiling, salted water until just tender. Rinse well and drain.

2 Remove skin and bones from smoked haddock and flake the fish.

3 Chop whites of hard-boiled eggs.

4 Melt butter in a saucepan; toss rice in it. Then add flaked fish, chopped egg whites and diced ham. Stir in tomato ketchup and toss lightly over heat until hot. Stir in coarsely chopped watercress and season with salt and freshly ground black pepper.

5 Grate or sieve yolks of hard-boiled eggs over kedgeree and serve immediately.

SPINACH SALAD WITH CROUTONS

1 pound spinach
6 tablespoons olive oil
  Lemon juice
2 cloves garlic, finely chopped
  Coarsely grated lemon rind
  Salt and freshly ground black pepper
  Sautéed croutons (see page 31)

1 Wash spinach, removing thick stalks, and gently dry with paper towels.

2 Heat olive oil and 2 tablespoons lemon juice in a large saucepan; add garlic and grated rind of 1 lemon.

3 Add spinach and toss over moderate heat until it is hot and each leaf is thoroughly coated. Season to taste with salt and pepper.

4 Arrange leaves on a hot serving dish; garnish with croutons and a little coarsely grated lemon rind.

GRANITA DI CAFFE

4 to 6 tablespoons instant coffee
2½ to 3 cups water
½ to ¾ cup sugar
4 to 6 ice cubes
  Whipped cream

1 Combine coffee and 1⅓ to 1¾ cups water in a saucepan, adding sugar to taste. Bring to a boil, stirring constantly. Reduce heat and simmer for 5 minutes. Remove from heat. Add 1⅓ cups water and ice cubes; stir until ice is melted. Pour into an ice cube tray and freeze for 1½ to 1¾ hours, or until ice is firm around edges.

2 Turn ice into bowl of an electric mixer and mix at medium speed until mixture is smooth.

3 Turn into 2 ice cube trays and freeze until almost solid. This will take about 1 hour.

4 When ready to serve, stir ice and spoon into parfait or sherbet glasses. Top with whipped cream and serve at once.

 MENU

Stuffed Zucchini Appetizer
Spanish Pork and Rice Casserole
with
Quick-Fried Asparagus
Strawberries Romanoff
SERVES 4-6

RED WINES
Rioja Red
Serradayres
Cabernet Red
Gigondas

STUFFED ZUCCHINI APPETIZER

8 to 12 small zucchini, 4 inches long
  Salt
1 large onion, finely chopped
1 clove garlic, finely chopped
  French dressing (see page 146)
  Lettuce
3 tomatoes, peeled and chopped
1 green pepper, finely chopped
1 tablespoon capers
1 tablespoon each parsley and basil
  Freshly ground black pepper

1 Simmer unpeeled zucchini in salted water for about 5 minutes. Cut them in half lengthwise and carefully scoop out seeds. Lay zucchini, cut sides up, in a flat dish.

2 Combine half the onion with the garlic and cover zucchini with this mixture. Sprinkle half the French dressing over them, cover with aluminum foil and marinate in the refrigerator for at least 4 hours.

3 When ready to serve, remove onion and garlic and drain off marinade.

4 Arrange zucchini halves on crisp lettuce leaves and fill the hollows with remaining French dressing combined with remaining onion and tomatoes, green pepper, capers, parsley, basil, salt and pepper, to taste.

SPANISH PORK AND RICE CASSEROLE

    4 large pork chops
      Olive oil
      Salt and freshly ground black pepper
    1 green pepper, coarsely chopped
    1 onion, coarsely chopped
    1 cup rice, uncooked
    2 cups chicken stock
    1 large (35 ounces) can Italian peeled tomatoes
      Paprika

1 In a large frying pan brown chops well on both sides in olive oil. Remove from pan and trim off excess fat with a sharp knife. Arrange chops in a shallow ovenproof baking dish or casserole. Season generously with salt and pepper.

2 Fry green pepper and onion in fat remaining in frying pan until golden.

3 Add rice and continue to cook, stirring constantly, until rice is golden, adding a little olive oil to the pan if mixture gets too dry.

4 Moisten vegetables with chicken stock and tomatoes. Cover chops with this mixture; season with salt and pepper and sprinkle top with paprika.

5 Cover tightly with a piece of aluminum foil if baking dish has no cover and bake in a preheated 350°F oven for 40 to 50 minutes, or until rice tastes done and pork is tender.

A quick-fried vegetable in the Chinese manner—asparagus, broccoli or green beans—is one of the simplest vegetable accompaniments I know. Sauté the sliced vegetable for 2 to 3 minutes in a little seasoned oil; add 4 tablespoons chicken stock and a dash of soy sauce or lemon juice; and steam until just tender.

QUICK-FRIED ASPARAGUS

    2 pounds fresh asparagus
      Vegetable oil
      Salt and freshly ground black pepper
      Monosodium glutamate
    4 tablespoons chicken stock or water
      Soy sauce or lemon juice

1 Cut stalks of asparagus diagonally, making thin, slant-edged slices about 1½ inches long.

2 Heat oil in a large frying pan; add asparagus; sprinkle lightly with salt, pepper and monosodium glutamate to taste and cook over high heat, stirring, for 2 or 3 minutes.

3 Add chicken stock; cover pan and cook over medium heat for 3 to 5 minutes, shaking pan frequently.

4 Season to taste with soy sauce or lemon juice. Serve immediately.

STRAWBERRIES ROMANOFF

    4 to 5 cups fresh strawberries
    6 tablespoons confectioners' sugar
    3 tablespoons rum
    3 tablespoons Cointreau
  1¼ cups heavy cream
    3 tablespoons kirsch

1 Wash, drain and hull strawberries, and place in a bowl.

2 Toss with 4 tablespoons of the sugar. Pour over rum and Cointreau and chill in refrigerator for at least 1 hour.

3 An hour before serving, whip cream until stiff; add remaining 2 tablespoons sugar, flavor with kirsch and mix with the strawberries, tossing until thoroughly blended.

4 Chill until serving time.

Breakfast and Brunch Parties

Doctors and nutritionists agree that the first meal of the day should provide from one-quarter to one-third of our daily intake of calories and proteins. Measure this against your cup of black coffee and toasted English muffin and you'll have a fair idea of why the mornings do not go as smoothly for you as they might. Breakfast should be as important, or almost as important, as the other two meals we normally eat every day—so why not make the most of it? All the trite excuses—"in a hurry," "not hungry," "too sleepy," "no time"—are worse than flimsy when the facts prove that non-breakfasters lag behind the big-breakfast league in energy by the time mid-morning arrives.

Make breakfast one of the most rewarding meals of the day by using individual recipes from the breakfast and brunch menus in this book to spark off your weekday mornings. And why not invite friends over to join the family for informal breakfast parties at weekends or during vacations?

A good idea when planning a special breakfast party is to do everything possible the night before—even setting the table. In this way, when you get up all you have to do are the last-minute things like cooking the sausages and eggs and putting the coffeepot on to bubble.

The Sunday Brunch Party

Sunday is the day of the week when your friends are most likely to be free for breakfast.

Why not plan a brunch party—and invite friends around for an imaginative feast.

Sunday brunch should be an unhurried delight.

Make the invitation flexible. Invite your guests for "about noon" or "when you get up"—remember most people like to read the Sunday newspapers before they are ready to leave the house.

Plan to give guests simple things superbly served—grilled grapefruit with cinnamon, followed by a puffy bacon omelet with cheese sauce—or try that old familiar standby scrambled eggs, but brought up to date for the occasion with the addition of thin slivers of smoked salmon and snippets of chopped chives.

Paper-thin slices of hot toast spread with sweet butter, homemade croissants and a dollop of your own fresh fruit preserves, or piping hot butter scones will add much to the occasion.

Grilled Grapefruit with Cinnamon, Puffy Bacon Omelets with Cheese Sauce, and Butter Scones

If you are planning to serve hot breads for breakfast, make the dough the night before so that all you have to do is pop it into the oven as your family or guests sit down to the table. I have included several delicious recipes for delectable hot breads: popovers, butter scones that melt in your mouth, and fabulous French brioches and croissants. It took me weeks to perfect my "can't-fail" croissant recipe, and its foolproof method is described at length on pages 103–104.

Some Breakfast and Brunch Suggestions

For a really glamorous breakfast or brunch, start off with a thick slice of chilled fresh melon topped with strawberries or raspberries, and follow with pan-fried trout, hot from the frying pan, accompanied by tiny new potatoes.

Offer guests a choice of hot coffee or chilled white wine—and see which they choose!

A summer breakfast or brunch might begin with a compote of fresh fruits, or orange and grapefruit sections in lemon juice, followed by a simple little dish of eggs cooked *en cocotte* (cooked in cream in individual ramekins or soufflé dishes). Or try fried eggs with sausages and bacon, accompanied by popovers—just right when served with homemade strawberry preserve and fresh unsalted butter.

For a winter breakfast or brunch, start off with a compote of dried fruits, particularly delicious when spiked with tangy lemon juice or a splash of port for late Sunday morning guests. Follow with a kedgeree made of chunks of poached salmon, rice and hard-boiled eggs in a creamy sauce and deviled kidneys and bacon.

Why not sit down and plan a Sunday morning breakfast or brunch right now?

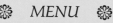 *MENU*

Grilled Grapefruit with Cinnamon
Puffy Bacon Omelets with Cheese Sauce
Butter Scones

SERVES 4-6

COFFEE OR TEA

GRILLED GRAPEFRUIT WITH CINNAMON

- 5 **large grapefruit**
- 6 **tablespoons brown sugar**
- 2 **teaspoons ground cinnamon**
- 2 **tablespoons butter**

1 Cut each grapefruit in half. With a sharp-pointed spoon scoop out each half-segment over a bowl to catch the juices, leaving behind the membranes dividing the segments. Take care not to crush the segments, so that pieces remain as large as possible.

2 Take 6 of the best half-shells and cut out all the pith and membranes from the center.

3 Mix sugar and cinnamon together. Drain grapefruit segments, reserving juices; toss segments with cinnamon-sugar and divide evenly among the 6 half-shells.

4 Arrange shells side by side in a broiling pan or an ovenproof baking dish that will fit under your broiler. Fill them to the brim with reserved grapefruit juice and dot with butter.

5 Have the broiler preheated to hot. Run grapefruit under the broiler; reduce heat to moderate and broil steadily for 5 to 7 minutes, or until grapefruit are thoroughly hot and bubbling brown on top.

PUFFY BACON OMELETS WITH CHEESE SAUCE

- 1/2 **pound bacon**
- 6 **eggs, separated**
- 2 **tablespoons cold water**

Salt and freshly ground black pepper
2 **tablespoons butter**

Cheese Sauce:

- 2 **tablespoons butter**
- 2 **tablespoons flour**
- 2 1/2 **cups milk**
- 1 **to 1 1/2 cups grated cheddar cheese**
- 2 **teaspoons Worcestershire sauce**
  Salt and freshly ground black pepper

1 **To make sauce:** melt butter in a small, heavy pan; add flour and cook over very low heat for 2 minutes, stirring constantly. Add milk gradually, beating vigorously to avoid lumps; bring to the boil, stirring, and simmer for 8 to 10 minutes, stirring occasionally.

2 Remove from heat; stir in cheese and beat until smooth. Season to taste with Worcestershire sauce, salt and pepper.

3 Cover surface of sauce with a piece of waxed paper brushed with water to prevent a skin forming; keep hot.

4 **To make omelets:** fry bacon until crisp, then crumble.

5 Beat egg yolks with cold water until light and frothy. Season lightly with salt and pepper.

6 Preheat broiler at highest temperature.

7 Beat egg whites until stiff but not dry, and gently fold into egg yolk mixture.

8 Cook mixture in two batches one after another, using two 8- to 9-inch omelet pans simultaneously: melt 1 tablespoon butter in each pan; pour in half the omelet mixture and, swirling lightly with a fork, allow base to set over a steady heat. Slip omelets under broiler just long enough to puff and set tops.

9 Scatter half the crumbled bacon over half of each omelet and carefully fold in two.

10 Remove omelets to heated serving dishes, cover with hot cheese sauce and serve.

BUTTER SCONES

(For the recipe, see page 106.)

❀ *MENU* ❀

Breakfast Apple Rings
Scrambled Eggs with Mushrooms
or
Scrambled Eggs with Smoked Salmon
and Chives
Croissants
SERVES 6

COFFEE OR TEA

❀

2 Beat eggs lightly in a bowl with cream —just enough to mix them. (Water will make extremely fluffy eggs; cream gives a richer, smoother texture.)

3 Put prebaked patty shells into a 350°F oven to heat through.

4 Melt remaining 6 tablespoons butter in a large, heavy skillet (about 8 inches in diameter). When butter is hot but not brown, pour in eggs and cook over low heat, stirring constantly with a wooden spoon, until eggs are just on the point of setting. Add sautéed mushrooms and salt and pepper, to taste.

5 Remove pan from heat. Divide mixture between patty shells and serve immediately.

BREAKFAST APPLE RINGS

    6 tart eating apples
    6 tablespoons sugar (white or brown)
 1½ teaspoons ground cinnamon
    6 tablespoons melted butter

1 Wash and core apples, and slice them crosswise into rings ½ inch thick. Mix sugar with cinnamon.

2 Place apple rings on a cookie sheet, brush with melted butter and sprinkle with half the cinnamon-sugar.

3 Broil for about 5 minutes, or until rings are golden brown on one side. Then turn carefully with a spatula, brush with butter, sprinkle with remaining cinnamon-sugar and broil for 5 minutes longer. Serve hot.

SCRAMBLED EGGS WITH MUSHROOMS

    6 ounces button mushrooms
    8 tablespoons butter
  12 eggs
    6 tablespoons cream, milk or water
    6 (3-inch) patty shells, prebaked
       Salt and freshly ground black pepper

1 Wash or wipe mushrooms clean; trim stems and slice. Sauté in 2 tablespoons of the butter for 5 minutes until softened.

SCRAMBLED EGGS WITH SMOKED SALMON AND CHIVES

1 Combine eggs with cream, milk or water as above.

2 Melt 6 tablespoons butter in a large, heavy skillet. Add 6 ounces smoked salmon, cut into thin strips. Sprinkle with 1 or 2 teaspoons lemon juice and heat through for a few seconds until strips change color. Pour in eggs and scramble them as above.

3 Just before removing pan from heat, season mixture to taste with salt and freshly ground black pepper. Stir in 2 to 3 tablespoons finely chopped chives (or scallion tops or parsley), and serve immediately in hot patty shells as above.

CROISSANTS

(For the recipe, see pages 103–104.)

Summer Breakfast Compote,
Fried Eggs with Sausages and Bacon,
and Whole Strawberry Preserves

SUMMER BREAKFAST COMPOTE

- 4 **tablespoons lemon juice**
- 2 **tablespoons honey**
- 2 **oranges**
- 1 **grapefruit**
- 1 **eating apple**
- 1 **banana**
- ½ **pint strawberries**

1 Combine lemon juice and honey in a glass serving bowl.

2 Peel oranges and grapefruit and divide into segments, discarding seeds and every scrap of pith and membrane. Toss with honey and lemon juice.

3 Quarter apple; remove core and dice (unpeeled) apple.

4 Peel and slice banana.

5 Add apple and banana to the bowl and toss thoroughly until all surfaces are coated with juices to prevent them turning brown. Cover and chill until ready to serve.

6 Just before serving, hull strawberries and add them to the bowl.

FRIED EGGS WITH SAUSAGES AND BACON

Fried Eggs

Do not attempt to fry more than 4 eggs at a time in the average frying pan, and always make sure they are fresh—a stale egg has a "watery" white that will run all over the frying pan instead of remaining firm and rounded. To test an egg for freshness, hold it upright between your thumb and forefinger and shake it gently up and down. If you can feel the yolk thudding lightly against the shell, the egg is stale.

For 4 eggs, heat 2 tablespoons butter in a frying pan until sizzling. Break 1 egg at a time into a cup; season with salt and freshly ground black pepper and slide into pan. Fry eggs very slowly until done to your liking; then lift out carefully with a spatula, drain and serve on hot plates.

Grilled Sausages

Prick sausages lightly all over with a fork and lay them side by side in the bottom of a pan. Brush with melted butter and broil under a moderate heat for 6 to 8 minutes, turning sausages to brown them evenly.

Fried Sausages

Melt about 1 tablespoon butter or bacon grease in a heavy frying pan; prick large sausages all over and arrange them in the pan in one layer.

Cook them over moderate heat until they just begin to brown. When they sizzle, pour in 1 tablespoon water, cover tightly and continue to cook over moderate heat until water has been absorbed and sausages are crisp on the underside. Continue adding water and cooking sausages in this manner until they are brown and crisp all over. Drain and serve.

Bacon

Broil or fry bacon until done to your liking. Halved tomatoes, lightly seasoned, may be slipped into the broiling pan a few minutes before bacon is ready, but do not let them reduce to a mush. Fried tomatoes should always be cooked in a separate pan.

OEUFS EN COCOTTE

    Butter
8 fresh eggs
    Salt and freshly ground black pepper
1 to 2 tablespoons light cream

1 Butter 4 ovenproof ramekins. Break 2 eggs into each ramekin; season with a pinch of salt and a few turns of the peppermill.

2 Arrange ramekins side by side in a wide pan with a lid. (If you do not have a large enough pan, use a roasting pan and cover it with a sheet of foil.) Pour in boiling water to come one-third of the way up sides of ramekins. Cover pan tightly and simmer very gently for about 8 minutes for soft eggs, a minute or two longer if you prefer them on the firm side.

3 As soon as eggs are cooked to your taste, remove ramekins from water and swirl about 1 teaspoon cream round the top edge of each one. Serve immediately.

HOT POPOVERS
(For the recipe, see page 105.)

WHOLE STRAWBERRY JAM

  2 to 2½ cups small, hard strawberries
  2 to 2½ cups sugar
    Juice of 1 lemon

1 **The day before you intend to make jam:** wash strawberries quickly, drain them thoroughly on paper towels and hull them. Pile strawberries up slightly on a wide, flat dish and cover completely with a layer of sugar taken from the total amount.

2 **The following day:** pour juices drawn from strawberries by the sugar into a pan. Add remaining sugar and set pan over very low heat. Allow sugar to melt, stirring and brushing down any sugar grains stuck to sides of pan with a little cold water. Then bring to the boil once and skim off any foam that collects on the surface.

3 Slide strawberries into pan; add lemon juice and simmer very gently for 5 to 8 minutes, or until strawberries are plump and soft but not disintegrating. They must not be stirred with a spoon while they are simmering. As flecks of white foam appear on the surface, shake the whole pan back and forth very gently so that foam collects in the center; skim it off with a sterilized spoon.

4 When syrup just begins to set, remove pan from heat. Allow jam to cool in the pan, swirling the latter gently from time to time so that strawberries remain suspended in syrup and do not sink to the bottom.

5 Pour into a dry sterilized jar and seal.

Breakfast Bakery

CROISSANTS

MAKES 12

    6 **tablespoons lukewarm milk mixed with**
        3 **tablespoons lukewarm water**
    1 **tablespoon sugar**
    ½ **package active dry yeast**
    2 **cups sifted flour**
    1 **teaspoon salt**
    3 **tablespoons melted butter**
    6 **tablespoons unsalted butter, chilled**
       Egg yolk beaten with a little water for glaze

1   The day before you wish to serve croissants: put 3 tablespoons of the lukewarm milk and water mixture in a cup. Add 1 teaspoon sugar and stir until dissolved. Sprinkle yeast over the surface; beat lightly with a fork and set aside for about 10 minutes, or until liquid is frothy and yeast granules have completely dissolved.

2   Meanwhile, sift flour, salt and remaining sugar into a warmed bowl and set aside for 10 minutes.

3   Make a well in the center of the flour; pour in dissolved yeast. Rinse cup out with remaining milk and water and add this to the flour. Knead into a smooth dough that is quite soft, but firm enough to roll into a ball.

4   When dough is smooth, gradually add melted butter, kneading vigorously until dough is smooth and springy again.

5   Roll dough into a ball; place in a buttered mixing bowl and cover with a sheet of buttered waxed paper or foil; then cover bowl with a cloth and set in a warm place to rise to 3 times its original bulk. This will take approximately 3½ hours.

6   When dough has risen, scoop it out on to a very lightly floured surface. Press it gently with the palm of your hand to deflate it; then fold it over onto itself to make a ball again; return to the bowl, cover as before and leave to rise again. This time it should take about 2 hours to double its bulk.

7   Punch dough down once again. Pat it into a rectangle, 8 × 4 inches, and seal in foil. Chill for 30 minutes.

8   Toward the end of this time, take chilled butter and work it with your fingertips until softened but not oily. If your hands are warm, hold them under cold running water for 1 or 2 minutes to cool them.

9   Unwrap dough and place on a lightly floured surface. Roll out into a rectangle 12 × 8 inches. Take small pats of butter; pinch them out paper thin between your fingertips and dot upper two-thirds of rectangle with them so that the entire surface is evenly covered, with just a ¼-inch border around the 3 outer sides unbuttered.

10   Fold unbuttered third of rectangle up over the center; then fold the top (buttered)

third down, making a neat rectangle composed of 3 layers of dough sandwiched with 2 layers of butter.

11 Dust board and rolling pin lightly with flour again if necessary and roll dough out once more into a rectangle 12 × 8 inches. Use short, light strokes to avoid overstretching the dough, or it will tear and allow butter to seep through. Fold in thirds as before, wrap in foil and chill for 15 minutes.

12 Unwrap foil and give dough a quarter-turn to the right, i.e., so that top now faces right. Repeat rolling and folding twice more, giving dough another quarter-turn to the right each time and chilling it for 15 minutes in between. After the last rolling and folding, seal tightly in foil and chill overnight (or for at least 2 hours).

13 **To shape croissants:** on a lightly floured board, roll dough into a rectangle 15 × 5 inches. Cut in thirds to make three 5-inch squares and return two of them to the refrigerator.

14 Roll remaining square into a rectangle 10 × 5 inches. Cut it in half to make two 5-inch squares again and cut each square into 2 triangles.

Croissants

15 Roll each triangle up quite tightly from the broadest end to the tip. Pull into a horseshoe shape, twisting ends slightly, and place on an ungreased baking sheet, with the tip of the triangle underneath.

16 Repeat with the 2 remaining squares of pastry, taking them from the refrigerator one at a time.

17 Cover croissants with a cloth and let rise again until doubled in bulk, about 30 minutes.

18 Preheat oven to 425°F.

19 When croissants are well risen, brush all over with beaten egg yolk. Bake for 8 to 10 minutes, or until light and crisp with a rich golden glaze.

20 Serve them lukewarm, or heat gently just before serving.

BRIOCHES

MAKES 12

    1 package active dry yeast
    8 tablespoons lukewarm water
    5 cups sifted flour
    4 tablespoons sugar
  1/2 teaspoon salt
    4 eggs
    8 tablespoons lukewarm milk
    1 teaspoon vanilla
    8 tablespoons softened butter
      Melted butter for molds
    1 egg yolk beaten with a little water for glaze

1 **The day before you wish to serve brioches:** dissolve yeast in a small bowl with lukewarm water.

2 Sift flour, sugar and salt into a warmed bowl and make a well in the center.

3 Beat eggs with lukewarm milk; stir in vanilla and add to flour, together with dissolved yeast. Mix well.

4 Add half the softened butter, diced, and beat with a wooden spoon until dough is smooth. It should be very soft at this stage.

Brioches

5 Dot surface of dough with remaining butter; cover bowl with a clean cloth and set aside in a warm place to rise until doubled in bulk, about 1½ hours.

6 Punch dough down and beat vigorously by hand for 5 minutes, or until it no longer sticks to sides of bowl (flour your hands from time to time while beating).

7 Cover bowl tightly with a sheet of foil and refrigerate overnight. Brioche dough is very rich and sticky, and chilling makes it easier to handle.

8 **The following day:** brush 12 individual brioche molds with melted butter.

9 Turn dough out on to a lightly floured surface and knead until smooth.

10 Weigh dough and cut off a quarter, making two balls. Divide each ball into 12 pieces of equal size. Roll the larger pieces into balls and place them in prepared molds. Roll each of the smaller pieces into a ball; snip top of each larger ball twice with scissors to form a cross and set one of the smaller balls on top.

11 Place molds on a baking sheet and let brioches rise again until doubled in bulk, about 30 minutes.

12 Preheat oven to 400°F.

13 When brioches have risen, brush tops with egg yolk beaten with a little water and bake for 15 to 20 minutes, or until firm and a rich golden color.

14 Turn out and cool on a wire rack.

HOT POPOVERS

MAKES 12

    Melted butter (about 5 tablespoons)
2 eggs
7 ounces milk
    Generous pinch of salt
1 cup sifted flour

1 Preheat oven to 400°F.

2 Put a teaspoon of melted butter in the bottom of each of 12 heavy cast-iron muffin pans. Place on a baking sheet and put into the oven to heat through for 5 to 6 minutes.

3 Combine eggs with milk, salt and 1 tablespoon melted butter in a bowl, and beat until well mixed. Add flour gradually, beating vigorously until batter is smooth and has the consistency of thick cream.

4 Divide batter between hot molds and bake for 25 to 30 minutes, or until well puffed and golden brown.

5 Turn out and serve immediately.

SCOTTISH BUNS

MAKES 12

2 cups milk and water, mixed
4 tablespoons lard
2 teaspoons sugar
1½ teaspoons salt
1 package active dry yeast
5 cups sifted flour

1 Heat milk and water until lukewarm. Add lard, sugar and ½ teaspoon salt; stir until dissolved.

2 Dissolve yeast according to instructions on package using some of the measured liquid.

3 Sift flour and remaining salt into a large, warmed bowl; make a well in the center and pour in dissolved yeast. Work into flour by hand, adding enough of milk mixture to make a soft but manageable dough. Depending on quality of flour, you may need up to 4 tablespoons more or less liquid.

4 Knead dough vigorously until shiny and pliable. Roll into a ball; place dough in a buttered mixing bowl; cover bowl with a damp cloth and set aside in a warm place until dough has doubled in bulk, about 1½ hours.

5 Preheat oven to 475°F.

6 Punch dough down; knead lightly and divide into 12 even-sized balls. Arrange them, well spaced apart, on 2 or 3 baking sheets. Flour palms generously and flatten rolls into flat disks; then press a hole in the center of each with your thumb—this is a characteristic feature of the Scottish bap.

7 Leave baps to rise again until puffy, about 20 minutes; then bake for about 10 minutes, so that they are just golden. Serve very fresh.

BUTTER SCONES

MAKES 8

   3 **cups sifted flour**
   2 **teaspoons baking powder**
   ½ **teaspoon salt**
   10 **tablespoons butter**
   2 **eggs, well beaten**
   7 **tablespoons very cold milk**

1 Preheat oven to 475°F.

2 Sift flour, baking powder and salt into a bowl. Rub in butter with fingertips until mixture resembles very coarse bread crumbs.

3 Make a well in the center and pour in eggs and milk. Combine lightly with a fork until dough holds together.

4 Turn dough out onto a floured board and roll lightly and quickly into a rectangle about ½ inch thick. Fold in three as you would puff pastry and roll out again. Repeat procedure twice more, handling dough as little as possible and working very quickly.

5 After folding dough for the third time, roll it out just under ½ inch thick and cut into 2½-inch rounds with a floured cookie cutter.

6 Arrange scones on an ungreased baking sheet and bake for 10 to 15 minutes, or until well risen and a rich golden color. Serve warm.

 MENU
Dried Fruit Compote
or
Stewed Apricots and Prunes
Deviled Kidneys and Bacon
or
Grilled Kippers
or
Poached Salmon Casserole
Scottish Buns
SERVES 6

RED WINES
Brouilly
Pomerol
Beaujolais

DRIED FRUIT COMPOTE

   ¾ **pound mixed dried fruit: apricots, peaches, apples, figs, prunes, raisins**
   5 **cups boiling water**
   3 **tablespoons sugar**
   1 **tablespoon grated orange rind**
   Juice of 1 lemon
   1 **orange, peeled and sliced**
   Blanched almonds, slivered

1 Preheat oven to 350°F.

2 Rinse fruit and place in a baking dish with boiling water. Cover tightly and bake for 1 to 1½ hours, or until fruit is plump and soft.

3 Pour off cooking juices into a saucepan. Add sugar, orange rind and lemon juice, to taste, and simmer for 5 minutes.

4 Pour syrup over fruit in a serving dish. Add orange slices and chill until ready to serve.

5 Just before serving, sprinkle with slivered almonds.

STEWED APRICOTS AND PRUNES

  6 ounces plump prunes
1¼ to 2 cups strong hot tea
1¼ to 2 cups hot water
  6 ounces dried apricots
  3 to 4 tablespoons sugar

1 Cover prunes with hot tea, and apricots with hot water, in separate bowls; soak overnight, or at least for several hours.
2 Slit prunes carefully and remove pits.
3 Transfer prunes and apricots to a pan, together with their soaking liquids. Sweeten to taste and simmer for 10 to 15 minutes, or until fruits are tender and syrup slightly thickened.
4 Cool; chill and serve with a pitcher of chilled cream.

GRILLED KIPPERS

6 plump kippers
3 tablespoons melted butter

1 Preheat broiler at maximum setting.
2 Remove heads, tails, fins and as many large bones as possible from the kippers; place the fish flat in a large, deep dish (a roasting pan is ideal). Pour over boiling water to cover; leave for just 1 minute, then drain thoroughly.
3 Grill kippers as follows, two or three at a time, brush them liberally on both sides with melted butter and arrange them, skin side down, in the pan. Place under broiler; reduce heat to moderate and broil kippers for 3 minutes, or until thoroughly hot, without turning them.
4 Remove each kipper to a heated plate and serve immediately.

DEVILED KIDNEYS AND BACON

 18 lamb kidneys
    Milk and water
 12 tablespoons softened butter
  1 tablespoon dry mustard
1½ teaspoons curry powder
  1 tablespoon lemon juice
    Tabasco sauce
    Cayenne pepper
    Salt and freshly ground black pepper

  6 tablespoons coarse stale bread crumbs, toasted
    Fried bacon for garnish

1 Trim kidneys of excess fat and discolored bits; slice each kidney lengthwise through the core so that it lies flat, without separating halves. Remove thin outer skins. Soak in milk and water for 1 hour (or overnight).
2 **When ready to cook kidneys:** combine butter with mustard, curry powder, lemon juice, several drops of Tabasco, cayenne, salt and pepper, to taste, and blend thoroughly.
3 Drain kidneys and pat dry. Make small incisions on both sides of each one with the point of a sharp knife. Place them flat in a roasting pan, cut sides up. Spread each with about 2 teaspoons deviled butter.
4 Place pan under a moderately hot, preheated broiler. After 3 or 4 minutes, turn kidneys over, baste and broil for 3 minutes longer. Then turn kidneys again; baste once more and sprinkle with toasted bread crumbs (1 teaspoon per kidney).
5 Turn broiler up to maximum temperature and broil for a final 3 to 4 minutes until kidneys are just cooked.
6 Serve immediately, sprinkled with pan juices and accompanied by crisp bacon slices.

POACHED SALMON CASSEROLE

  1 cup long-grain rice
    Salt
1½ pounds poached salmon
  3 hard-boiled eggs
  6 tablespoons butter
1½ teaspoons curry powder
    Freshly ground black pepper
  2 cups hot béchamel sauce (see page 140)
  6 to 8 tablespoons heavy cream
  2 tablespoons lemon juice
  3 tablespoons chopped parsley

1 Cook rice in boiling salted water until each grain is tender but still very firm. Drain thoroughly and keep warm.

2   Dice or flake fish coarsely, discarding any bones or pieces of skin.

3   Shell hard-boiled eggs; separate yolks from whites and chop the latter finely.

4   Melt butter in a wide, heavy pan; blend in curry powder; add fish and cook, stirring, over very gentle heat until hot and golden.

5   Add rice and egg whites and toss lightly until well mixed taking care not to crumble fish.

6   Season to taste with salt and pepper; remove from heat and keep hot.

7   Combine the béchamel sauce with cream and lemon juice.

8   Fold sauce into rice mixture, together with parsley.

9   Turn casserole into a heated serving dish. Sieve hard-boiled egg yolks over the top and serve very hot.

SCOTTISH BUNS

(For the recipe, see page 105.)

Fried Trout with New Potatoes and Parsley Butter

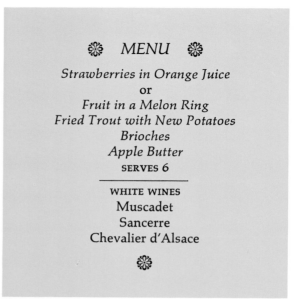

❀   *MENU*   ❀

Strawberries in Orange Juice
or
Fruit in a Melon Ring
Fried Trout with New Potatoes
Brioches
Apple Butter
SERVES 6

WHITE WINES
Muscadet
Sancerre
Chevalier d'Alsace

❀

STRAWBERRIES IN ORANGE JUICE

3 cups strawberries
Juice of 2 oranges, strained
Sifted confectioners' sugar
Whipped cream (optional)

1   Choose small strawberries. Toss with orange juice and sugar to taste. Chill in the refrigerator for at least 1 hour.

2   Serve in individual cups or bowls, garnished with a little whipped cream, if desired.

FRUIT IN A MELON RING

1 large, ripe cantaloupe or honeydew melon
2 cups soft fruit: strawberries, raspberries, etc.
Sifted confectioners' sugar
Lemon juice

1   Cut 6 thick slices across the widest part of a well-chilled, large, ripe melon. Scoop out seeds to make neat rings.

2   Toss fruit with sugar and lemon juice, to taste, and pile in center of melon rings. Serve immediately.

FRIED TROUT WITH NEW POTATOES

  6 (½-pound) trout
    Salt and freshly ground black pepper
    Milk
    Flour
  2 to 3 tablespoons olive oil
  4 to 6 tablespoons butter
  6 slices lemon
    Small bunch of parsley
1½ pounds small new potatoes, cooked

Parsley Butter:

4 tablespoons softened butter
2 to 3 tablespoons finely chopped parsley
  Lemon juice
  Salt and freshly ground black pepper

1 Wash and dry trout thoroughly both inside and out. Season with salt and pepper. Dip trout in milk, shake off excess, then coat with flour, patting it on gently so that it sticks to the skin.

2 Melt half the oil and butter in each of 2 large frying pans. When it is hot and sizzling, lay 3 trout, side by side, in each pan. Fry over moderate heat for 8 to 10 minutes, turning trout carefully with a spatula halfway through.

3 **To make parsley butter:** combine softened butter with parsley and blend until smooth. Season to taste with lemon juice, salt and black pepper. Chill until firm again.

4 Transfer trout to a large heated serving platter. Garnish with lemon slices and tiny sprigs of parsley and serve accompanied by hot boiled new potatoes tossed with diced parsley butter.

BRIOCHES

(For the recipe, see page 104.)

APPLE BUTTER

MAKES ABOUT 1 POUND:

  2 pounds tart apples
  ½ cup water
2½ cups sweet cider
    Juice of 1 lemon
  1 cup sugar
  ¼ teaspoon ground cloves
  ¼ teaspoon ground cinnamon
  ¼ teaspoon freshly grated nutmeg

1 Wash apples; slice them without coring or peeling and put them in a heavy saucepan. Add water, bring to a boil and cover tightly. Simmer for 10 to 15 minutes, or until apples are soft and fluffy.

2 Drain apples and rub them through a sieve.

3 While apples are cooking, simmer cider in a heavy pan until reduced to about 6 tablespoons.

4 Combine sieved apples with reduced cider, lemon juice, sugar and spices. Cook, stirring, over low heat until sugar has dissolved; then simmer, stirring occasionally, for about 20 minutes, or until puree is thick and glossy with the consistency of thick jam.

5 Pour into a hot, sterilized jar and seal.

Luncheon Parties Are Fun

Invite friends around for a meal and ten times out of ten they will assume that you mean dinner or supper. Lunches seem to have been relegated to the realms of expense account living, or a quick salad and coffee on a shopping trip in town.

True, with husbands away from dawn till dusk and wives shopping frantically among the office lunchhour crowds or coping at home with endless snacks of baked beans, fish sticks or hamburgers as the children bundle in and out, there seems little place in our modern way of life for the leisurely late luncheon parties of our grandparents' day.

It helped, of course, in those days, to have a kitchenful of cooks and maids hard at work preparing the feast from the early morning.

You may think that weekday lunch parties in suburban deserts devoid of menfolk are a pleasure you can do without—but every week has its oasis, and it is then that the weekend luncheon with its comfortable pattern of unhurried food in a free-and-easy setting comes into its own.

What about those friends who live just that little bit too far away to make driving back after a late dinner party feasible? Ask them over for Sunday lunch instead. You can read the papers over coffee before you start putting the food together (especially if you've done some of the preparation the evening before), and they can still get back home in time to prepare themselves for the stark realities of Monday morning.

A weekend lunch party is a great idea for a group of friends who are planning to go on to some other activity together—be it a football game, baseball, cards or just lazy chatter in the afternoon sun; for friends that you like well enough for you not to mind if they linger on into the evening (an occupational hazard for weekend lunch-party givers); or for friends with late-night babysitting problems (children are bright and relaxed enough early on in the day to enjoy you and your guests at the lunch table).

Some of my best lunch parties have been given in my house in the south of France. There we can sit fourteen around the huge farmhouse table, and it's a sort of cook-as-you-eat pattern where guests help to string the beans and carry away the dishes as I produce the next course. Great fun.

Lunch parties should be informal. That's really why they are such a pleasure to go to or to give.

Don't treat a lunch party like a poor relation of a dinner party. For, while the kind of food one serves is more or less elastic it is wise to keep it on the light side, and the drink as well: save your heavier, more full-bodied wines for leisurely evenings when you can give yourself up to them fully without fear of the consequences. Our menus for lunch parties are mainly three-course affairs—a light appetizer, a main course with a vegetable or salad, and an inspired dessert.

One of my favorite luncheon first courses—an avocado, tomato and onion appetizer—was created when I myself was a weekend guest in the country and was asked to make something out of what was available. To make it, peel avocados, cut them crosswise into thickish rings and combine them with thick slices of tomato and thin rings of onion; toss in French dressing for a deliciously light luncheon appetizer.

Try the recipe for salade de moules au kari (a fresh-tasting salad of curried mussels) or crab Louis with cucumber (tomato, cucumber and crab salad) to start your luncheon feast off with a flourish.

The main dishes in this section—sauté of veal with asparagus, little "tournedos" of lamb, and omelette Arlésienne—all bring a note of lightness to the menus.

As do the desserts—pineapple ambrosia, cold lemon soufflé, angel food cake, and glazed apple tart.

Get all the shopping done the day before—your three-course lunch will probably take up all of your time after clearing away breakfast, unless advance preparation has been seen to the previous evening.

Lunchtime entertaining doesn't mean roughing it in the kitchen—so polish up the silver and let your best china see the light of day.

❀ *MENU* ❀

Pâté Liégeois
German Veal with Almonds
with
Quick Hollandaise Sauce
and
Gratin Dauphinois
Italian Bean Salad
Grapefruit Sorbet
SERVES 6

———————

WHITE WINES
Chablis
Muscadet

❀

Gratin Dauphinois

PATE LIEGEOIS

- **1 pound chicken livers**
- **Salt**
- **½ pound sweet butter**
- **4 tablespoons grated onion**
- **2 teaspoons dry mustard**
- **½ teaspoon freshly grated nutmeg**
- **¼ teaspoon ground cloves**
- **Freshly ground black pepper**

1 Cover livers with salted water; bring to the boil; reduce heat and simmer, covered, for 20 minutes. Drain livers, pat dry and puree in an electric blender.

2 Return livers to pan and cook over moderate heat for 1 minute to evaporate excess moisture.

3 Work butter with a wooden spoon until soft and creamy. Add onion, mustard, nutmeg and cloves; then beat in livers. Season to taste with salt and pepper.

4 Pack pâté firmly into one or two small earthenware pots or terrines and chill until ready to use. Serve with hot toast.

GERMAN VEAL WITH ALMONDS

    2 **cups thinly sliced button mushrooms**
    4 **tablespoons butter**
    4 **tablespoons olive oil**
       Salt and freshly ground black pepper
    2 **tablespoons Madeira**
    6 **veal cutlets, about 4 to 5 ounces each**
    6 **ounces cooked tongue**
    1 **to 2 eggs**
    1 **cup fine dry bread crumbs**
  ½ **cup flaked almonds**
       Flour

1 Sauté mushrooms in 1 tablespoon *each* butter and olive oil until soft. Add salt and pepper. Sprinkle with Madeira and allow to cool.

2 Pound veal as thinly as possible.

3 Cut tongue into thin strips; divide into 6 portions and place one in the center of each cutlet. Spoon mushrooms on top and fold each cutlet into an envelope.

4 Beat egg(s) lightly with a little water. Toss bread crumbs with almonds.

5 Dust veal birds with flour; dip into egg and coat with almond-bread crumb mixture, patting it on firmly. Chill.

6 **To cook veal:** melt remaining 3 tablespoons butter and oil and fry veal slowly on both sides until golden brown, about 10 minutes. Serve immediately accompanied by **quick hollandaise sauce.**

GRATIN DAUPHINOIS

    2 **pounds potatoes**
  2½ **cups milk**
       Salt and freshly ground black pepper
    4 **tablespoons butter**
  1¼ **cups light cream**
    8 **tablespoons grated Gruyère cheese**
    3 **tablespoons grated Parmesan cheese**

1 Preheat oven to 375°F.

2 Peel and slice potatoes thinly into a bowl of cold water. Drain slices thoroughly and arrange in a 6-cup gratin dish.

3 Add milk; season to taste with salt and pepper.

4 Bake for 20 to 30 minutes, or until potatoes are half cooked. Remove from oven and reduce temperature to 325°F.

5 Drain potatoes. Rinse and dry gratin dish, then grease it with 2 tablespoons of the butter.

6 Layer potato slices in buttered dish and add cream. Sprinkle with grated cheese and dot with remaining 2 tablespoons butter.

7 Return to the oven for 30 minutes longer, or until potatoes are tender, with a golden crust. (Cover dish with foil if they brown too quickly.) Serve very hot.

QUICK HOLLANDAISE SAUCE

  12 **tablespoons butter**
    6 **egg yolks**
       Lemon juice
       Salt and white pepper

1 Melt butter in a small pan, taking care that it does not bubble or sizzle.

2 Warm container of an electric blender and in it combine egg yolks with 1½ teaspoons lemon juice, 1½ tablespoons water and a pinch of salt and white pepper.

3 Switch blender to moderate speed and, when yolks are well mixed, remove lid and pour in butter in a thin stream. If butter is poured in slowly enough, sauce will thicken into a genuine Hollandaise. However, if it remains too liquid, transfer to the top of a double boiler and cook, stirring, over hot water for a few seconds to thicken it; conversely, an overly stiff sauce may be thinned by beating in a tablespoon or two of very hot water.

4 Add more salt, pepper or lemon juice if necessary and keep sauce warm over warm water until needed.

ITALIAN BEAN SALAD

(For the recipe, see page 178.)

GRAPEFRUIT SORBET

1½ cups sugar
2½ cups fresh grapefruit juice
    Finely grated rind of 1 lemon

1 Turn refrigerator down to its lowest temperature.

2 In a heavy saucepan, combine sugar with 3 cups water. Bring to the boil, stirring until sugar has dissolved, and boil for 5 minutes.

3 Remove pan from heat. Cool syrup slightly.

4 Stir in grapefruit juice and the finely grated rind of 1 lemon. Leave to cool.

5 Pour mixture into freezing trays or into a container shallow enough to fit into your freezing compartment.

6 Freeze mixture for 4 hours, or until firm.

7 Transfer water ice to the main cabinet of the refrigerator at least 1 hour before serving to allow it to soften slightly.

8 Serve water ice in individual dishes. If you like, you can decorate each portion with fresh grapefruit segments or a sprinkling of

 MENU

Avocado, Tomato and Onion Appetizer
Sauté of Veal with Asparagus
and
Plain Boiled Rice
Pineapple Ambrosia
SERVES 6

WHITE OR ROSE WINES
Vouvray
Saumur Blanc
Tavel Rosé

AVOCADO, TOMATO AND ONION APPETIZER

4 to 6 slices large onion
2 large ripe avocados
6 firm, ripe tomatoes
1 to 2 tablespoons chopped parsley
    Finely chopped fresh herbs: basil, tarragon
    or chives

Vinaigrette Dressing:

3 tablespoons olive oil
1 to 2 tablespoons wine vinegar
    Salt and freshly ground black pepper
    Pinch of dry mustard
    Pinch of sugar

1 **To make vinaigrette:** beat olive oil and vinegar with a fork; season generously with salt and pepper and add a pinch *each* of mustard. and sugar.

2 Separate onion rings and use only the ones between 1½ inches and 2 inches in diameter. Soak them in ice water for 15 minutes, then drain thoroughly.

3   Peel avocados and cut into rings cross-wise, slipping each ring off the pit as you slice it.

4   Toss avocados with vinaigrette, coating each ring thoroughly to prevent it discoloring. Arrange in a deep serving dish.

5   Slice tomatoes and add them to the avocados, together with onion slices. Toss lightly; sprinkle with parsley and fresh herbs, to taste, and toss again. Serve very cold.

SAUTE OF VEAL WITH ASPARAGUS

- 2   **pounds asparagus**
-     **Salt**
- 1   **(2-pound) boned loin of veal**
- 6   **tablespoons butter**
-     **Freshly ground black pepper**
- 4   **scallions or shallots, finely chopped**
- 6   **tablespoons flour**
- ⅔   **cup heavy cream**
- 1   **teaspoon lemon juice**

1   Clean asparagus carefully, trimming root ends. Cut stalks in two, separating tips and stems. Cook tops and stems until tender in separate pans of simmering salted water: tips for about 8 minutes, stems 3 to 5 minutes longer. Drain well, reserving cooking liquids; keep hot.

2   Cut veal into 2-inch cubes.

3   Melt butter in a wide, heavy pan or casserole and sauté veal gently until golden on all sides. Do not let brown. Season to taste with salt and pepper.

4   Add scallions and sauté for a few minutes longer.

5   Sprinkle veal and scallions with flour and simmer gently until flour is cooked, taking care as before not to let ingredients brown.

6   Stir in 1¾ to 2⅔ cups reserved asparagus liquid; cover and simmer for 15 to 20 minutes, or until veal is tender.

7   Puree asparagus tips in a blender. Stir puree into veal, together with cream and lemon juice. Taste for seasoning, adding more salt, pepper or lemon juice if necessary. (Asparagus liquid will already have contributed some salt.) Simmer for 7 to 8 minutes longer.

8   Heat a large, deep serving dish. Transfer veal to dish and pour over sauce. Arrange asparagus stems attractively in small bunches around sides of dish and serve immediately, accompanied by a bowl of **plain boiled rice** (see page 89).

PINEAPPLE AMBROSIA

- 3   **small, ripe pineapples, about 1 pound each**
- 2   **oranges**
- 2   **bananas**
-     **Juice of ½ large lemon**
- 1   **cup fresh strawberries**
- ½   **cup confectioners' sugar**
- 1   **cup freshly grated or shredded coconut**

1   Using a very sharp knife, slice each pineapple in half vertically through the flesh and leafy stem. Carefully scoop out flesh, leaving a firm shell; cut flesh into small dice and place in a bowl.

2   Peel oranges and remove pith. Slice oranges into thin rounds, discarding seeds.

3   Peel and slice bananas. Toss in lemon juice to prevent discoloring.

4   Hull strawberries.

5   Layer fruit in pineapple shells, sifting a little confectioners' sugar to taste between each layer. Sprinkle with coconut and chill.

❊ *MENU* ❊
Salade de Moules au Kari
Shepherd's Pie
with
Quick Brown Sauce
and
Sautéed Zucchini and Tomatoes
Cold Lemon Soufflé
with
Langues de Chat
SERVES 6

WHITE WINES
Muscadet
Sancerre
RED WINES
Côtes-du-Rhône
Beaujolais

❊

SALADE DE MOULES AU KARI

    1 cup long-grain rice
       Salt
    2 quarts mussels
1¼ cups dry white wine
    1 large onion, finely chopped
    2 teaspoons curry powder
    ¼ pound shrimp, peeled and deveined
    2 firm tomatoes, sliced
    1 to 2 tablespoons chopped parsley
       Vinaigrette dressing (see step 6)
       Crisp lettuce leaves for garnish

1 Boil rice in salted water until tender but still firm. Drain thoroughly; cool.

2 Scrub mussels clean and remove beards. Place them in a heavy pan with wine, onion, and curry powder; cover tightly and cook over high heat, shaking pan frequently, until mussels have all opened. (Discard any that don't open.)

3 Shell mussels over pan to catch any liquor trapped inside. Strain liquor through cheesecloth and return to rinsed-out pan; add shrimp and simmer for 15 minutes.

4 Drain shrimp, reserving liquor, and com-

bine with rice and mussels in a bowl; add tomatoes and parsley.

5 Simmer shrimp liquor until reduced to about 3 tablespoons.

6 Make a highly seasoned vinaigrette, using 2 tablespoons wine vinegar, 5 tablespoons olive oil, 1 finely chopped shallot, salt and pepper, and beating with a fork until ingredients are well blended. Stir in reduced shrimp liquor and pour over salad; toss lightly and chill before serving piled in a lettuce-lined bowl.

SHEPHERD'S PIE

       Butter
    1 large onion, finely chopped
    2 tablespoons olive oil
    2 cups cooked roast beef, coarsely diced
    1 cup rich beef gravy or quick brown sauce
       (see below)
    2 teaspoons Worcestershire sauce
    1 tablespoon chopped parsley
    ¼ teaspoon each thyme, oregano, and rosemary
       Salt and freshly ground black pepper

Potato Topping:

    6 tablespoons heavy cream
    3 tablespoons melted butter
    2 eggs, lightly beaten
    2 pounds potatoes, peeled, boiled and mashed
       Salt and freshly ground black pepper

1 Generously butter a deep, 3-pint baking dish.

2 Preheat oven to 400°F.

3 Sauté onion in olive oil until soft and transparent. Stir in beef, gravy or **quick brown sauce** (see below), Worcestershire sauce, parsley and herbs, and season to taste with salt and pepper. Remove from heat.

4 **To make potato topping:** beat cream, 2 tablespoons of the melted butter and eggs into hot mashed potatoes, and season to taste with salt and pepper.

5 Spread meat mixture evenly in the baking dish. Top with mashed potatoes and brush with remaining 1 tablespoon melted butter.

6 Bake for 20 to 25 minutes, or until potatoes are puffed and golden brown.

7 Serve with **sautéed zucchini and tomatoes** (see page 67).

QUICK BROWN SAUCE

2 tablespoons butter
1 onion, coarsely chopped
1 carrot, coarsely chopped
½ bay leaf
3 sprigs parsley
1 sprig of fresh thyme or pinch of dried thyme
2 tablespoons flour
1 tablespoon tomato paste
2 cups hot beef stock
   Freshly ground black pepper

1 Melt butter in a heavy pan. Add onion, carrot, bay leaf, parsley and thyme. Brown vegetables thoroughly, stirring occasionally with a wooden spoon and scraping bottom of pan. Sprinkle in flour and continue to cook until this has browned as well.

2 Stir in tomato sauce and beef stock, scraping bottom of pan vigorously to dislodge crusty brown bits. Season lightly with pepper and simmer for 45 minutes, stirring occasionally.

3 Strain sauce through a fine sieve, pressing vegetables against sides of sieve to extract all their juices. Correct seasoning.

Note: The sauce can be used immediately, or stored for 2 days in an airtight container in the refrigerator.

Shepherd's Pie with Quick Brown Sauce and Sautéed Zucchini and Tomatoes

COLD LEMON SOUFFLE

3 eggs, separated
½ cup and more sugar
  Finely grated rind and strained juice of
    3 large lemons
1 envelope gelatin
1¼ cups heavy cream
  Whipped cream for decoration (optional)

1 Tie a double layer of waxed paper around the outside of a 1 quart soufflé dish to come at least 3 inches above the rim.

2 Place egg yolks in a bowl; add sugar and beat over hot water until very light, white and fluffy.

3 Gradually add lemon rind and juice, beating constantly, until mixture thickens; then remove from heat and beat until cool.

4 In a small cup, soften gelatin in 3 to 4 tablespoons cold water; place cup in a pan of hot water and stir gently until gelatin has completely dissolved.

5 Beat egg whites until stiff but not dry.

6 Beat cream until barely stiff enough to hold its shape.

7 Beat dissolved gelatin into egg and lemon mixture (for a completely smooth texture, they should both ideally be at the same temperature). Carefully fold in cream, followed by egg whites and more lemon juice or sugar, if desired.

8 Pour mixture into prepared soufflé dish and chill until set.

9 **To serve:** carefully peel off paper collar from dish and serve soufflé decorated with more piped whipped cream if desired, and accompanied by a plate of crisp **langues de chat.**

LANGUES DE CHAT

MAKES ABOUT 24

  Butter and flour for cookie sheets
4 tablespoons softened butter
½ cup sugar
2 egg whites
½ cup sifted flour

1 Preheat oven to 425°F. Butter and flour 2 or 3 cookie sheets, shaking off any excess flour.

2 In a small bowl, beat butter until creamy. Add sugar and beat vigorously until mixture is very pale and fluffy again. (This will take several minutes; the success of the cookies largely depends on adequate beating.)

3 Put egg whites in a shallow dish. Then, with a teaspoon, add them (unbeaten) to the butter mixture a little at a time, beating vigorously after each addition.

4 Sift flour over mixture and fold in lightly but thoroughly.

5 Spoon mixture into a pastry bag fitted with a plain ¼-inch nozzle and pipe out in 3-inch lengths, spacing them about 2 inches apart, as they spread considerably. If you do not have enough cookie sheets to take all the dough at once, these may be baked in batches.

6 Bake for 5 minutes, or until cookies are very thin and tinged with brown around the edges.

7 Quickly transfer to wire cooling racks with a spatula and allow to become quite cool and crisp before serving or storing in an airtight container.

2   Stir in olives and chill for at least 1 hour, preferably 2, before serving.

3   When ready to serve, fold flaked crabmeat into sauce.

4   Decorate outer edge of 4 or 6 individual plates with a ring of overlapping cucumber slices, and lay a large, crisp lettuce leaf in the center. Pile with crabmeat mixture and serve, garnished with chopped chives.

"TOURNEDOS" OF LAMB

     1   onion, finely chopped
     1   clove garlic, finely chopped
     2   tablespoons butter
     2   tablespoons olive oil
     1   cup soft white bread crumbs
     3   to 4 tablespoons cold milk
  1¼   pounds lean ground lamb
     3   tablespoons chopped parsley
     ¼   teaspoon dried oregano
     2   teaspoons Worcestershire sauce
     1   egg
          Salt and freshly ground black pepper
          Flour
     6   to 8 slices bacon

1   Sauté onion and garlic in half the butter and oil until soft; cool. Soak bread crumbs in milk; then squeeze out excess moisture.

2   Place lamb in a large bowl. Add onion and garlic, bread crumbs, herbs, Worcestershire sauce and egg, and mix well. Season with salt and pepper.

3   Divide mixture into 6 portions. Shape into balls; roll in flour and flatten into patties 2 inches in diameter.

4   Stretch each bacon slice to meet around the middle of a patty, using extra slices of bacon if necessary, and tie securely with string.

5   Heat remaining butter and oil in a large frying pan, or 2 smaller pans, and fry patties slowly on all sides until cooked through, about 30 minutes.

6   Discard strings, transfer patties to a heated serving dish and serve very hot.

CRAB LOUIS WITH CUCUMBER

     1   cup homemade mayonnaise (see page 141)
     2   tablespoons ketchup
     3   tablespoons olive oil
     1   tablespoon wine vinegar
     2   tablespoons grated onion
     2   tablespoons finely chopped parsley
     6   tablespoons heavy cream, whipped
          Tabasco or Worcestershire sauce (optional)
          Salt and freshly ground black pepper
          Cayenne
     1   to 2 tablespoons chopped, stuffed or ripe
          pitted olives
     2   cups flaked cooked crabmeat
          Thinly sliced unpeeled cucumber, lettuce
          leaves and 2 tablespoons chopped chives
          for garnish

1   Blend first 7 ingredients together. Season with Tabasco or Worcestershire sauce, if used, salt, pepper and a dash of cayenne, to taste.

POTATOES O'BRIEN

    2 to 2½ pounds potatoes, peeled
      and finely diced
    1 large green pepper, cored, seeded
      and finely chopped
    1 large onion, finely chopped
    1 tablespoon flour
    4 tablespoons chopped parsley
    1 cup freshly grated gruyère
      Pinch of cayenne
      Salt and freshly ground black pepper
    ½ cup hot milk
    ¾ cup heavy cream
    2 tablespoons butter

1 Preheat oven to 400°F.

2 Place potatoes, green pepper and onion in a bowl. Toss lightly.

3 Sprinkle vegetables with flour, parsley and gruyère and toss again. Then season to taste with a pinch of cayenne, salt and a little pepper, bearing in mind that the mixture may already be quite peppery because of the green pepper.

4 Spread potato mixture evenly in an 8-cup ovenproof dish; moisten with milk and cream, dot with butter and bake for 1 hour, or until potatoes are soft, with a crisp, golden topping.

ANGEL FOOD CAKE

    ¾ cup sifted flour
    ¼ cup sifted cornstarch
    ½ teaspoon salt
    1 cup sugar
   10 egg whites
    1 tablespoon lemon juice
    1 tablespoon water
    1 teaspoon cream of tartar
    1 to 1½ teaspoons vanilla

1 Preheat oven to 350°F.

2 Prepare a greased 9-inch tube pan, making sure that it is spotlessly clean, as otherwise the delicate cake will not rise properly.

3 Sift flour with cornstarch and salt. Sift ½ cup sugar separately, then resift flour mixture 3 times with 3 ounces of the sugar.

4 Mix egg whites with lemon juice and 1 tablespoon water; beat until foamy. Add cream of tartar and beat until stiff but not dry.

5 Beat in remaining sugar, a tablespoon at a time. **Note:** If you are using an electric mixer, start adding sugar earlier to avoid overbeating.

6 Flavor with vanilla.

7 Sift 2 to 3 tablespoons flour mixture over egg whites and fold in quickly and gently but thoroughly. Fold in remaining flour mixture gradually in the same way.

8 Turn mixture into prepared pan; bake for about 45 minutes, or until cake springs back when lightly pressed with a finger.

9 Remove cake from oven and immediately invert pan upside down, so that the cake hangs free—a bottle is good for this. Leave cake hanging for 1½ hours, or until set and cold.

10 Then gently shake cake out of the pan on to a serving dish. Serve with **orange sauce.**

ORANGE SAUCE

    Juice of 4 large oranges and ½ lemon
    Finely grated rind of 2 oranges
    2 tablespoons arrowroot
    3 tablespoons sugar
    2 tablespoons butter
    2 egg yolks, lightly beaten
    1 to 2 teaspoons Grand Marnier

1 Combine orange and lemon juice with orange rind in a measuring cup. There should be 1⅓ cups liquid. Add water to measure 2⅔ cups liquid.

2 Mix arrowroot with a little juice into a smooth paste, then combine with remaining juice and pour into pan.

3 Bring to a boil, stirring, and simmer for 2 to 3 minutes, until sauce is thick and translucent.

4 Beat in sugar and butter over low heat until dissolved.

5 Pour hot sauce over lightly beaten egg yolks, beating constantly.

6 Return to pan and cook, stirring, over low heat for a minute or two longer until sauce thickens slightly, taking care not to let it boil.

7 Strain sauce; cool slightly and flavor to taste with a little Grand Marnier.

8 Serve warm or cool.

❀ *MENU* ❀

Smoked Trout Appetizer
Omelette Arlésienne
Glazed Apple Tart
SERVES 4-6
———————
WHITE OR ROSE WINES
Chablis
Tavel Rosé

❀

OMELETTE ARLESIENNE

A rich, thick omelette that makes a substantial summer luncheon dish. Follow with a fresh green salad.

  3 **medium eggplants**
     Salt
½ **cup olive oil**
  1 **large onion, finely chopped**
  2 **pounds ripe tomatoes, peeled, seeded and diced**
     Freshly ground black pepper
  1 **clove garlic, finely chopped**
  4 **tablespoons finely chopped parsley**
  8 **eggs**
  1 **to 2 tablespoons melted butter**

1 Peel eggplants and dice pulp. Soak in a bowl of salted water for at least half an hour.

2 Heat half the olive oil in a deep, heavy frying pan. Add onion and tomatoes and sauté gently for a few minutes.

3 Drain eggplant thoroughly, squeezing out as much of its bitter juices as possible between the palms of your hands. Add eggplant to the simmering tomato mixture and mix well.

Omelette Arlésienne

SMOKED TROUT APPETIZER

  3 **smoked trout**
  6 **slices white bread**
  6 **tablespoons heavy cream**
  1 **to 2 tablespoons grated horseradish, or to taste**
     Finely chopped parsley

Garnish:

  6 **crisp lettuce leaves**
  6 **slices firm tomato**
  6 **large black olives, pitted and halved**
  6 **lemon wedges**

1 Skin and fillet smoked trout, and cut each fillet in two.

2 Toast bread slices and remove crusts.

3 Beat heavy cream; add 1–2 tablespoons iced water and beat again until firm. Fold in grated horseradish, to taste.

4 Spread each slice of toast with horseradish whipped cream and arrange pieces of trout on top. Sprinkle with a pinch of finely chopped parsley. Cut each slice of toast in half diagonally.

5 Serve 2 toast triangles per person on individual plates garnished with lettuce, tomato, black olives, and lemon wedges to squeeze over the trout.

4 Season to taste with salt and pepper and cook gently for about 25 minutes, stirring occasionally with a wooden spoon.

5 Add garlic and parsley, mix well and cook for a minute longer. Remove from heat and keep warm.

6 Beat eggs lightly with a fork. Season to taste with salt and pepper.

7 Heat remaining oil in a large omelet pan; pour in eggs and stir over a moderate heat until they begin to thicken and have set underneath.

8 Spoon eggplant mixture down center, reserving 2 or 3 tablespoons for garnish.

9 Continue to cook omelet until firm and golden brown on the underside but still creamy on top; then slide it up one side of the pan and fold it over on itself.

10 Slip folded omelet out carefully on to a heated serving dish. Brush with melted butter and garnish with remaining eggplant mixture. Serve immediately.

Glazed Apple Tart

GLAZED APPLE TART

You will need: 1 tart shell, **crème pâtissière** filling, tart apples, sliced thinly (enough to cover tart), lemon juice and apricot glaze.

Tart Shell:

> 2 **cups sifted flour**
> **Pinch of salt**
> 2 **tablespoons confectioners' sugar**
> 10 **tablespoons cold butter (1¼ sticks)**
> 1 **egg yolk**
> 2 **teaspoons lemon juice**
> **Ice water**

1 Sift the flour, salt and sugar into a large bowl.

2 Cut cold (not chilled butter) into ¼-inch cubes. Add to bowl.

3 Using a pastry blender (or two knives) cut butter into flour mixture until it resembles coarse bread crumbs.

4 Set aside pastry blender. Scoop up some of the mixture in the palms of both hands and let it shower back lightly through your fingers, gently rubbing out the crumbs of fat between your fingertips. You should only need to do this 6 or 7 times for the mixture to be reduced to fine bread crumbs.

5 Beat egg yolk in a small bowl. Add lemon juice and 1 tablespoon ice water, and beat lightly until well mixed.

6 Sprinkle this over flour mixture, tossing and mixing with a fork. Rinse out bowl with another tablespoon of ice water and mix this into the pastry in the same way. Continue tossing and mixing with the fork until about three-quarters of the pastry is holding together. Then use your hand, cupped, to press the pastry lightly into one piece.

7 Shape pastry into a round. Wrap in a sheet of waxed paper, followed by a dampened towel, and chill for at least 1 hour before using.

8 If chilled dough is too firm for handling, let it stand at room temperature until it softens slightly. Then turn on to a floured board, knead or pat lightly into a round, roll out and use as required.

9 Bake "blind" (see page 125) in a pre-heated 425°F oven for 15 minutes; lower heat to 350°F and bake for 30 minutes.

Crème Pâtissière Filling:

The magic trick of a French fruit tart is the sweet, creamy filling hidden underneath the fruit. Crème pâtissière holds its shape when cold, yet is soft and never stiff in texture.

MAKES 1¾ CUPS
  2 **cups milk**
  2-inch piece vanilla bean, split
  5 **egg yolks**
  ½ **cup sugar**
  2 **tablespoons flour**
  1 **tablespoon cornstarch**
  1 **tablespoon butter**
    A few drops of vanilla and/or flavoring according to specific recipe

1 Pour milk into a medium-sized pan and add vanilla bean, split to give out maximum flavor. Bring to boiling point over a low heat. Cover pan and put aside until needed.

2 In a bowl, beat egg yolks with sugar until thick and light. Gradually beat in flour and cornstarch.

3 Discard vanilla bean and gradually pour milk into egg yolk mixture, beating until well blended.

4 Pour mixture back into pan. Bring to a boil over a moderate heat, stirring constantly.

Then simmer for 3 minutes longer, beating vigorously with a wooden spoon to disperse lumps. (These lumps invariably form, but they are easy to beat out as the cream thickens.)

5 Remove pan from heat. Beat in butter and continue to beat for a minute or two longer to cool the pastry cream slightly before adding flavorings.

6 Strain cream, if necessary. Put in a bowl and cover with lightly buttered waxed paper to prevent a skin forming on top.

7 Allow to become quite cold; then chill until required.

8 **To assemble tart:** Half fill baked pastry shell with **crème pâtissière**; peel and slice apples thinly and brush with lemon juice to prevent discoloration. Arrange apple slices on **crème pâtissière** bed in overlapping rows. Coat with apricot glaze.

To Make Apricot Glaze:
(MAKES ENOUGH FOR 1 TART)
  ½ **cup apricot jam**
  4 **tablespoons water**
  1 **to 3 tablespoons rum, brandy or kirsch (optional)**

1 Heat apricot jam and water in a small saucepan, stirring constantly, until mixture melts. Strain.

2 If desired, stir in rum, brandy or kirsch. Keep warm over hot water, until ready to use.

3 Brush surface of fruit to give a shiny glaze.

Come for a Quiche and a Salad

One of the most delicious dishes I know is quiche Lorraine. This is a custard mixture of eggs and cream, sometimes thinned with a very little chicken, veal or beef stock. This savory mixture is poured over sautéed bacon bits and thin slices of Gruyère cheese. (I have often used cheddar in the country, when Gruyère was unavailable—not quite as delicate perhaps, but absolutely delicious in its own right.) You will find that the variations on this masterly recipe are practically limitless once you have perfected the basic custard mixture—and the pastry shell.

From this basic—but delicious—quiche recipe, it is just a simple step to a host of variations on the quiche theme. Tiny ones serve as cocktail canapés; larger ones as the main course for luncheon or supper, with a crisp salad as an accompaniment.

Quiches are a great boon to the busy host or hostess, as the pastry can be prepared the day before and chilled; the shells baked "blind" (see page 125) before they are filled and then put into the oven just 30 minutes before the guests sit down to dinner.

Ideally, quiches should be served warm, not too hot. I like to bake them in special large pastry pans with loose bottoms to make the turning out operation simple and painless.

It took me just four days to perfect the foolproof "fingertip" pastry that I use for all the quiches, tarts and flans that I serve daily in my restaurant, and that I have made for public demonstrations and parties all over the world.

Make the quiche your speciality. It's a wonderful "secret weapon" in the cook's arsenal for using up leftovers discreetly and elegantly. For a pastry shell filled with a custard mixture and your choice of garnish—bacon and cheese (quiche Lorraine); smoked salmon, shrimp, crab or lobster (seafood quiche); sliced mushrooms or zucchini simmered in butter and oil (vegetable quiche); spinach, cottage cheese and Parmesan (cheese and spinach quiche); or homely leeks and sausages—makes some of the best eating imaginable.

All you need to make the fabulous crumbly butter-rich pastry is 2 cups sifted flour, 1 tablespoon confectioners' sugar, a generous pinch of salt, 1¼ sticks slightly softened butter, 1 beaten egg yolk and an equal amount of ice water.

The custard mixture is easier still: 4 eggs, 2 cups milk or heavy cream (or a combination of the two) and salt, pepper and nutmeg or cayenne to taste.

A Lesson in Making Perfect Pastry

Make pastry in as cool a place as possible; the colder it is kept during the preparations, the lighter it will be.

See that all utensils used—pastry board, bowl, rolling pin, etc.—are clean and chilled. The board or marble should be smooth and perfectly flat. Use it for pastry making only.

Clean, dry hands are a must for pastry making. In the summer, when hands are apt to be warm, mix the pastry as much as possible with a knife or a pastry cutter to keep it cool.

Liquid should be added to the flour as quickly and lightly as possible. Some cooks do this on the board or slab by making a well in the center of the flour and pouring the water into the center as they mix. I find that mixing it in a large mixing bowl is much easier.

When handling pastry, never rub little pieces off the fingers on to the pastry or the pastry board as these tend to form hard lumps when cooked.

Pastry should always be wrapped in foil or a damp cloth and refrigerated for at least half an hour before it is used.

To Roll Out Dough

Sprinkle the pastry board with flour; place the dough on it and work lightly with the hands until free from cracks. Flour a rolling pin; press down the pastry and then with sharp, quick strokes roll pastry out to the thickness required.

Roll lightly and try to press equally with both hands.

Never allow dough to stick to the board; lift it occasionally on the rolling pin and dust some flour underneath. If any has stuck to the board, scrape it off carefully with a knife before beginning to roll again.

Always sprinkle flour over board and dough through a sifter to make it finer and lighter, using as little flour as possible for this, as too much tends to make the pastry hard.

If the rolling pin sticks to the pastry, dust with a little flour and brush it off again lightly with a small brush kept for this purpose.

To Bake Pastry

A fairly hot oven is required for pastry, for if it is not hot enough the butter will melt and run out before the starch grains in the flour have had time to burst and absorb it. If the oven is too hot, however, the pastry will burn before it has risen properly.

Pastry should never be baked in an oven in which meat is being roasted, or with any other dish that generates steam, as moist heat is apt to destroy its crispness. When baking pastry, open and close the door as gently as possible and never more often than is absolutely necessary.

If pastry becomes too brown before it has cooked sufficiently, cover it over with a piece of aluminum foil. If the pastry is not to be used at once when taken from the oven, allow it to cool slowly in the warm kitchen. Light pastry tends to become heavy when cooled too quickly.

To Bake "Blind"

Pastry that is going to be cooked with its filling should be prebaked in a hot oven for a while just to keep it from going soggy. To protect pastry during this process, professional cooks bake it "blind" in the following manner.

Line a pie plate with pastry, fluting the edges; chill. Prick bottom with a fork; cover bottom of pastry with a piece of waxed paper or aluminum foil, and cover this in turn with dried beans; then bake in a hot oven (450°F) for about 15 minutes, just long enough to set the crust without browning it. Remove beans and paper or foil and allow to cool. Then fill as desired and bake in a slow oven (325°F) until done. The beans can be reserved in a jar and used again.

However, if your tart or pastry shell is to be filled with a filling that is already cooked, it is imperative to continue cooking it as below.

To Bake Pastry Shell Only

Bake "blind" as above for 15 minutes; remove beans and foil; lower heat to 375°F and bake for 10 to 15 minutes longer. If crust becomes too brown at the edges, cover rim with a little crumpled foil.

FINGERTIP PASTRY

ENOUGH FOR A 9- TO 10-INCH PIE SHELL

1 Combine 2 cups sifted flour and 1 tablespoon confectioners' sugar in a large mixing bowl. Add a generous pinch (¼ teaspoon) salt and 10 tablespoons diced, slightly softened butter to the ingredients in the bowl. Lift flour gently over the butter cubes with your hands and then rub in the butter gradually with the tips of your fingers—lifting flour and butter out of bowl each time—until the mixture resembles fine bread crumbs. Do this very gently and lightly

Italian Antipasto Salad

or the mixture will become greasy and heavy. (More pastry has been ruined by overhandling than by underhandling.)

2 Place 1 egg yolk in a measuring cup or small bowl and add 4 tablespoons ice water. Mix well and add to pastry, working in lightly with your fingers.

3 Shape moist dough lightly into a slightly flattened round; wrap in aluminum foil, a clean dish towel or a plastic wrap and put it in the refrigerator for at least ½ hour to "ripen" and become firm.

If chilled dough becomes too firm for easy handling, let it stand at room temperature until it softens slightly. Then turn out on to a floured board and roll as required.

4 Press into a pie plate with your fingers and prick with a fork.

MENU

Italian Antipasto Salad
Smoked Haddock Quiche
Baked Apple Compote
SERVES 4-6

WHITE WINES
Chianti Ruffino
White
Mâcon-Viré
Bourgogne Aligoté

ITALIAN ANTIPASTO SALAD

1 **head lettuce**
4 **heads chicory, sliced lengthwise**
2 **fennel roots, cut into sections**
1 **green pepper, sliced in rings**
1 **red pepper, sliced in rings**
1 **large onion, very coarsely diced**
4 **anchovy fillets, coarsely chopped**
2 **tablespoons capers**
   Parsley sprigs for garnish

Italian Dressing:

6 **tablespoons olive oil**
2 **tablespoons lemon juice**
½ **clove garlic, finely chopped**
2 **tablespoons finely chopped parsley**
   Salt and freshly ground black pepper

1 Wash and dry the lettuce leaves and arrange in the bottom of a large, shallow salad bowl.

2 Arrange chicory, fennel, peppers and onion in groups on the lettuce.

3 Mix the anchovies with capers and place in the center of the salad.

4 **To make dressing:** combine the first 4 ingredients and season to taste with salt and pepper.

5 Sprinkle salad with dressing and garnish with sprigs of parsley.

SMOKED HADDOCK QUICHE

½ **pound fingertip pastry (see above)**
½ **pound smoked haddock**
⅔ **cup milk**
4 **eggs**
⅔ **cup heavy cream**
   Salt and freshly ground black pepper
   Freshly grated nutmeg
   Butter

1 Soak smoked haddock in water for 1 hour. Drain, place in a small saucepan, cover with equal amounts of milk and water and bring to a fast boil. Remove from heat and allow to stand for 15 minutes. Drain, reserving stock. Remove skin and bones; break fish into pieces.

2 Beat eggs together with cream, ⅔ cup milk and ⅔ cup reserved haddock stock. When well mixed, flavor to taste with salt, freshly ground black pepper and freshly grated nutmeg.

3 Line a large pastry tin (or 6–8 individual tins) with pastry; prick bottom with a fork and bake "blind" in a 450°F oven for 10–15 minutes, or just long enough to set pastry without browning it. Allow to cool.

4 Arrange flaked cooked haddock in bottom of pastry case (or cases) and fill with custard mixture. Dot with butter. Bake in a 325°F oven for 30–40 minutes and serve immediately.

Note: Unless you use a very large pastry tin (one with a removable bottom), you will have surplus custard mixture. Use for baked fish custard with any leftover fish.

BAKED APPLE COMPOTE

2 **pounds cooking apples**
   Rind and juice of 1 lemon
1 **cup brown sugar**
4 **tablespoons butter**
   Heavy cream

1 Slice peeled and cored cooking apples into a buttered baking dish.

2 Sprinkle with lemon juice, lemon rind and brown sugar and dot with butter.

3 Bake, uncovered, in a 375°F oven for 30 minutes, or until tender. Serve with cream.

MENU

Quiche Lorraine
Tossed Green Salad with Herbs
Fresh Pineapple with Kirsch
SERVES 4-6

WHITE OR ROSE WINES
Sylvaner d'Alsace
Touraine Sauvignon
Chablis
Tavel Rosé

QUICHE LORRAINE

> **Fingertip pastry for 10-inch pie**
> **(see page 125)**
> 1 **egg, beaten**
> 4 **egg yolks**
> 1¼ **cups light cream**
>   **Salt and freshly ground black pepper**
>   **Freshly grated nutmeg**
> 6 **to 8 slices bacon**
> 2 **tablespoons butter**
> 1 **cup diced Gruyère cheese**

1 Line a pie plate with pastry. Prick bottom with a fork; brush with a little beaten egg and bake "blind" at 450°F for 15 minutes.

2 Beat egg yolks in a bowl; add cream and beat until thick and lemon-colored. Season to taste with salt, pepper and nutmeg.

3 Fry bacon until crisp.

4 Arrange bacon and cheese in pastry shell. Pour over cream and egg mixture and bake in a 375°F oven for about 30 minutes. Serve hot.

TOSSED GREEN SALAD WITH HERBS

(For the recipe, see **green salad and variations,** page 146.)

FRESH PINEAPPLE WITH KIRSCH

> 8 **to 12 thin slices fresh pineapple**
>   **Sugar**
>   **Kirsch**

1 Trim cores and rinds from pineapple and arrange slices in overlapping circles in a flat serving dish.

2 Sprinkle with sugar and kirsch to taste.

Four Summer Meals from the Continent

Summer Food– Italian Style

One of the most delicious pasta dishes I know —and one of the quickest and easiest to prepare —is tagliatelle alla crema, egg noodles in a creamy, cheese-flavored sauce. The noodles are cooked in boiling, well salted water until they are tender, but not mushy, drained and then tossed in a sauce made of heavy cream and egg yolks, well seasoned with salt and freshly ground black pepper. You will find that the heat of the tagliatelle cooks the delicate sauce as you toss it. But make sure that the serving bowl, dishes and tagliatelle are piping hot before you start operations. To finish the dish, add a lump of butter and some freshly grated Parmesan cheese and serve immediately. Our second course—breaded baby lamb chops—is an Italian innovation that might have come right out of an eighteenth-century cookbook. The lamb chops should be tiny—they're no bigger than your finger in Italy. They are dipped in egg yolk and then in grated bread crumbs before being pan-fried. The crisp, golden covering and the moist meat within make a perfect combination of taste and texture. Italians often serve them after a pasta dish. I like them with well drained fresh spinach simmered in butter or, for an even better contrast, a peppery watercress and radish salad tossed in a mustard-flavored vinaigrette sauce. Orange ice, with a touch of lemon, ends this light summer meal with a clean, sharp flavor.

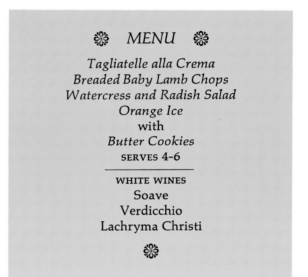

❊ *MENU* ❊

Tagliatelle alla Crema
Breaded Baby Lamb Chops
Watercress and Radish Salad
Orange Ice
with
Butter Cookies
SERVES 4-6

WHITE WINES
Soave
Verdicchio
Lachryma Christi

❊

TAGLIATELLE ALLA CREMA

  1 **pound tagliatelle**
    Salt
    Butter
  4 **egg yolks**
 ⅔ **cup heavy cream**
    Pinch of nutmeg
    Freshly grated Parmesan cheese

1 Bring 3 to 4 quarts well salted water to a boil in a large saucepan. Add tagliatelle and cook until tender but still firm.

2 Melt 4 tablespoons butter in a large saucepan. Drain the pasta and, while it is still very hot, toss in the butter.

3 Pour the egg yolks beaten with cream over the pasta; add a grating of nutmeg. Stir for a minute; remove from heat and add an addi-

Tagliatelle alla Crema

tional 4 tablespoons butter. The sauce and eggs should not begin to solidify. Serve with freshly grated Parmesan cheese and additional butter.

BREADED BABY LAMB CHOPS

    4 to 6 tender baby lamb chops
      Salt and freshly ground black pepper
      Flour
    2 eggs, well beaten
      Fresh bread crumbs
    4 to 6 tablespoons clarified butter
      Béarnaise sauce (see page 142)

1 Trim lamb chops and flatten with the side of a cleaver. Season with salt and pepper to taste. Roll in flour; dip in beaten eggs and then roll in bread crumbs.

2 Heat clarified butter in a thick-bottomed frying pan and sauté cutlets for 5 minutes on each side, or until golden brown and tender.

3 Serve with a béarnaise sauce.

WATERCRESS AND RADISH SALAD

    1 head lettuce
    1 bunch watercress
    1 bunch radishes

1 Wash and trim lettuce and watercress. Dry thoroughly.

2 Wash and trim radishes, then slice paper thin. Chill lettuce, watercress and radishes.

3 **To assemble salad:** arrange lettuce leaves in a salad bowl and spread watercress on top. Scatter radishes over the top.

4 Make **French dressing** (see page 146) and just before serving add dressing and toss until every ingredient glistens.

ORANGE ICE

 1½ **cups sugar**
  3 **pints water**
  2 **cups orange juice**
 ½ **cup lemon juice**
    Finely grated rinds of 1 orange
      and 1 lemon
    Orange segments
    Slivered orange rind

1 Bring sugar and water to the boil; boil for 5 minutes.

2 Cool slightly and add juices and grated rinds.

3 Cool, strain and freeze.

4 Serve in individual dishes, garnished with orange segments and slivered orange rind simmered in a little syrup.

BUTTER COOKIES

  3 **cups sifted flour**
  2 **teaspoons baking powder**
  1 **teaspoon salt**
 12 **tablespoons butter**
  1 **cup sugar**
  2 **eggs**
  1 **teaspoon vanilla or almond extract**

1 Sift flour with baking powder and salt into a bowl. Beat butter, sugar and eggs until creamy. Add vanilla or almond extract and continue to beat until well mixed. Blend in flour mixture. Divide dough into two parts and chill until it can be easily handled.

2 Preheat oven to 400°F.

3 Roll out half the dough on a lightly floured surface, about ⅛ inch thick. Cut into desired shapes with floured cookie cutters.

4 Place cookies on ungreased baking sheets about 1 inch apart. Bake for 6 to 8 minutes, or until firm and slightly browned. Repeat steps **3** and **4** with remaining dough.

Summer Luncheon in Provence

The easiest way to take yourself back to some well-remembered holiday place is to recreate at home the dishes you enjoyed there. This menu takes us to Provence, where you can eat in some of the most famous restaurants in the world or have a three-course meal in a charming back-street café for a very modest sum—with the wine and service thrown in. No matter where you choose to eat, you will find the cuisine is based on the fresh vegetables (often dressed in olive oil) and fruit that are the blessings of Provençal markets, or the region's specialities, such as black olives, and on recipes designed to bring out the subtle flavors of the ingredients.

One of the best ways to reproduce a Provençal meal is to start off with a typical selection of hors d'oeuvres: roasted pepper and fresh tomato salads, tuna fish, anchovies and a cold ratatouille served in individual terrines, bowls or *raviers* (those oblong, porcelain hors d'oeuvre dishes used by French restaurants the world over).

The main course is an earthy daube of beef, flavored with finely chopped onions, bacon, garlic and herbs.

You'll find that this recipe uses no liquids. It is the juices of the vegetables and meat, slowly simmered in a cast-iron or enameled casserole, that give richness to the dish. For extra flavor, I sometimes boil a quarter of a bottle of red wine to a quarter of its original quantity and stir it into the juices just before serving.

Serve the daube with boiled new potatoes or rice. Follow with a green salad and then end the meal with a tart, mouth-freshening lemon sherbet.

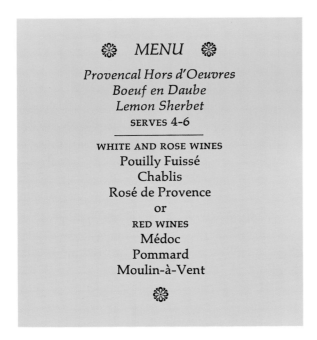

❀ *MENU* ❀

Provencal Hors d'Oeuvres
Boeuf en Daube
Lemon Sherbet
SERVES 4-6

WHITE AND ROSE WINES
Pouilly Fuissé
Chablis
Rosé de Provence
or
RED WINES
Médoc
Pommard
Moulin-à-Vent

❀

PROVENÇAL HORS D'OEUVRES

1: Peppers

Choose sweet peppers—both yellow and green —and brush with olive oil. Drain and put them under the broiler until they begin to change color. Then slice them and toss with a **vinaigrette sauce** (see page 146) to which you have added a little finely chopped garlic and parsley.

2: Sardine Salad

Open 2 cans of sardines packed in oil. Remove sardines and drain off surplus oil. Combine 2 tart, diced apples, 1 medium-sized, finely chopped onion, 2 tablespoons finely chopped parsley and 4 thin lemon slices in a bowl. Add 6 tablespoons olive oil and 2 tablespoons lemon and mix well. Add sardines and freshly ground pepper to taste, and marinate for at least 2 hours before serving. Toss carefully just before serving to amalgamate flavors.

3: Tomatoes

Choose large, ripe tomatoes; slice them in half and arrange in a dish. Top with thinly sliced shallots or raw leeks and finely chopped parsley. Serve with a **vinaigrette sauce** (see page 146).

4: Green and Black Olives

5: Tuna Fish

Flake canned tuna fish and arrange in an hors d'oeuvre dish. Top with slices of hard-boiled egg, thinly sliced scallions and finely chopped parsley. Dress with a **vinaigrette sauce** (see page 146).

BOEUF EN DAUBE

  1 **pound Canadian bacon (1 piece)**
  3 **onions, sliced**
  3 **tablespoons olive oil**
  3 **tablespoons butter**
  3 **pounds bottom round, cut into 2-inch cubes**
     Flour
     Coarse salt and freshly ground black pepper
  1 **to 2 cloves garlic**
  1 **strip dried orange rind**
  2 **cloves**
     Bouquet garni: 2 sprigs thyme,
       4 sprigs parsley, 2 bay leaves

  1 Cut bacon into large cubes; combine with onions, olive oil and butter and sauté until onions are transparent.

  2 Sprinkle beef cubes with flour; add to casserole and continue to cook, stirring constantly, until brown.

  3 Then add coarse salt, pepper, garlic, dried orange rind, cloves and bouquet garni. Place casserole in a preheated 275°F oven and cook for 2½ to 3 hours.

LEMON SHERBET

  1 **cup sugar**
  3 **cups water**
 1¼ **cups lemon juice**
     Finely grated rind of 1 large lemon

  1 Bring sugar and water to the boil; boil for 5 minutes. Cool slightly and add lemon juice and rind.

  2 When cold, strain through a fine sieve and freeze in a rectangular aluminum loaf pan. Stir sherbet from time to time. It will take 2 to 3 hours to freeze.

A Continental Summer Luncheon for Four

❀ MENU ❀

Tomato and Eggplant Casserole
Saltimbocca
Italian Bean Salad
Baked Pears in White Wine
SERVES 4

WHITE WINES
Soave
Verdicchio
Lachryma Christi

Summer meals should be comparatively easy to fix. The French and Italians often solve the problem of warm weather food with casseroles, which save standing at a hot stove. This summer lunch begins with a simple, satisfying dish made of tomatoes and eggplants—substantial enough to stand alone as a main course, yet just right as a prelude to the superlight rolls of veal and prosciutto which follow.

TOMATO AND EGGPLANT CASSEROLE

A bubbling casserole of sliced tomatoes and golden-fried eggplants in alternate layers, high-lighted with cheese and cream. Served right from the cooking pot, it has a melting texture and smooth, rich flavor.

> 4 to 6 eggplants
> Salt
> 2 tablespoons olive oil
> Butter
> Freshly ground black pepper
> ½ cup freshly grated Parmesan cheese
> ⅔ cup heavy cream
> 4 to 6 tomatoes, thickly sliced
> 4 tablespoons bread crumbs

1 Peel the eggplants; cut in thin slices; sprinkle with salt and let them "sweat" in a dish for 2 hours. Drain slices, wipe and fry lightly in olive oil until soft and golden, but not quite cooked. Drain again.

2 Butter a deep ovenproof casserole; place a layer of eggplant slices in the bottom; season with pepper and sprinkle generously with grated cheese and fresh cream.

3 Add a layer of sliced raw tomatoes; add

pepper and a little more cream and cheese, then another layer of eggplant slices and so on until the dish is full.

4 Finish with cream on top, cover with bread crumbs and grated Parmesan, dot with butter and cook in a 375°F oven for 45 minutes.

SALTIMBOCCA

Wine-glazed rolls of veal and Parma ham—as easy to make as they are to serve. They are sautéed in butter before guests arrive and then simmered gently on top of the stove until ready to serve. Accompany them with a chilled **Italian bean salad**—*cooked green beans with a French dressing and a little finely chopped garlic and fresh parsley (see page 178).*

> 4 thin slices veal
> 8 to 12 small fresh sage leaves or ½ to 1
>   teaspoon crumbled sage
> Freshly ground black pepper
> 4 thin slices prosciutto (Parma ham)
> Flour
> Melted butter
> 2 tablespoons Marsala or dry white wine

1 Flatten veal into thin pieces; cut each slice into 2 or 3 pieces. Place 1 sage leaf (or

pinch of crumbled sage) on each slice, and add pepper, to taste (no salt, the prosciutto will flavor meat). Cover each slice of veal with prosciutto cut to the same shape; make each into a small roll and secure with a toothpick.

2   Dredge rolls in flour and cook in melted butter until golden all over; then add Marsala.

3   Cook over a high heat for a moment; then reduce heat, cover the pan and simmer gently until the veal and ham rolls are quite tender. Remove toothpicks from each roll and transfer meat to a hot serving platter. Serve immediately.

BAKED PEARS IN WHITE WINE

    4 pears
       Dry white wine to cover
       Sugar
    2 tablespoons chilled kirsch (optional)
       Whipped cream

1   Peel pears and place in an ovenproof baking dish with dry white wine and sugar.

2   Cover and bake in a 375°F oven for 45 minutes.

3   Serve warm with chilled kirsch and/or whipped cream.

Tortellini in Brodo

A Simple Italian Dinner

 MENU

Tortellini in Brodo
Liver and Onions, Italian Style
with
Buttered Spinach
Cold Orange Soufflé
or
Peach Sherbet
SERVES 4-6

RED WINES
Chianti Ruffino Red
Valpolicella
Barolo

TORTELLINI IN BRODO

    1 pound shin of beef with bone
   7½ cups water
    1 beef bouillon cube
    2 celery stalks, coarsely chopped
    1 onion, coarsely chopped
    6 carrots, peeled and chopped
    3 tomatoes, peeled, seeded and chopped
       Salt and freshly ground black pepper
    ½ pound tortellini noodles
       Finely chopped parsley

1   Ask your butcher to cut through the shin bone in 2 or 3 places.

2   Place the meat and bones in water; add the bouillon cube and bring to the boil. Remove surface scum; add the vegetables; cover and simmer for 1 hour.

3   Remove the meat and strain the broth. Season to taste with salt and pepper.

4   Add the tortellini to the broth and cook for 20 minutes longer.

5   Serve in a heated soup tureen, garnished with a little chopped parsley.

LIVER AND ONIONS, ITALIAN STYLE

The Italians are past masters at cooking liver. Their secret is to cut it almost paper thin and then sear the slices in butter and oil over high heat so that they remain meltingly pink and tender inside. It is overcooking that causes liver to toughen and lose its flavor.

> 1 pound calves' liver
> ½ to ¾ teaspoon crumbled sage
> Salt and freshly ground black pepper
> 4 tablespoons butter
> 2 tablespoons olive oil
> 1 pound onions, thinly sliced
> Lemon juice
> 2 tablespoons finely chopped parsley

1 Cut the liver into very thin slices, or have this done by your butcher.

2 Dredge liver in crumbled sage and season with salt and pepper.

3 In a large frying pan, melt butter with olive oil. Add onions and sauté until soft and a rich golden color. Remove onions with a slotted spoon and keep hot.

4 Add a little more butter and oil to the pan if necessary. Raise the heat and fry liver slices quickly for just 1 or 2 minutes on each side. Then return onions to the pan and toss together with liver for a few seconds longer.

5 Sprinkle a few drops of lemon juice over the entire pan; garnish with parsley and serve immediately with **buttered spinach** (see page 35).

COLD ORANGE SOUFFLE

> 3 eggs
> 5 medium-sized oranges
> 1 envelope gelatin
> 3 to 6 tablespoons sugar
> 1 teaspoon cornstarch
> Juice of 1 to 2 lemons
> ½ teaspoon vanilla
> 2 tablespoons orange-flavored liqueur (optional)
> ⅔ cup heavy cream

To Decorate:

> Orange segments
> Whipped cream

1 Separate the eggs. Place the egg yolks in the top of a double boiler and beat well. Place the whites in a round-bottomed bowl.

2 Squeeze the oranges and strain the juice into an enameled saucepan. Add gelatin and set aside for 30 minutes. Then add sugar and cornstarch and cook over gentle heat, stirring constantly, until mixture comes to a boil. As soon as it starts to boil, remove from heat and pour through a fine sieve into egg yolks. Beat well and place double boiler over hot, but *not* boiling water. Cook the orange mixture, stirring constantly, until the sauce coats the back of a spoon. (**Note:** Do not allow the sauce to come to a boil, or it will curdle.) Add lemon juice to taste, vanilla and orange-flavored liqueur, if desired.

3 Whip the cream until stiff; beat the egg whites until stiff; fold both gently into the orange cream. Spoon into 4 individual soufflé dishes around which you have tied a piece of aluminum foil to make a collar about 2 inches high—or use 1 large soufflé dish. Refrigerate until set.

4 **When ready to serve:** remove the foil and decorate the tops of the soufflés with orange segments and a swirl of whipped cream.

PEACH SHERBET

> 1⅓ cups peach puree
> 1⅓ cups syrup for ices
> Juice of 1 lemon
> 2 to 3 drops almond extract
> 2 to 3 drops red food coloring

1 Peel peaches and blend in an electric blender to obtain 1⅓ cups puree.

2 Add syrup to the fruit puree together with strained lemon juice and almond extract. Tint mixture slightly with red food coloring. Cool and then freeze, stirring the mixture up vigorously with a fork every half-hour, until half frozen, then leaving it for a further 2 or 3 hours until frozen hard. Transfer from freezer to refrigerator about 1 hour before serving.

A water ice should not be served when it is still hard. It is best served scooped into frappé or parfait glasses just one stage harder than slushy—i.e., firm enough to hold a shape in scoop.

Note: It is the absence of any fat in the syrup that permits large ice crystals to form. In order to break these down, the mixture must be beaten vigorously with a fork at regular intervals before being allowed to freeze hard.

Syrup for Sherbet:

MAKES 3 CUPS

> 2 **cups sugar**
> 2½ **cups water**
>   **Juice of ½ lemon**

Combine sugar and water in an enameled saucepan; bring to the boil and boil for 10 minutes, removing any scum that rises. Add lemon juice and strain through a cheesecloth-lined sieve.

Fundamentals

Drinks

Drinks—the right kind—can spark a party. Of course, there is always champagne or gin and tonic, whiskey and soda, or the ubiquitous Bloody Mary. But for my money nothing beats one or two specially prepared cocktails for getting people quickly into a party mood.

The quantities given below are for one drink.

BACARDI COCKTAIL

Combine the juice of ½ a large lime, or 1 small lime, with ½ teaspoon granulated sugar and 1½ ounces Bacardi rum. Mix thoroughly and then strain through crushed ice.

PERNOD DAIQUIRI

Combine the juice of ½ a large lime, or 1 small lime, with 1½ ounces white rum and add a dash of Pernod and confectioners' sugar, to taste. Strain through crushed ice.

RYE SNIFTER

Crush 1 small lump of sugar with a dash of Angostura bitters and 2 tablespoons water in bottom of brandy snifter. Add ice cubes, 1½ ounces rye and 1 piece lemon peel. Finish with a generous squirt of soda water and top with a slice of orange or lemon and a maraschino cherry.

ORANGE GIN FLING

Combine 1½ ounces gin with 1 tablespoon *each* Italian vermouth and French vermouth. Add 3 ounces fresh orange juice and strain through crushed ice.

MANHATTAN COCKTAIL

Put 2 or 3 ice cubes into an old-fashioned glass. Add 1½ ounces bourbon, 1 tablespoon Italian sweet vermouth and a dash of Angostura bitters and stir. Top with a slice of orange and a maraschino cherry.

WHITE LADY

Combine 1½ ounces gin with 1 tablespoon *each* lemon juice and Cointreau. Strain through crushed ice.

SPANISH BLOODY MARY

Combine 1½ ounces vodka with tomato juice, a little Tabasco and Worcestershire sauce, celery salt and freshly ground black pepper, to taste, and add a dash of La Ina sherry.

CHAMPAGNE COCKTAIL

Rub half a sugar cube with angostura bitters; add a shot of cognac and a slice of orange and top with chilled champagne.

CHAMPAGNE ORANGE

Cut the peel from 1 orange in a long spiral. Arrange the strip of peel in a balloon glass and fill with ice cubes. Add 1½ ounces gin and enough chilled champagne almost to fill glass. Gently spoon in 2 tablespoons cognac.

Hors d'Oeuvres

Interesting hors d'oeuvres—fingers of toast spread with steak tartare, or bacon and chutney and cream cheese—can make your reputation as the best party giver in town. Try one, or more, at your next cocktail party.

STEAK TARTARE

Grind 1 pound lean beef twice and combine with 1 egg yolk, 4 tablespoons finely chopped onion, 2 cloves garlic, finely chopped, salt, freshly ground black pepper, 1 tablespoon Worcestershire sauce, 2 tablespoons finely chopped parsley and 4 tablespoons cognac in a mixing bowl. Mix thoroughly and chill until ready to serve.

Spread on rounds of rye, toast, or fingers of pumpernickel bread. Top with chopped onion and hard-boiled egg, parsley, capers or caviar.

SOUSED CAMEMBERT CANAPES

Remove outer skin from ½ pound Camembert cheese, cut in quarters and marinate in 1⅓ cups dry white wine at room temperature for at least 6 hours, turning cheese several times. Drain cheese, discarding wine, and mash through a coarse strainer; blend in 8 tablespoons softened butter; add cayenne pepper to taste and chill. Spread rounds of bread or toast with cheese mixture and dust generously with finely chopped almonds.

BACON AND CHUTNEY CANAPES

Dice 8 slices lean bacon finely and fry until crisp. Pour off fat and stir in 1 small jar mango chutney, finely chopped. Spread bread fingers with cream cheese. Top with chutney mixture.

PROVENÇAL CANAPES

Combine 4 to 6 tablespoons of mayonnaise with 2 tablespoons olive oil and 1 tablespoon Dijon mustard and beat until smooth. Add 1 onion, 10 anchovies and 2 hard-boiled eggs, all finely chopped. Season with the juice and grated rind of 1 lemon and freshly ground black pepper. Spread on buttered rounds of French bread.

The same basic mixture used for Provençal canapes can serve for both spreads and dips. Just add a little more cream, sour cream or lemon juice to thin the spreads to a dippable consistency.

Use spreads with thin fingers or rounds of toasted white or dark bread, rye bread, brioches or pumpernickel.

Serve dips in small bowls with a platter of crisp crackers, toasted fingers of white or dark bread, rye, brioches or pumpernickel. Greek pita bread and Mexican tortillas make good "dippers," as do potato chips, or crisp raw vegetables —julienne slices of carrot, green or red pepper, celery, cucumber, trimmed radishes and cauliflowerets—kept ice cold in bowls of ice.

OLIVE CHEESE MIX

Combine 8 ounces cottage cheese, 6 tablespoons chopped ripe olives and 6 tablespoons chopped walnuts. Add just enough heavy cream or sour cream—or a combination of the two—to make a smooth spread for canapés. Add a few tablespoons more cream to make a smooth dip. Season with salt, pepper, lemon juice or cayenne pepper.

CURRIED CHEESE MIX

Combine 8 ounces cottage cheese, 2 tablespoons chopped Indian chutney and 1 teaspoon curry powder. Add enough heavy cream or sour cream —or a combination of the two—to make a smooth spread. Add more cream to make a dip. Season as above.

MEXICAN CHEESE MIX

Combine 8 ounces cottage cheese, 2 tablespoons *each* chopped green pepper, chopped pimento and chopped onion. Add enough heavy cream or sour cream—or a combination of the two— to make a smooth spread. Add more cream for dip. Season as above.

ROQUEFORT CHEESE MIX

Combine 8 ounces cottage cheese, 4 tablespoons crumbled Roquefort cheese and ½ teaspoon dry mustard. Add enough heavy cream or sour cream—or a combination of the two—to make a smooth spread. Add more cream for dip. Season as above.

PROVENÇAL HERB AND GARLIC MIX

Combine 8 ounces cottage cheese, 4 tablespoons finely chopped fresh basil or tarragon, 2 tablespoons finely chopped chives, 1 tablespoon finely chopped parsley and 1 mashed garlic clove. Add heavy cream and lemon juice to taste. Add more cream and lemon juice for dip. Season as above.

PROVENÇAL ANCHOVY MIX (ANCHOIADE)

In a blender combine 1 can of anchovy fillets in oil, 1 large clove garlic, 1 tablespoon olive oil and 1 tablespoon softened butter. Blend to a smooth paste. Season to taste with a few drops of lemon juice or cognac and a little freshly ground black pepper.

PROVENÇAL OIL MIX (TAPENADE)

In a blender combine 36 pitted ripe olives, 12 anchovy fillets, 1 small can tuna fish, 1 tablespoon Dijon mustard and 4 tablespoons chopped capers. When the mixture has been blended to a smooth paste, transfer to a bowl and whisk in 12 tablespoons olive oil a little at a time. Add 2 tablespoons cognac and 2 hard-boiled eggs, finely chopped; blend well and season with freshly ground black pepper.

GUACAMOLE

Peel 2 ripe avocados and mash them lightly with a wooden spoon. Add the juice of 1 lemon, 1 crushed clove garlic, 4 tomatoes, peeled, seeded and coarsely chopped, ½ onion, finely chopped, and 4 tablespoons finely chopped celery or green pepper. Stir in 1 tablespoon finely chopped coriander leaves or parsley, 2 to 4 tablespoons olive oil, and salt and freshly ground black pepper to taste. Leave the avocado pits in the mixture until ready to serve to keep it from discoloring.

Stocks

REAL CHICKEN STOCK
(Quick Method)

Place 1 (4-pound) chicken and 1 pound veal knuckle in a large kettle with 3 quarts water and bring to the boil, skimming until the scum no longer rises to the surface. Simmer for 1 hour. Add 2 leeks (white parts only), 1 large onion stuck with cloves, 2 coarsely chopped carrots, 2 stalks celery, tops included, 1 large clove garlic and 4 sprigs parsley; add salt and pepper to taste and continue to simmer for 1 hour. Correct seasoning and strain the stock through a fine sieve. Cool, remove fat and reheat, or store in the refrigerator.

REAL BEEF STOCK
(Quick Method)

Have 1 pound veal knuckle and 1 pound shin of beef coarsely chopped by your butcher; brush with 4 tablespoons meat fat (beef, veal or pork) or oil and brown them in the oven. Place in a large kettle with 2 pounds lean stewing beef, 2 leeks (white parts only), 1 large onion stuck with 2 cloves, 2 stalks celery, tops included, 2 coarsely chopped carrots, 4 sprigs parsley and 1 large clove garlic. Cover with 3 quarts cold water and bring slowly to the boil, removing the scum as it accumulates on the surface. Simmer gently for 1 hour; add salt and pepper and continue to simmer for another hour, or until the meat is tender. Correct seasoning and strain the stock through a fine sieve. Cool, remove fat and reheat, or store in the refrigerator for later use.

FISH STOCK
(Quick Method)

Ask for some fish heads, fish bones and trimmings. Wash them well, discarding any black looking skin, and break the bones in pieces. Put them in an enameled saucepan with 1 pound haddock, cod, halibut or flounder, 3 to 4 parsley stalks, 1 sliced onion, 2 sliced carrots, 1 bay leaf, a few white peppercorns and a little salt. Cover with equal parts water and dry white wine and simmer for 30 minutes. Strain before using.

Other options for a more flavorful stock: ½ chicken bouillon cube, a little canned clam juice, a lobster shell, or the shells of shrimps.

CHICKEN CONSOMME

Strain 2½ to 3 quarts rich chicken stock into a large saucepan. Add whites and crushed shells of 2 eggs and bring to the boil. Simmer for 1 hour; strain through a fine cloth and cool. Skim.

BEEF CONSOMME

Strain 2½ to 3 quarts beef stock into a large saucepan; add ½ pound ground beef, 2 chopped leeks, ½ chopped onion, the whites and crushed shells of 2 eggs and bring to the boil. Simmer for 1 hour; correct seasoning and strain through muslin lined sieve. Cool and skim.

FISH CONSOMME

Strain 2½ to 3 quarts fish stock into a large saucepan; add ½ pound chopped fish, 2 chopped leeks, ½ chopped onion, ½ chicken bouillon cube and a little saffron. Simmer for ½ hour. Add lemon juice and salt and freshly ground black pepper, to taste. Strain, cool and skim.

Sauces

BECHAMEL SAUCE

Melt 2 tablespoons butter for the roux in the top of a double boiler. In the butter, sauté ½ onion, finely chopped, and 1 stalk celery, finely chopped, over a low heat until onion is soft but not browned. (For a fuller flavor, I sometimes add 4 tablespoons chopped cooked ham or chopped raw veal to the onion and celery mixture.) Remove pan from heat, stir in 2 tablespoons flour, return to heat and cook gently for 3 to 5 minutes, stirring constantly, until flour is cooked through. Add ½ cup milk, heated to boiling point, and cook over hot water, stirring vigorously. As the sauce begins to thicken add a further 2 cups hot milk, stirring constantly with a wooden spoon until sauce bubbles. Add 1 small sprig thyme, ½ bay leaf, white peppercorns and freshly grated nutmeg to taste, and simmer sauce gently for 15 minutes. Strain through a fine sieve and dot surface with butter. Makes about 2½ cups.

Variations:

Cream Sauce

For fish, poultry, eggs and vegetables:
Add 4 tablespoons heavy cream to 2½ cups

hot béchamel and bring to boiling point. Add a few drops lemon juice.

Mornay Sauce

For fish, vegetables, poultry, poached eggs, noodle and macaroni mixtures:
Mix 2 slightly beaten egg yolks with a little cream and combine with 2½ cups hot béchamel sauce.
Cook, stirring constantly, until it just reaches boiling point. Add 2 tablespoons butter and 2 to 4 tablespoons freshly grated cheese (Parmesan or Swiss cheese is best).

Aurora Sauce

Excellent with eggs, chicken or shellfish:
Add 2 to 3 tablespoons tomato paste to 2½ cups hot béchamel sauce.

Velouté Sauce

Melt 2 tablespoons butter in a saucepan; add 2 tablespoons flour and cook for a few minutes to form a roux blond. Add 2½ cups boiling white stock (chicken or veal), salt and white peppercorns and cook, stirring vigorously with a whisk. Add 4 chopped button mushrooms and cook slowly, stirring occasionally and skimming from time to time, until the sauce is reduced to two-thirds of its original quantity and is very thick but light and creamy. Strain through a fine sieve.

French Onion Sauce

Chop 1 onion finely; cover with water and parboil for 3 to 5 minutes. Drain and sauté onion in butter until soft. Add 2½ cups hot béchamel sauce and cook 15 minutes longer. Strain sauce through a fine sieve; return to heat; beat in 4 tablespoons heavy cream and flavor with nutmeg, lemon juice, salt and white pepper, to taste.

ESPAGNOLE SAUCE

Melt 3 tablespoons beef or bacon fat in a large, heavy saucepan; add 3 ounces, diced fat salt pork, 3 carrots, 1 onion and 2 stalks celery, all coarsely chopped, and cook until golden. Sprinkle with 3 tablespoons flour and cook gently over very low heat, stirring frequently, until well browned. Divide 8 cups of boiling homemade beef stock into 3 parts; add first third together with bouquet garni and 1 clove garlic to flour mixture and cook, stirring frequently, until sauce thickens.

Add the second third of stock and cook very slowly over a very low heat, uncovered, stirring the sauce occasionally, for about 1½ to 2 hours. Skim off scum and fat rising to surface as it cooks. Add ⅔ cup rich tomato sauce (or 3 to 4 tablespoons tomato paste) and cook for a few minutes longer. Then strain through a fine sieve into a bowl, pressing the vegetables against the sieve to extract all their juices.

Clean the saucepan; return the mixture to it; add remaining stock and continue cooking slowly until the sauce is reduced to about 5 cups, skimming the surface from time to time.

Strain again. Cool, stirring occasionally. Store in a covered jar in the refrigerator until ready for use.

Variations:

Madeira Sauce

Reduce 2½ cups Espagnole sauce until it is half the original quantity. Add 6 tablespoons Madeira. Heat the sauce through but do not let it boil or the flavor of the wine will be lost.

Sauce Bordelaise

Cook 2 finely chopped shallots in ⅔ cup red wine until liquid is reduced to a third of its original quantity. Add 2 cups Espagnole sauce and simmer gently for 10 minutes.

Remove the marrow from a split beef bone; cut it into small dice and poach it in boiling salted water for 1 or 2 minutes. Drain, and just before serving sauce add 2 tablespoons diced beef marrow and a little finely chopped parsley.

Sauce Lyonnaise

Sauté ½ onion, finely chopped, in 2 tablespoons butter until golden. Add 6 tablespoons dry white wine and simmer until reduced to half the original quantity. Add 2 cups Espagnole sauce; cook gently for 15 minutes; add 1 tablespoon chopped parsley and finish by swirling in 1 tablespoon butter.

Sauce Fines Herbes

Remove leaves from 3 sprigs *each* parsley, tarragon and chervil. Chop stems and sauté in butter with a few chopped shallots and mushrooms. Add 2 chopped tomatoes and ½ cup dry white wine and cook until reduced to half original quantity. Add 2½ cups Espagnole sauce and simmer for 20 minutes. Strain. Heat sauce with reserved leaves, juice of ½ lemon and 1 tablespoon butter.

HOW TO MAKE PERFECT MAYONNAISE

Place 2 egg yolks (with no trace of whites) in a small mixing bowl with ½ teaspoon Dijon mustard and salt and freshly ground black pepper to taste. Twist a cloth wrung out in very cold water around the bottom of the bowl to keep it steady and cool. Use a wire whisk, fork, wooden spoon or hand beater, and beat the yolks to a smooth paste. Add a little lemon juice and, drop by drop, beat in about ¼ cup of the oil. Add a little more lemon juice; then, rather faster now, add more oil, beating constantly. Continue adding oil and beating until the sauce is of a good thick consistency (you will need about 2½ cups oil in all). Then correct the seasoning, adding more salt, pepper, and lemon to taste.

If mayonnaise curdles, break another egg yolk into a clean bowl and gradually beat curdled mixture into it.

When mayonnaise is to be used in a fish or potato salad, thin it down considerably with dry white wine, champagne, vinegar or lemon juice. If it is to be used for coating meat, poultry or fish, add a little liquid gelatin to stiffen it.

If you are keeping mayonnaise a day before using, stir in 1 tablespoon boiling water. This will prevent it turning or separating. Cover the bowl with a cloth wrung out in very cold water to prevent skin forming.

Blender Mayonnaise

Combine in electric blender 2 whole eggs, ⅔ cup olive oil, 4 tablespoons lemon juice or vinegar, ½ teaspoon *each* dry mustard and salt, with freshly ground black pepper to taste. Cover the container and turn the motor to high. When blended, remove cover and add 1⅓ cups olive oil in a thin steady trickle, as you blend continuously. Correct seasoning.

Horseradish Mayonnaise

For eggs, egg salads or seafood:

Add juice of ½ lemon and salt to taste to 2 cups mayonnaise. Just before serving, stir in 2 to 3 tablespoons freshly grated horseradish.

Russian Mayonnaise Dressing

For eggs, cooked vegetable salads and seafood:

Add 3 tablespoons ketchup, a dash of Tabasco or Worcestershire sauce and 1 teaspoon *each* chopped canned pimentos and chives to mayonnaise.

Cucumber Mayonnaise

Add ¼ cucumber, finely chopped, and 2 tablespoons finely chopped parsley to mayonnaise.

Mustard Mayonnaise

Add Dijon or dry mustard to mayonnaise.

Sauce Tartare

Add 1 to 2 teaspoons *each* chopped parsley, tarragon, chervil, capers and gherkins to mayonnaise.

BEARNAISE, HOLLANDAISE AND VARIATIONS

The two great French sauces—béarnaise and hollandaise—are served hot to add a fillip to dishes of broiled meats and broiled or poached fish. Hollandaise is used, too, to add interest to cooked egg and vegetable dishes—and as a delicious golden sauce for those aristocratic vegetables, artichokes and asparagus.

Professional chefs also use hollandaise to add body and richness to gratin sauces. It helps them "stand up" under the heat.

Both sauces are quite easy to achieve in minutes if you are careful with the heat over which they are cooked.

Sauce Béarnaise

1   Chop leaves and stems of 2 sprigs tarragon and 3 sprigs chervil coarsely and combine with 1 tablespoon chopped shallots, 2 crushed peppercorns, 2 tablespoons tarragon vinegar and ⅔ cup dry white wine in the top of a double boiler. Cook over a high flame until liquid is reduced to about 1 tablespoon. Reducing the sauce in this way to almost a glaze on the bottom of the pan seems to make the following steps easier.

2   Add 3 egg yolks and 1 tablespoon water to the herb and wine mixture in the top of double boiler, and place it over hot, but not boiling water. Whisk until light and fluffy. *Never let water in bottom of double boiler begin to boil, or sauce will not "take."* Add 8 tablespoons soft butter gradually to egg mixture, whisking briskly all the time as sauce begins to thicken. Continue adding butter gradually (about 8 tablespoons more) whisking continuously until sauce is thick. Season to taste with salt and cayenne pepper. Strain through a fine sieve and serve.

Choron Sauce

Make a béarnaise sauce as above and flavor to taste with tomato paste.

Hollandaise Sauce

1   Combine 1 teaspoon lemon juice, 1 tablespoon cold water, salt and white pepper in the top of a double boiler. Divide ½ pound soft butter into 4 equal pieces. Add 4 egg yolks and a quarter of the butter to the liquid in the saucepan and whisk the mixture over hot, but not boiling, water until the butter is melted and the mixture begins to thicken. Add the second piece of butter and continue whisking. As the mixture thickens and the second piece of butter melts, add the third piece of butter, stirring from the bottom of the pan until it is melted. *Be careful not to allow the water over which the sauce is cooking to boil at any time.* Add rest of butter, beating until it melts and is incorporated in the sauce.

2   Remove top part of the double boiler from the heat and whisk sauce for 2 to 3 min-

utes longer. Replace over hot, but not boiling water for 2 minutes more, beating constantly. By this time your sauce should be rich and creamy. Finish sauce with a few drops of lemon juice, strain and reserve.

If at any time in the operation the mixture should curdle, beat in 1 or 2 tablespoons cold water to rebind the sauce.

Mustard Hollandaise

Make a hollandaise sauce as above, and flavor to taste with Dijon mustard.

Sauce Mousseline

Make in the same way as hollandaise sauce, adding 4 to 6 tablespoons whipped cream just before serving.

Wine Magic

You will find cooking with wine is as easy as opening the bottle and taking a sip. If like some of my friends, you are a little inhibited in your use of this magic cook's aid, don't be: think of it as just another good ingredient, like butter, olive oil, fresh herbs or cream. First, remember: the alcohol evaporates in cooking. Second, you don't have to use great quantities. Even a tablespoon or two, a quarter bottle, or at the most a half bottle, will work wonders for a delicious dish to feed four to six people.

Easy-to-prepare casserole recipes with wine are literally as old as time. The manner of cooking fish and shellfish, and meat, poultry and game in a combination of wine and stock or wine and cream probably originated centuries ago on the sun-washed hillsides of southern France when the early Romans were first teaching the natives of the region how to cultivate the local grapes to make wine. In those days, the casserole was undoubtedly cooked in the ashes. Today, we use modern electricity and gas to make our task even easier. But two magic "constants" remain:

Slow, Even Cooking

All wine-simmered casseroles—vegetables as well as meats, poultry, fish and game—respond wonderfully well to "low heat" cookery.

Over the many years I have been experimenting with heat, I have gradually lowered the temperature at which I like to cook stews, daubes, ragouts and casseroles to cool (225°F or 250°F). And when cooking this type of dish on top of the stove, I always use an asbestos or wire mat to help keep the cooking down to a faint, barely perceptible simmer. It is a good idea, the first few times you follow this method of cooking, to check up on your casserole frequently. Thermostats vary, and you may find you have to adjust the setting slightly to keep the casserole at its low, "barely simmering" point. And always make sure that you bring the ingredients up to a bubble on top of the stove before you put the casserole into the oven.

The Reduction of Wine to Give Added "Fillip"

Wine "reduced" to a quarter of its original quantity by fast boiling over a high heat is one of the best ways of adding flavor to a casserole. Professional cooks often use this method of seasoning to "correct" and intensify the depth of flavor of their wine cooked dishes. I like to reduce stock, too, in the same manner, adding a combination of the two separate reductions— stock and wine—to the dish at the last minute to give hidden depth and interest to a ragout of meat, poultry or game. Try adding separate reductions of fish stock and dry white wine in this way to add excitement to a fish soup, casserole, or fish-based cream or velouté sauce.

Small Quantities of Wine Can Make a Great Difference to Your Cooking

1 Add 2 tablespoons dry white wine to your usual salad dressing; add a little finely chopped scallion, onion or garlic and mix with sliced, boiled new potatoes for a delicious potato salad. Always remember to toss the potato slices with the dressing when potatoes are still a little warm.

2 Combine 6 tablespoons *each* olive oil and dry white wine with 2 crumbled bay leaves, a little finely chopped onion and parsley and salt and freshly ground black pepper, to taste. Use to marinate brochettes of lamb, chicken or fish before broiling. Good, too, for marinated lamb chops. This is one of the best and easiest marinades I know.

3 Combine 1 cup red wine with 1 clove crushed garlic, ¼ teaspoon dried marjoram or thyme (or a combination of both), ¼ chicken bouillon cube and freshly ground black pepper, to taste. Reduce these ingredients over a high heat to half the original quantity and use this sauce with a little butter swirled in to baste lamb, veal or chicken.

4 Always add 2 or more tablespoons of red wine just before serving a casserole of meat or game which you have marinated or simmered in red wine. You will find it helps the flavor of the finished dish.

5 Toss fresh strawberries in a few tablespoons of red wine. Chill before serving.

6 Spike a fresh fruit salad with half a quarter bottle of champagne. Leave just enough champagne for a glass for the cook! A double delight.

Choosing Your Wine

Wine is a living thing with its own distinctive character. Wine knowledge comes from drinking. The more wines you taste, the more you will enjoy them, the more you will know about them. White wines, except the sweet ones which can live for many years, should be drunk when young. Red wines such as Beaujolais and the lighter Burgundies are almost always drunk when young. Red wines of quality need a little time to be at their best. Serve red wines with red meats, game and even some of the richer fish dishes such as salmon. And in the summer —when the weather is at its hottest—drink a light red Beaujolais or Fleurie "on the rocks" as a refreshing accompaniment for any meal.

Choosing the right wine for the right dish is not as difficult as you may think. First of all, a fresh, dry white wine served slightly chilled— a flinty Chablis, a light Muscadet or Sancerre, a fuller flavored Pouilly Fuissé, Pouilly Fumé or Puligny Montrachet—provides the perfect accompaniment to most first courses, quiches, and all fish and chicken dishes. Serve a chilled dry white wine or rosé, too, in the hot summer

months to accompany cold or broiled meats and veal and lamb dishes. You'll find the cooling light freshness of dry whites and rosés the perfect foil for summer dining.

WINE GUIDE

Low-Priced White Wines

Bourgogne Aligoté	Retsina
Cabernet Blanc	Riesling
Chablis	Sancerre
Chevalier d'Alsace	Saumur Blanc
Chianti Ruffino White	Soave
Lachryma Christi	Sylvaner d'Alsace
Mâcon Blanc	Touraine Sauvignon
Mâcon-Viré	Verdicchio
Médoc	Vinho Verde
Muscadet	Vouvray
Pouilly Blanc Fumé	

Low-Priced Rosé Wines

Rosé d'Anjou
Rosé de Provence
Tavel Rosé

Low-Priced Red Wines

Barolo	Fleurie
Beaujolais	Gigondas
Beaujolais Fleurie	Mâcon Rouge
Beaujolais Villages	Médoc
Bordeaux Supérieur	Pomerol
Cabernet Red	Pommard
Châteauneuf-du-Pape	Rioja Red
Chianti Ruffino Red	Serradayres
Chinon	Valpolicella
Côtes-du-Rhône	

Medium-Priced White Wines

Chablis	Puligny Montrachet
Meursault	Riesling d'Alsace
Pouilly Blanc Fumé	Sancerre
Pouilly Fuissé	

Medium-Priced Rosé Wines

Rosé de Provence
Tavel Rosé

Medium-Priced Red Wines

Aloxe Corton	Mercurey
Barolo	Morgon
Beaune	Moulin-à-Vent
Brouilly	Nuits-St.-Georges
Côtes de Bourg	Pomerol
Côtes-du-Rhône	Pommard
Côte-Rôtie	St. Emilion
Médoc	

Expensive White Wines

Bâtard-Montrachet
Clos Vougeot Blanc
Corton-Charlemagne
Montrachet

Expensive Red Wines

Bonnes Mares	Moulin-à-Vent
Chambertin	Musigny
Chambolle-Musigny	Petrus
Clos de Vougeot	Richebourg
La Tache	Savigny-les-Beaune

CHOOSING THE RIGHT WINE

Cold Hors d'Oeuvres: Muscadet, Sancerre, Chablis/Pouilly, Mâconnais, Champagne, Alsace, White Burgundies, Rosé

Hot Hors d'Oeuvres: Chablis/Pouilly, Champagne, White Burgundies

Oysters, Mussels, etc.: Muscadet, Sancerre, Chablis/Pouilly, Mâconnais, Champagne, Alsace

Caviar: Chablis/Pouilly, Champagne

Smoked Salmon: Muscadet, Sancerre, Chablis/Pouilly, Champagne

Foie Gras, Pâtés, etc.: Chablis/Pouilly, Champagne

Cooked Egg Dishes and Omelets: Muscadet, Sancerre, Chablis/Pouilly, Champagne, Alsace, Vouvray, Saumur, Rosé

Cooked Fish, Shellfish—Hot: Muscadet, Sancerre, Chablis/Pouilly, Mâconnais, Champagne, Alsace, Graves Sècs, White Burgundies, Entre-Deux-Mers, Rosé

Cooked Fish and Shellfish—Cold: Muscadet, Sancerre, Chablis/Pouilly, Champagne, Graves Sècs, White Burgundies, Rosé

Tripe, Sweetbreads: Muscadet, Sancerre, Chablis/Pouilly, Mâconnais, Champagne, Alsace, White Burgundies, Côtes-du-Rhône, Bourgueil/Chinon, St. Emilion, Rosé

Roast Chicken, Turkey, etc.: Chablis/Pouilly, White Burgundies, Côtes-du-Rhône, Beaujolais Fleurie, Côtes de Bordeaux, Médoc, St. Emilion

Roast Duck and Game Birds: Côtes-du-Rhône, Beaujolais Fleurie, Côtes de Bordeaux, St. Emilion, Côtes de Beaune, Red Burgundy, Côtes-Rôties

Roast Game: Côtes-du-Rhône, Beaujolais Fleurie, Côtes de Bordeaux, St. Emilion, Côtes de Beaune, White Burgundies, Côtes-Rôties

Beef—Grilled and Roast: Côtes-du-Rhône, Beaujolais Fleurie, Côtes de Bordeaux, Médoc, St. Emilion, Côtes de Beaune, Red Burgundies, Côtes-Rôties

Beef—Sauced: Beaujolais Fleurie, Côtes de Bordeaux, Médoc, St. Emilion

Veal—Grilled and Roast: Chablis/Pouilly, Mâconnais, Champagne, St. Emilion, Rosé

Lamb—Grilled and Roast: Côtes-du-Rhône, Côtes de Bordeaux, Médoc, St. Emilion

Veal and Lamb—Sauced: Côtes de Bordeaux, St. Emilion

Pork: Côtes-du-Rhône, Médoc, St. Emilion, Côtes de Beaune, Côtes-Rôties

Ham: Côtes-du-Rhône, Médoc, St. Emilion, Rosé

Cheese, Fermented: Beaujolais Fleurie, Côtes de Bordeaux, Médoc, St. Emilion, Côtes de Beaune, Red Burgundies, Côtes-Rôties

Cheese, Fresh: Muscadet, Sancerre, Chablis/Pouilly, Champagne, White Burgundies, Côtes de Bordeaux

Sweets, Puddings, Cakes, etc.: Champagne, Graves Doux, Vouvray, Saumur, Côtes de Bordeaux, Rosés, Sauternes, and Dessert Wines

Salads

GREEN SALAD

A crisp green salad, tossed at the table with a classic dressing of olive oil and wine vinegar or fresh lemon juice, can be one of the highlights of a meal.

The very word "salad" evokes a vision of green lettuce leaves, carefully washed and dried, bathed with fruity olive oil and flavored with a touch of wine vinegar, a hint of garlic and a dusting of salt and freshly ground black pepper. Sometimes, too, I add a little Dijon mustard and a sprinkling of finely chopped fresh herbs—basil, tarragon and chives. On second thought, not too finely chopped after all. We want to see them. And taste them.

Tossed Green Salad

Wash the leaves of 1 to 2 heads of lettuce well in a large quantity of water. They should be left whole, never cut. Drain well and dry thoroughly so that there is no water on them to dilute the dressing.

To serve: pour **French dressing** into salad bowl; arrange prepared lettuce leaves on top. Check seasoning. Then, before serving at the table, give a final toss to the ingredients to ensure that every leaf is glistening with dressing. This salad will serve 4 to 6.

Variations:

Add other salad greens in season—romaine lettuce, endive, chicory, young spinach leaves, and watercress.

Add finely chopped garlic or shallots, or a combination of both, to salad dressing.

Add fresh green herbs—finely chopped chervil, basil, tarragon, chives or mint—to the dressing.

For crunch appeal, add diced celery, green pepper or fennel.

FRENCH DRESSING

Vinaigrette Sauce

Mix together 1 tablespoon lemon juice, 1 to 2 tablespoons wine vinegar and ¼ to ½ teaspoon Dijon mustard, and season to taste with coarse salt and freshly ground black pepper. Add 6 to 8 tablespoons olive oil, and beat with a fork until mixture emulsifies.

Special Vinaigrette Sauce

Make French dressing as directed. Add a little finely chopped parsley and onion or chives, finely chopped green olives, capers or gherkins, and the sieved yolk of a hard-boiled egg.

SALADE PAYSANNE

Wash and dry leaves from 2 heads of lettuce. Chill. Sauté 6 ounces diced fat salt pork in 2 tablespoons olive oil until golden. Arrange lettuce in bowl; add diced pork and hot fat, 2 hard-boiled eggs, chopped, 3 tablespoons finely chopped chervil, tarragon or basil, and salt, freshly ground black pepper and wine vinegar, to taste.

Cheeses

A GUIDE TO SERVING CHEESES

Cheese, like its natural partners, bread and wine, is made by a process of fermentation which can turn one substance, just as it is about to spoil, into something better than it was in the first place.

Cheese is one of the most versatile foods known to man. It can be soft and creamy, firm, or tangy and blue-veined; and it can be served at every course throughout the meal, from appetizer to dessert.

Bring out a cheese tray of three or four different kinds of cheese with crackers at cocktail time; serve it at the end of the meal with crusty French bread, fruit, nuts and wine; try a snack of cheese with pumpernickel, dark rye bread, crusty French loaf or stone-ground whole meal.

To bring out its full flavor, well-ripened cheese should be removed from the refrigerator at least two hours before serving.

Cheddar (English)

Most popular English cheese, close and buttery in texture, with a full, clean, slightly nutty flavor. Crumbles when aged. Cooks well, if a trifle too greasily, when fresh for soufflés and fine sauces. Good with beer and red wine.

Stilton (English)

Perhaps the world's most regal blue cheese. Its blue mold should be evenly distributed in wide-branching veins, the cheese itself being a rich cream, not anemic white. Best season is between November and April. Serve with port, nuts and raisins.

Cheshire (English)

Crumbly in texture, slightly salty in flavor and excellent with apple pie.

Leicester (English)

Crumbly and flaky, very like Cheshire in texture but a deep orange-red in color. A good keeper, but best when young and mild. Good with salads and watercress; excellent as one of the components of Welsh rarebit. Goes well with beer.

Havarti (Danish)

Mild, creamy, whipped milk cheese. Good with grapes or for sandwiches.

Danish Blue (Danish)

Blue-veined, white, creamy, sharp-flavored. Use it, creamed with butter and brandy, as a spread or to fill celery stalks; crumble a little into French dressing for salads.

Emmenthal (Swiss)

Comes in large wheels, aged to achieve a faintly waxy texture and huge "eyes." A perfect table cheese, and one of the great cooking cheeses. (Not to be confused with Gruyère, which has no eyes, and from which Swiss fondue is made.)

Edam (Dutch)

A red cannonball, mild or sharp according to age. Ideally, cut a "lid" from top and spoon out cheese, replacing "lid" to keep soft.

Gouda (Dutch)

A junior version of Edam. Melts well; use for toasted cheese sandwiches.

Camembert (French)

One of the world's favorite cheeses, "invented" by a farmer's wife in 1790. Best when pale yellow, rather runny and soft. Eat it with crusty French bread, claret or Burgundy, and a slice of ripe pear; try it soused in dry white wine.

Pont L'Evêque (French)

One of the noblest French cheeses, ripe and strong in flavor. Made in square molds and cured for four months to develop heavy crust and typical odor. Best avoided in its early stages and when past its prime. Goes with all red wines.

Brie (French)

Talleyrand called this soft, creamy cheese "the king of cheeses." Comes in thin, yellow-crusted wheels dusted with powdery white mold. Apt to be chalky when underripe; smells of ammonia when past its prime. Good with red Burgundy or Beaujolais.

Bel Paese (Italian)

Soft but firm, rich yet delicately flavored; delicious with fruit. Served almost entirely as a dessert cheese, it can be used instead of mozzarella in cooked dishes. Keeps well, sharpening with age. Serve it at room temperature.

Gorgonzola (Italian)

Originated in Gorgonzola, near Milan, more than 1,000 years ago. Riper in flavor than other blue cheeses, but softer and creamier in texture. Very good with fruit, and combines well with butter and oil for dips, spreads and sauces.

Picnics and Outdoor Meals

A Meal to Serve Out of Doors

The kitchen is a great place not to be when the weather is sizzling hot. Cold foods, of course, are appealing in this kind of weather, but every meal—unless it is a picnic or a buffet—should have one hot dish. The rest of the menu can be as simple and as quickly cooked as possible, to avoid spending hours over a hot stove. If you start with a chilled fruit juice or a chilled vegetable soup, have a hot meat or vegetable dish and then cool off again with a fresh fruit dessert.

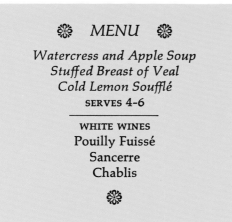

❄ *MENU* ❄

Watercress and Apple Soup
Stuffed Breast of Veal
Cold Lemon Soufflé
SERVES 4-6

WHITE WINES
Pouilly Fuissé
Sancerre
Chablis

❄

WATERCRESS AND APPLE SOUP

A chilled curried cream of chicken soup to which pureed watercress and apple add their individual flavors. Dark green watercress leaves and cubes of lemony apple add bite and texture to its creamy coldness.

> 2 tablespoons butter
> 1 onion, coarsely chopped
> 1 bunch watercress
> 2½ cups chicken stock
> 1 tablespoon curry powder
> 1 tablespoon cornstarch
> 2 egg yolks
> ½ to ¼ cups hot heavy cream
> 2 apples
> Salt and freshly ground black pepper
> Juice of ½ lemon
> Extra watercress leaves for garnish

1 Melt butter; add onion and cook until soft but not brown. Stir in watercress, chicken stock and curry powder; add cornstarch mixed with a little water. Bring to the boil, then simmer for 8 minutes.

2 Add egg yolks to hot cream and stir gradually into soup.

3 Remove from heat immediately and transfer mixture to electric blender with 1 apple, peeled, cored and sliced. Blend until smooth. Season to taste with salt and pepper. Chill.

4 Peel, core and dice remaining apple and marinate in lemon juice to prevent discoloration.

5 Just before serving, stir in diced apple and enough watercress leaves to garnish.

STUFFED BREAST OF VEAL

Sausage meat, finely chopped onion, parsley and spinach are combined for the stuffing of this green and pink veal roll. Season it generously with the herbs and spices of your choice. I like fresh tarragon when available, or failing this, a combination of dried thyme, crumbled bay leaf and rosemary. Serve it with tomatoes stuffed with the same mixture (they can be baked at the

A Picnic for Hot Summer Days:
Roast Chicken, a Green Salad,
Olives and Fresh Fruit and Cheeses

same time) or with **boiled rice** (see page 89). Any leftovers are excellent cold.

> 3 to 4 pounds breast of veal
> Lemon juice
> Salt and freshly ground black pepper
> Flour
> 2 tablespoons butter
> 2 tablespoons olive oil

Stuffing:

> ½ pound sausage meat
> ½ large onion, finely chopped
> 2 tablespoons butter
> 1 tablespoon finely chopped parsley
> 1 egg, beaten
> ½ pound spinach, chopped and sautéed
>   in butter
> ½ teaspoon rosemary
> ½ teaspoon marjoram
> 2 bay leaves, crumbled
> ¼ teaspoon cayenne pepper
> ¼ teaspoon nutmeg
>   Salt, freshly ground black pepper

1 Wipe veal on both sides with a damp cloth; sprinkle with lemon juice and season with salt and pepper.

2 To make stuffing: combine sausage meat, onion sautéed in butter, parsley, egg, spinach, salt, pepper and herbs or spices. Mix well.

3 Place this stuffing in the center of the veal; make into a neat roll and sew up with fine string. Dust with flour; place in a roasting pan with butter and olive oil and roast in a 325°F oven for about 1½ to 2 hours, basting frequently with pan juices.

COLD LEMON SOUFFLE

One of the freshest, tartest sweets imaginable —serve it in a soufflé dish or in sherbet glasses.

> 6 egg yolks
> ¾ cup sugar
>   Juice of 2 lemons
>   Grated rind of 1 lemon
> 6 egg whites, stiffly beaten
> ½ tablespoon gelatin
>   Angelica "leaves," for decoration
>   Red currant jelly
>   Kirsch (optional)

1 Beat egg yolks well with sugar, lemon juice and rind.

2 Transfer mixture to the top of a double boiler and cook over hot but not boiling water, stirring constantly with a whisk until mixture thickens.

3 Remove from heat; let it cool slightly and then fold in the egg whites.

4 Fold in gelatin which you have dissolved in ½ cup water. Pour the mixture into a serving bowl and chill. Decorate with angelica "leaves."

5 Whisk red currant jelly with a little kirsch to taste, if desired, and serve separately.

Portable Feast

There's nothing easier than packing a basket full of cheeses wrapped in foil, fruits, wines, rolls, a thermos of chilled soup and a cold dish of chicken and setting out in the car for a portable feast.

For events like this, I like to bring the salads washed but not yet prepared, selecting all sorts of greens in season; romaine, iceberg, Boston, Bibb, limestone, arugula, watercress, tender baby spinach leaves and sprigs of fresh basil and tarragon if available. Always keep salad greens wrapped in foil, of course, complete with bowl, and with a separate cocktail shaker or screw-top jar of dressing. Butter in foil can be kept chilled in a portable ice chest.

❧ MENU ❧

My Favorite Gazpacho
Cold Roast Chicken
Green Salad with Roquefort Dressing
Apple Streusel Tart
Cheese and Fresh Fruits
SERVES 4-6

WHITE AND ROSE WINES
Sylvaner d'Alsace
Pouilly Blanc Fumé
Tavel Rosé

❧

MY FAVORITE GAZPACHO

- 6 large ripe tomatoes
- ½ large onion, thinly sliced
- 1 green pepper, seeded and thinly sliced
- ½ cucumber, peeled and thinly sliced
- 1 clove garlic, finely chopped
   Salt, Tabasco and freshly ground black pepper
- 6 tablespoons olive oil
- 3 tablespoons wine vinegar
- ¾ to 1¼ cups chilled chicken consommé (see page 139)
   Finely chopped chives or parsley
   Gazpacho accompaniments

1 Seed tomatoes and dice; combine in a soup or salad bowl with onion, green pepper and cucumber. Season to taste with garlic, salt, pepper and Tabasco. Marinate in olive oil and vinegar in the refrigerator for at least 30 minutes.

2 Just before serving, add chilled chicken consommé and chives or parsley. Serve with traditional gazpacho accompaniments: diced tomato, green pepper, onion, cucumber and garlic croutons.

COLD ROAST CHICKEN

(For recipe, see **roast chicken with watercress stuffing,** page 54.)

Serve with a **green salad** with a **Roquefort dressing** (see **Delmonico salad,** page 194.)

APPLE STREUSEL TART

- 6 tart eating apples
   Juice of 1 lemon
- 1 unbaked pie shell
   sugar
- ¼ teaspoon cinnamon
- ¼ teaspoon nutmeg or allspice

Streusel Topping:

- ½ cup brown sugar
- ¾ cup sifted flour
   Grated rind of 1 lemon
- 6 tablespoons softened butter

1 Peel and core apples; cut into eighths and toss in lemon juice. Arrange apples in an unbaked pie shell. Combine sugar and spices and sprinkle over apples.

2 To make streusel topping: combine brown sugar, flour and lemon rind. Cut softened butter into mixture until crumbly, using a pastry blender or 2 knives. Sprinkle mixture over apples and bake in a 450°F oven for 15 minutes. Reduce oven temperature to 350°F and bake for 30 minutes.

CHEESE AND FRESH FRUITS

(For **cheeses,** see pages 146–147.)

Gazpacho

Beach Picnic for the Younger Generation

When I was a boy, we used to like to bring a simple picnic basket to the beach. Easy to carry on a bicycle, or in the car, this light lunch was a winner during many a summer vacation. I've repeated it since accompanied by cold beer for more adult tastes. For the weight conscious, who prefer their portable lunches without bread or rolls, just double the quantities of cooked chicken and bacon, tomatoes and mayonnaise, and serve on individual plates.

The ingredients: red peppers, tomatoes and hard-boiled eggs; 1 jar of mustard salad dressing; 1 jar of homemade mayonnaise; rolls or French bread; cooked chicken and bacon; and lettuce leaves, fresh fruit and cookies.

Equipment needed: a sharp knife for vegetables and bread; a bowl for the pepper appetizer; a bread board on which to make the sandwiches; plates; pepper and salt mills; and paper cups and napkins.

Red Pepper Salad with Mustard Dressing

 ❀ MENU ❀
Red Pepper Salad with Mustard Dressing
Hard-Boiled Eggs
Club Sandwich Rolls
Hot Coffee
Fresh Fruit
Gingerbread Cookies
SERVES 4

WHITE WINES
Soave
Lachryma Christi
Cabernet Blanc

RED PEPPER SALAD WITH MUSTARD DRESSING

4 red peppers

Mustard Dressing:

1 to 2 teaspoons Dijon mustard
1 to 2 tablespoons wine vinegar
Salt and freshly ground black pepper
3 to 6 tablespoons olive oil
1 tablespoon finely chopped parsley and/or chives

1 Wash the peppers and place them under the broiler as close to the heat as possible. Cook, turning the peppers frequently, until the skin on all sides has charred. Remove charred skin under cold running water.

2 Cut peppers lengthwise—4 to 6 pieces to each pepper—and remove all the seeds and excess fiber. Drain the peppers on paper towels.

3 **To make mustard dressing:** Combine the mustard and wine vinegar. Add salt and pepper to taste. Beat in olive oil. Finally, as a garnish, sprinkle over chopped parsley and/or chives.

HARD-BOILED EGGS

4 to 8 eggs
Water

1 Fill a pan with enough water to cover the eggs thoroughly. Bring to the boil and lower eggs into it gently, using a spoon. Lower heat until water is barely bubbling, and cook for about 10 minutes.

2 Remove eggs from water at once and rinse under cold water to stop further cooking.

CLUB SANDWICH ROLLS

       4 large flat rolls (or 1 loaf French bread
             cut in quarters)
     ⅔ cup homemade mayonnaise
             (see page 141)
       1 pound sliced cooked chicken
       4 ripe tomatoes, sliced
       8 slices bacon, cooked
       4 lettuce leaves
             Salt and freshly ground black pepper

1 Cut each roll, or piece of French bread, horizontally. Spread bottom slice lavishly with mayonnaise. Cover with a layer of chicken; a layer of tomato; top with 2 slices bacon and 1 lettuce leaf. Season with salt and pepper.

2 Spread top half of roll, or French bread, with mayonnaise and assemble sandwich.

FRESH FRUIT AND HOT COFFEE

GINGERBREAD COOKIES

MAKES ABOUT 36 COOKIES
       3 cups sifted flour
       1 teaspoon allspice
       1 teaspoon ginger
       1 teaspoon cinnamon
       1 teaspoon salt
     ½ teaspoon baking soda
             Butter
       4 tablespoons brown sugar
     ½ cup corn syrup
       6 tablespoons milk

1 Sift together flour, spices, salt and soda. In another bowl, blend 12 tablespoons butter, sugar and corn syrup. Add sifted dry ingredients alternately with milk. Mix well. Chill overnight in the refrigerator.

2 Roll out dough and cut out shapes with cookie cutters. Place cookies on a well-buttered cookie sheet, and bake in a 400°F oven for 10 to 12 minutes.

Seafood Picnic

There's something festive about eating in the great outdoors, even when your horizons are limited to the confines of your own backyard. Weather permitting, focus your next outdoor meal around a summer spectacular—one of these delicious fish salads from the south of France. With these recipes, I suggest the following wines.

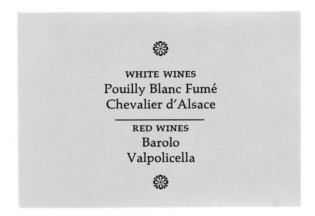

❁

WHITE WINES
Pouilly Blanc Fumé
Chevalier d'Alsace

─────────

RED WINES
Barolo
Valpolicella

❁

BOUILLABAISSE SALAD

(SERVES 6-8)
     ½ pound shrimp, peeled, deveined and cooked
     ½ pound cooked lobster meat, diced
     ½ pound cooked halibut or sole, diced
     ½ pound cooked crabmeat, flaked
             French dressing (see page 146)
       1 head lettuce, washed and chilled
       1 head romaine lettuce, washed and chilled
       4 ripe tomatoes
       8 large ripe black olives
             Finely chopped parsley

1 Marinate shrimp, lobster, fish and crab in French dressing in individual bowls.

2 When ready to serve: line salad bowl with lettuce leaves. Arrange shrimp, lobster, fish and crabmeat in clusters on a bed of salad greens.

3 Garnish with colorful wedges of tomato, ripe black olives and parsley. Serve with additional dressing.

PROVENÇAL FISH SALAD IN TOMATOES

(SERVES 6)

  6 large ripe tomatoes
1⅓ cups homemade mayonnaise (see page 141)
  1 clove garlic, finely chopped
  1 to 2 anchovy fillets, finely chopped
  1 tablespoon finely chopped basil or tarragon
  2 tablespoons finely chopped parsley
  1 tablespoon finely chopped capers
    Lemon juice, to taste
1½ pounds cold poached fish, diced
    Salt and freshly ground black pepper
    Finely chopped parsley

1 To prepare tomatoes: plunge tomatoes into boiling water one by one, and remove their skins. Slice cap off each and carefully scoop out all pulp and seeds. Cover loosely with foil and chill in refrigerator until ready to use.

2 Combine mayonnaise, garlic, anchovy fillets, herbs, capers and lemon juice, to taste; toss fish lightly in sauce until well coated; season with salt and pepper, to taste; pile mixture into tomatoes and garnish with parsley.

PROVENÇAL SEAFOOD SALAD

(SERVES 6)

  1 head iceberg or Boston lettuce
  1 head romaine lettuce, washed and chilled
  1 pound poached fish
  ½ pound cooked shrimp
  6 ripe tomatoes
 12 black olives
    French dressing (see page 146)

1 Line salad bowl with lettuce and Boston lettuce.

2 Combine ingredients for **provençal fish salad** mixture (see recipe above). Toss well and arrange in center of bowl with greens.

3 Garnish with cooked shrimp and wedges of ripe tomato and black olives. Serve with a French dressing.

Barbecue Parties

Eating outdoors has been revolutionized. Thanks to modern equipment that allows us to cook right at the table in our own backyard, and new portable barbecue units that can be carried in the car for cooking chops, steaks and skewers, it has become one of life's finest pleasures. Add to this a selection of specially insulated carriers and thermoses to keep food at the right temperature and your outdoor meal can be as informal, or as elaborate, as you choose.

If you embrace the full scope of the barbecue instead of limiting your repertoire to steaks and chops, you will find that you have opened up a whole new range of tastes to your palate, for every dish cooked over charcoal seems to improve in flavor and alter subtly as it cooks to crusty doneness.

It's not just a trick of the imagination that makes food taste better in the open air. The fire in the grill, the freshness of the air and the beauty of the surroundings add flavor and interest to every dish, whether it is served in a garden, on a terrace, or on a lonely stretch of sandy beach. Skewer cookery can be great fun and delicious, and skewers can be made with practically any food imaginable. Try beef, lamb or pork kebabs, cubes of tender meat marinated in olive oil, lemon juice and soy sauce, seasoned with finely chopped shallots, garlic or onions and a bay leaf or two. Let your guests prepare their own kebabs, alternating cubes of marinated meat with fresh vegetables, a bay leaf or two, even cubes of bread, brushed with melted butter and finely chopped garlic.

This is a perfectly easy formula for a summer party with a difference. And the choice of combinations is legion: serve bowls of small onions, either raw or poached, strips of green or red pepper, cubes of poached potato, mushroom caps, thin wedges of apple or tomato wrapped in bacon, whole small tomatoes, rum-soaked apricots and port-soaked prunes wrapped in bacon, and cubes of fat salt pork.

❀ *MENU* ❀

Gazpacho Salad
Barbecued Hamburgers
or
Barbecued Sausages with Mustard
with
Barbecued Corn on the Cob
Fruit Brochettes in Foil
SERVES 12

RED WINES
Rioja Red
Serradayres
Cabernet Red
Gigondas

GAZPACHO SALAD

- **2 medium-sized onions**
- **1 large cucumber**
- **12 large ripe tomatoes**
- **1 large green pepper**
- **8 to 12 tablespoons dry French bread crumbs**

Dressing:

- **6 tablespoons olive oil**
- **2 to 3 tablespoons wine vinegar**
- **1 clove garlic, crushed**
  Generous pinch of dry mustard
  Salt and freshly ground black pepper

1 Slice onions thinly; soak in ice water for 1 hour; drain well.

2 Slice (unpeeled) cucumber thinly. Peel and slice tomatoes. Seed and core pepper, and cut into thin strips.

3 Layer onions, cucumber, tomatoes, green pepper and French bread crumbs alternately in a

Gazpacho Salad

Barbecued Hamburgers and Steak

large glass salad bowl until all ingredients are used up.

    4 Prepare a dressing with remaining ingredients. Pour over salad and chill until ready to serve.

BARBECUED HAMBURGERS

Try one of the following hamburger combinations, or devise your own. Quantities given are for 1 large hamburger.

ONE

  ¼ **pound lean ground beef**
   1 **teaspoon chopped parsley**
   1 **teaspoon finely chopped onion**
      Salt and freshly ground black pepper

TWO

  ¼ **pound lean ground beef**
   1 **teaspoon ketchup**
  ¼ **teaspoon Worcestershire sauce**
      Salt and freshly ground black pepper

THREE

    ¼ **pound lean ground beef**
    ¼ **teaspoon soy sauce**
     2 **drops Tabasco**
        Salt and freshly ground black pepper

1 Combine beef with remaining ingredients. Mix well and shape into 1 large hamburger.

2 Spread hamburger with softened butter and grill over very hot coals until underside is brown and crisp; then brush uncooked side with a little more butter, turn over carefully and continue to grill until done to your taste, about 15 minutes in all.

3 Serve immediately, accompanied by Dijon mustard and tomato ketchup.

BARBECUED SAUSAGES WITH MUSTARD

At their best piping hot, but also good cold.

    24 **large sausages**
        Dijon mustard

1 With the point of a sharp knife, make 3 or 4 diagonal slits on both sides of each sausage. Spread generously with mustard, pushing it into slits with the side of the knife blade.

2 Arrange sausages on grill and cook for 10 to 15 minutes, or until brown and crisp on the outside and hot through. Turn several times to ensure even cooking.

BARBECUED CORN ON THE COB

Serve 1 cob per person. When cooking corn, always remember that overcooking will make it tough and hard again.

1 Turn back husks; strip away silk. Brush cobs with softened butter; sprinkle with coarse salt and black pepper; pull husks back into position. Lay cobs on grill and cook for 15 to 20 minutes, or until done, turning frequently.

2 Strip off papery brown husks and serve corn with plenty of butter and coarse salt.

To barbecue corn in foil: remove husks; spread each ear with 2 tablespoons butter, sprinkle with salt and freshly ground black pepper and wrap tightly in foil. Grill, turning frequently, for about 20 minutes.

FRUIT BROCHETTES IN FOIL

     3 **bananas**
        Juice of 3 lemons
     3 **pears**
     3 **oranges**
     3 **peaches**
     6 **plums**
    ½ **to ¾ cup sugar**
     2 **teaspoons ground cinnamon**
        Grand Marnier (optional)

1 Peel and quarter bananas; toss with lemon juice in a large bowl.

2 Peel, quarter and core pears. Add to bananas and toss with lemon juice.

3 Peel oranges, removing every bit of pith. Cut in quarters and add to bowl.

4 Pour boiling water over peaches in a strainer one at time and quickly peel off skins. Quarter peaches, discarding pits, and add to the bowl, making sure they are well coated with lemon juice to prevent discoloration.

5 Halve and pit plums and add to the bowl. Sprinkle fruit with sugar and cinnamon; toss lightly. Cover bowl tightly with foil and refrigerate for 1 hour.

6 **To assemble skewers:** drain pieces of fruit thoroughly, reserving juices, and divide evenly between 12 7- or 8-inch skewers.

7 Wrap each skewer in a rectangle of double-thickness foil, sealing carefully. Keep cool until needed.

8 **When ready to cook:** lay parcels on grill and cook for 10 to 15 minutes, turning occasionally.

9 Meanwhile, pour reserved juices into a small pan and simmer until reduced by half. Remove from heat and add a little Grand Marnier, if desired.

10 Fold back foil wrappings. Spoon a little sauce over fruit and serve immediately.

MENU

Orange, Onion and Tomato Salad
Chinese Barbecued Spareribs
Charcoal-Baked Cod Steaks with Lemon
with
Baked Potato Slices in Foil
SERVES 6

WHITE OR ROSE WINES
Touraine Sauvignon
Verdicchio
Pouilly Fuissé
Rosé d'Anjou

ORANGE, ONION AND TOMATO SALAD

1 crisp romaine lettuce
2 large onions
3 large firm tomatoes
2 large oranges
  Pitted black olives for garnish

Dressing:

4 tablespoons olive oil
2 to 3 tablespoons lemon juice
  Pinch of sugar
  Pinch of dry mustard
  Salt and freshly ground black pepper

1 Wash lettuce and pat each leaf dry with paper towels, wrap in a damp cloth and chill until needed.

2 Peel onions and cut 6 slices from the middle of each one about ¼ inch thick. Soak in ice water for 1 hour.

3 In the same way, cut 4 ¼-inch slices from the middle of each tomato.

4 Peel oranges and cut 6 ¼-inch slices from middle of each one.

5 **To assemble salad:** line a large, flat dish with lettuce leaves. Arrange onion slices in one layer on top; cover each slice with a slice of tomato and top with an orange slice.

6 Make a dressing with olive oil, lemon juice, sugar, mustard, salt and pepper; pour over salad. Garnish with black olives and serve at once.

CHINESE BARBECUED SPARERIBS

3 pounds spareribs
½ cup light soy sauce
3 tablespoons red wine
4 teaspoons sugar
1 teaspoon salt
1 clove garlic, crushed
4 tablespoons water

1 With a sharp knife, score meat between ribs on both sides without separating them completely.

2 Combine remaining ingredients in a flat dish, stirring until sugar and salt have dissolved. Coat ribs thoroughly and let marinate for 1 hour.

3 Drain ribs, reserving marinade; place them on the grill and barbecue for 30 to 40 minutes, turning frequently and brushing with remaining marinade. Pork should be thoroughly cooked, with a rich brown glaze.

4 Separate ribs and serve immediately.

Note: Ribs may also be roasted in 350°F oven. Allow 1 to 1½ hours for really well-cooked meat and baste frequently with marinade to glaze and prevent drying out.

CHARCOAL-BAKED COD STEAKS WITH LEMON

6 cod steaks
  Salt and freshly ground black pepper
6 lemons
8 tablespoons butter, melted
6 tablespoons dry white wine
2 cloves garlic, crushed
2 tablespoons chopped parsley

1 Season fish generously with salt and freshly ground black pepper.

2 Peel lemons; cut away skin and pith as though peeling an apple. Slice lemons thinly.

3 Cut 6 pieces of foil 10 inches square. Arrange ½ lemon in slices down center of each square. Put a cod steak on top and cover with remaining half of lemon in slices.

4 Combine remaining ingredients and spoon over fish.

5 Wrap each cod steak in foil and seal parcel securely.

6 Place parcels on a grid over glowing coals. The fish will be ready in 15 to 20 minutes.

7 Serve immediately, with foil folded back.

Note: Fresh swordfish or salmon in season may be substituted for cod in this recipe.

BAKED POTATO SLICES IN FOIL

1 Allow 1 large baking potato per person. Scrub thoroughly; dry; cut each unpeeled potato in three lengthwise.

2 Brush cut surfaces with 2 tablespoons melted butter, a few drops lemon juice and a generous sprinkling of salt and freshly ground black pepper.

3 Reassemble each potato and wrap securely in foil.

4 Bake over hot coals for 1 hour, or until potatoes feel soft when lightly squeezed.

BLUEBERRY CHEESECAKE

Fresh blueberries are one of the delights of summer. However, you can buy excellent canned or jarred blueberries packed in syrup with a near-fresh flavor. This recipe for blueberry cheesecake will let you capture a bit of summer even in the dead of winter.

> **1** deep 9-inch pastry shell, prebaked

Filling:

> **10** ounces cottage cheese, sieved
> **2** eggs
> **1¼** cups sour cream
> **4** to 6 tablespoons sugar
> **3** to 4 teaspoons lemon juice
> **1** teaspoon vanilla extract
> **3** drops almond extract
> Pinch of salt

Topping:

> **16** ounces of blueberries in syrup
> **1½** tablespoons cornstarch
> **2** teaspoons lemon juice
> Pinch of salt
> Pinch of cinnamon

1 Preheat oven to 375°F. Leave baked tart shell in tin.

2 **To make filling:** combine sieved cheese with remaining ingredients and beat vigorously with a wooden spoon until smooth and creamy. (If you use an electric blender, it is not necessary to sieve cheese; simply blend ingredients for 2–3 minutes.)

3 Pour filling into prepared shell and bake for 45 minutes, or until set. Remove from oven and allow to cool completely.

4 **To make topping:** drain blueberries. Dilute cornstarch with a few tablespoons of blueberry syrup and combine with remaining syrup in a small, heavy pan. Stir over moderate heat, stirring until smooth and thick, about 4 minutes from the time mixture comes to the boil. Allow to cool; then stir in blueberries and flavor with lemon juice, salt and cinnamon.

5 Pour blueberry topping over cheesecake and chill until firm.

Note: For a picnic barbecue, leave chilled (or frozen) cheesecake in its tin and wrap in foil or waxed paper and several sheets of newspaper to keep it cold.

> ❈ *MENU* ❈
> *Salami Appetizer Snack*
> *Barbecued Lamb Chops with Herbs*
> with
> *Vegetables in Foil*
> and
> *Baked Potatoes with Blue Cheese Dressing*
> *Tossed Green Salad*
> *Fresh Peaches with Macaroons*
> **SERVES 8**
> ───────────
> **RED WINES**
> **Beaujolais**
> **Moulin-à-Vent**
> **Côtes-du-Rhône**
> ❈

SALAMI APPETIZER SNACK

4 tablespoons each finely diced green pepper, cucumber and celery
2 tablespoons diced red pimento
24 large thin slices salami
   Stuffed green olives for garnish

Dressing:

½ teaspoon Dijon mustard
   Few drops of lemon juice
1 tablespoon olive oil
   Salt and freshly ground black pepper

1   Mix green pepper, cucumber and celery together.

2   Make a dressing with mustard, lemon juice, olive oil, salt and pepper.

3   Put a little vegetable mixture on each slice of salami and fold in half. Arrange in a tight ring on a round serving dish so that folded slices support each other. (Spear slices with toothpicks if they refuse to stay folded.)

4   Fill center of dish with stuffed olives and serve immediately.

BARBECUED LAMB CHOPS WITH HERBS

1 teaspoon each dried thyme, rosemary and marjoram or oregano
3 to 4 small bay leaves, crushed
   Generous pinch of paprika
   Finely grated rind and juice of 1 large lemon
8 double loin lamb chops
6 tablespoons olive oil
   Salt and freshly ground black pepper
   Butter
   Finely chopped parsley

1   Combine herbs with bay leaves, paprika and grated lemon rind. Mix well.

2   Rub herb mixture into chops. Place chops side by side in a large, shallow dish. Pour over lemon juice and olive oil; season lightly with salt and generously with pepper. Set chops aside in a cool place to marinate for 3 hours, turning occasionally.

3   **When ready to cook chops:** drain thoroughly and place on grill. Cook for 20 to 30

Vegetables in Foil

minutes, turning occasionally, until done to your liking.

4 Just before removing chops from grill, throw a good pinch of dried mixed herbs on to the coals, using any or all of the varieties from the marinade. The resulting smoke will impart a delicious flavor to the meat.

5 Serve topped with a pat of butter and sprinkled with finely chopped parsley.

VEGETABLES IN FOIL

MAKES 1 PORTION

    Salt
2 **thick slices eggplant**
2 **thick slices firm tomato**
2 **thin slices onion**
2 **thick slices zucchini**
2 **small mushrooms, halved**
    Freshly ground black pepper
    Pinch of oregano or marjoram
1 **teaspoon olive oil**
1 **teaspoon butter**

1 Rub salt into eggplant slices and let drain in a colander for about 30 minutes. Rinse slices well and squeeze dry between folds of paper towels.

2 Cut a double thickness of foil 10 to 12 inches square. Arrange eggplant slices side by side in the center; cover each slice with a slice of tomato, followed by a slice of onion and a slice of zucchini. Place halved mushrooms on top. Sprinkle with salt, pepper and oregano or marjoram; moisten with olive oil and top with butter. Fold over edges of foil and seal tightly. All this can be done in advance.

3 **When ready to cook:** lay foil package on grill and cook for 12 to 15 minutes, turning once or twice.

4 Serve package intact, with foil folded back to act as a plate.

BAKED POTATOES WITH BLUE CHEESE DRESSING

1 Scrub large baking potatoes thoroughly and bake them either wrapped in foil and arranged on the barbecue grill, or in the ashes of the fire.

2 For each potato blend 1 ounce blue cheese with 2 tablespoons sour cream and 1 tablespoon chopped chives or scallion tops.

3 Just before serving, slash tops of potatoes in crisscross fashion and squeeze gently to force them open. Fill with cheese mixture and serve immediately.

TOSSED GREEN SALAD

(For the recipe, see **green salad and variations,** page 146.)

FRESH PEACHES WITH MACAROONS

Macaroons:

MAKES 36

1½ **cups ground almonds**
¼ **cup confectioners' sugar, sifted**
1 **cup sugar**
3 **egg whites, unbeaten**
    Few drops of almond extract
36 **blanched almonds**

1 Preheat oven to 300°F.

2 Line 3 cookie sheets with greased aluminum foil.

3 Mix ground almonds with confectioners' sugar and 2 ounces superfine sugar.

4 Make a well in the center; add 1 egg white and work by hand to a stiff, smooth paste.

5 Gradually work in remaining superfine sugar and egg whites until paste is soft and smooth again. Add almond extract.

6 Put mixture in a pastry bag fitted with a plain ¾-inch nozzle and pipe out 36 rounds on prepared baking sheets. (Or drop on to baking sheets from a teaspoon.)

7 Sprinkle lightly with a little extra superfine sugar and decorate top of each macaroon with a blanched almond.

8 Bake macaroons for 25 to 30 minutes until firm and golden.

9 Cool macaroons slightly before removing them from prepared cookie sheets.

10 Then leave macaroons to cool on a rack before serving or storing in an airtight container.

❀ *MENU* ❀

Crudités with Bagna Cauda
and
Herbed Cheese Dip
Corn-Husk Barbecued Trout
with
Grilled Eggplant
Chocolate Beer Cake
SERVES 8

WHITE OR ROSE WINES
Chianti Ruffino
White
Riesling
Tavel Rosé

❀

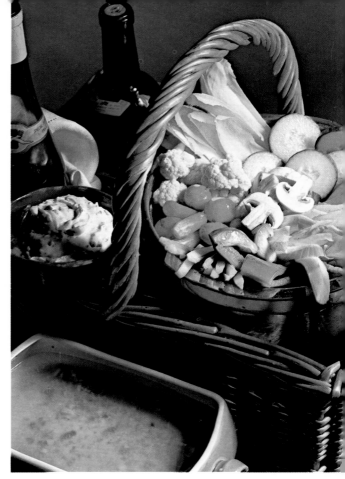

Crudités with Herbed Cheese Dip and Bagna Cauda

CRUDITES

Choose crisp raw vegetables—strips of carrot, celery and fennel, firm tomatoes and sweet peppers cut in wedges, thick slices of cucumber, scallions, cauliflowerets, tiny white mushrooms, radishes and leaves of chicory—enough to serve 8. Serve with **bagna cauda** and an **herbed cheese dip** (see below).

BAGNA CAUDA

½ **pound butter**
3 **to 4 tablespoons olive oil**
3 **to 4 cloves garlic, finely chopped**
6 **to 8 anchovies, crushed**
1 **small white truffle, thinly sliced (optional)**

1 This sauce is traditionally prepared in a flameproof earthenware dish with a short handle. Melt butter in it with olive oil and sauté garlic until golden.

2 Remove dish from heat; add anchovies and mix thoroughly. Return to low heat and simmer, stirring constantly, until anchovies have dissolved into a paste. Stir in sliced truffle, if used.

3 Serve in the pan, keeping it hot over a small burner.

HERBED CHEESE DIP

9 **ounces cream cheese**
2 **teaspoons lemon juice**
4 **tablespoons heavy cream**
1 **to 2 tablespoons milk**
½ **clove garlic, crushed**
Freshly ground black pepper
1 **to 2 tablespoons each finely chopped**
parsley, basil and chives
Dried thyme

1 Beat cream cheese with a wooden spoon until smooth.

2 Stir lemon juice into the cream; beat into softened cheese, together with milk.

3 Season to taste with garlic and a little pepper.

4 Finally, beat in finely chopped parsley, basil and chives and a generous pinch of thyme.

CORN-HUSK BARBECUED TROUT

- ½ cup softened butter
- 8 bay leaves, crushed
- 2 teaspoons lemon juice
  Salt and freshly ground black pepper
- 8 fresh trout, about ½ pound each, cleaned
- 2 tablespoons finely chopped parsley
- 1 teaspoon dried marjoram
- 16 slices bacon
- 8 corn husks
  Lemon wedges for garnish

1 Combine butter with bay leaves, lemon juice, salt and pepper, to taste. Divide into 8 equal portions.

2 Stuff a piece of butter into each trout. Season fish and sprinkle with parsley and marjoram.

3 Wrap 2 slices bacon around each trout. Put each fish inside a corn husk (in place of the ear of corn) and tie at the silk end.

4 Set husks in glowing embers and surround with live coals. Cook for 7 to 8 minutes on each side, or until fish flakes easily when tested with a fork.

5 Serve immediately, accompanied by a dish of lemon wedges.

GRILLED EGGPLANTS

- 4 large, long eggplants
  Salt and freshly ground black pepper
- 2 to 3 teaspoons oregano
  Olive oil

1 Cut eggplants into ½-inch slices. Sprinkle salt on both sides; place in a colander and leave for 1 hour to allow salt to draw out bitter juices.

2 Rinse slices thoroughly and press dry between folds of paper towels or a dishcloth.

3 Sprinkle slices with pepper and oregano; brush all over with olive oil.

4 Grill over hot ashes for 5 to 7 minutes, or until slices are soft and lightly browned, turning once.

CHOCOLATE BEER CAKE

  Butter
  Flour
- 2 ounces unsweetened chocolate
- ¼ teaspoon salt
- 1 teaspoon baking powder
- ¼ teaspoon bicarbonate of soda
- ¾ cup sugar
- 2 eggs
- 1 cup beer
- ½ cup walnuts, coarsely chopped (optional)

Filling:

- 4 tablespoons softened butter
- 1 cup confectioners' sugar, sifted
- 1 to 2 tablespoons beer
- 2 ounces unsweetened chocolate, melted and cooled

1 Butter and flour 2 8-inch cake pans. Preheat oven to 350°F.

2 Melt chocolate in the top of a double boiler and allow to cool to lukewarm.

3 Sift one-half pound flour, salt, baking powder and bicarbonate of soda into a bowl.

4 In another bowl, cream 8 tablespoons butter; add sugar gradually and beat until light and fluffy. Beat in eggs, 1 at a time, followed by melted chocolate. Then add flour mixture gradually, alternating it with beer (save 1 or 2 tablespoons for the filling) and beating vigorously until batter is well blended. Fold in walnuts, if used.

5 Pour batter into prepared pans and bake for 25 to 30 minutes, or until layers spring back when pressed lightly with the finger.

6 Remove cake from oven; allow to cool for 5 minutes, then turn layers out on wire racks and leave to become quite cold.

7 **To make filling:** cream softened butter with confectioners' sugar until very light. Add beer and lukewarm melted chocolate and beat vigorously until well blended. Chill until firm before using.

8 Spread chocolate filling between layers and cover top and side smoothly. (If you have not included nuts in the batter, you can decorate top of cake with walnut halves.)

❈ *MENU* ❈

Skillet Salad
Grilled Chicken
or
Grilled
Chicken with Honey Fruit Marinade
French Garlic Bread in Foil
Apple Turnovers
SERVES 12

WHITE OR ROSE WINES
Touraine Sauvignon
Verdicchio
Pouilly Fuissé
Rosé d'Anjou

❈

SKILLET SALAD

   4 pounds green peppers
   10 onions
   6 to 8 tablespoons olive oil
   12 ripe tomatoes
   2 (7-ounce) cans red pimentos
   Salt and freshly ground black pepper

1 Cut peppers in half lengthwise and remove pith and seeds. Slice lengthwise into strips ½ inch wide.

2 Peel onions and cut into slices ¼ inch thick.

3 Sauté green peppers and onions in olive oil over moderate heat, stirring frequently, for about 8 minutes, or until vegetables have lost some of their crispness and are slightly colored.

4 Cut tomatoes into slices ¼ inch thick. Drain pimentos and cut into ½-inch strips.

5 Add to peppers and onions, together with salt and pepper, to taste, and continue to cook for 4 or 5 minutes longer, until tomatoes are soft but not mushy. Serve hot.

Note: For a picnic barbecue, finish cooking the salad with tomatoes and pimentos in a large pan or skillet over the barbecue fire. Alternatively, cook salad completely at home and serve cold.

GRILLED CHICKEN

Nothing could be simpler or more delicious than a tender young chicken grilled over charcoal. Serve half a chicken per person, garnished with a generous dollop of butter and a squeeze of lemon.

   6 (2½-pound) chickens
   Olive oil
   Salt and freshly ground black pepper
   Paprika

1 Wipe chickens and split in half lengthwise. Break drumstick, hip and wing joints so that chickens will lie flat on the grill.

2 Brush each chicken generously with olive oil and season to taste with salt, pepper and a generous pinch of paprika per side.

3 Place on grill, cut side down, and cook for 10 to 15 minutes; then turn over, brush with more oil and continue to cook for 15 minutes longer, or until the juices run quite clear when chicken is pierced with a skewer through the thickest part of the leg.

For a more adventurous version, try the following:

GRILLED CHICKEN WITH HONEY FRUIT MARINADE

   6 (2½-pound) chickens

Marinade:

   6 tablespoons honey
   2 tablespoons Dijon mustard
   2 tablespoons oil
   1¾ cups pineapple juice
   1¾ cups orange juice
   ¾ cup ketchup
   Salt and freshly ground black pepper
   Cayenne pepper
   Ground ginger

1 To make marinade: bring the first 6 ingredients to the boil in a pan and simmer gently for about 40 minutes until slightly thickened. Season generously with salt, pepper and a generous pinch or 2 of cayenne and ground ginger.

2 Split chickens in half down the breast; break drumstick, hip and wing joints as above. Brush generously with marinade and set aside for at least 1 hour.

3 Drain chicken halves thoroughly and thread on spits (or place flat on a grill) over hot coals. Barbecue slowly, brushing occasionally with remaining marinade, for 15 to 20 minutes on each side, or until chickens are crisply browned on the outside, and juices run clear when a skewer is pushed into the thickest part of the leg.

FRENCH GARLIC BREAD IN FOIL

1 One long French loaf will serve 3, possibly 4. Cut each loaf on the slant into slices about 1½ inches thick, taking care not to cut through base at any point.

2 Spread each slice with **garlic butter** (see below).

3 Wrap loaf tightly in foil and grill over hot coals, turning frequently, for about 20 minutes, or until butter has melted and bread is crisp and hot.

Garlic Butter:

ENOUGH FOR 1 FRENCH LOAF ABOUT 16 INCHES LONG
- **8 tablespoons softened butter**
- **1 to 2 cloves garlic, crushed**
- **1 tablespoon finely chopped parsley**
  Salt and freshly ground black pepper

To make garlic butter: mash softened butter with garlic, parsley, salt and pepper, to taste, into a smooth paste.

APPLE TURNOVERS

MAKES 12
- **1 pound flaky pastry**
  Butter for cookie sheets
  Beaten egg for glaze

Filling:

- **1½ pounds cooking apples, peeled, cored and thinly sliced**
- **2 tablespoons granulated sugar**
- **2 tablespoons dark brown sugar**
- **¼ cup raisins, chopped**
- **1 tablespoon flour**
- **½ teaspoon freshly grated nutmeg**
- **½ teaspoon ground cinnamon**
  Grated rinds of ½ orange and ½ lemon
  Juice of 1 lemon
- **2 tablespoons orange juice**

1 Preheat oven to 400°F. Butter 2 large baking sheets.

2 Combine filling ingredients in a bowl and toss until well mixed.

3 Roll out pastry very thinly and cut into 12 circles 6 inches in diameter.

4 Heap filling on ½ of each pastry circle, leaving a ¼-inch rim clear. Brush edges lightly with water; fold each circle in half and seal tightly, turning edges over on themselves attractively.

5 Arrange turnovers on prepared cookie sheets. Cut 2 or 3 small slits on top with a sharp-pointed knife, and glaze with beaten egg.

6 Bake for 15 to 20 minutes, or until pastry is puffed and golden, and apples feel soft when pierced (through one of the slits) with a toothpick.

7 Serve hot, or reheat on a barbecue grill lined with foil.

Skillet Salad

Food After a Cocktail Party

If, like me, you are daunted by the terrors of a cocktail party at which no food is served, you might like to end your evening with something a little more substantial—perhaps a baked ham or a roast turkey, with a choice of salads and assorted breads. Or try a party idea from Alsace Lorraine: cold roast loin of pork with potato and sauerkraut salads.

For both informality and comfort, make it a buffet-cum-sit-down-dinner, where guests serve themselves from a candlelit sideboard, then move along to a set table. There is no first course, and raspberry and red currant tarts and coffee are arranged on a separate side table.

The main dish of cold roast loin of pork, flavored with thyme, bay leaf and mustard, is cooked on the day preceding the party. Cut it into chops and serve it on a bed of fresh watercress; and for additional effect garnish it with hollowed-out apples filled with homemade apple sauce spiked with a little grated horseradish or mayonnaise. Make sure you brush the interiors of the apples with lemon juice to keep their color fresh.

Serve this meal country-style—on thick white plates with red checked tablecloths and napkins—and accompany it with steins of beer or a wine.

 MENU

Cold Roast Loin of Pork
Potato Salad
and
Choucroute Salad
Raspberry and Red Currant Tarts
SERVES 6-8

ROSES
Tavel Rosé
Rosé de Provence

COLD ROAST LOIN OF PORK

1 **loin of pork (7 to 8 chops)**
4 **tablespoons softened butter**
  Crumbled thyme and bay leaf
  Dijon mustard
  Salt and freshly ground black pepper
  Sprigs of watercress
  Horseradish apple sauce or mayonnaise
    (see page 142)

1 Have your butcher remove rind but not fat from pork. Mix butter, thyme, bay leaf and mustard to a smooth paste and rub well into pork several hours before roasting. Sprinkle to taste with salt and pepper and let stand at room temperature to absorb flavors. Brown in a 450°F oven for 15 minutes, fat side up. Reduce heat to 350°F and continue to roast until meat is done, about 1¼ to 1½ hours. Cool.

2 Cut cold loin of pork into chops.

3 Serve on a bed of watercress with choice of salads and **horseradish apple sauce** or mayonnaise.

POTATO SALAD

3 **pounds new potatoes**
Salt
1 **to 2 tablespoons sugar**
3 **tablespoons wine vinegar**
6 **slices bacon**
Olive oil
1 **green pepper, finely chopped**
3 **tablespoons finely chopped onion**
3 **tablespoons finely chopped parsley**
Lemon juice
Cayenne pepper

1 Scrub new potatoes; cook in boiling salted water until just tender, 15 to 20 minutes; drain, peel and slice. Place potatoes in a bowl and sprinkle with sugar and vinegar. Toss gently.

2 Sauté bacon in a little oil until crisp. Drain well, pouring fat over potatoes. Crumble bacon or chop finely and add to potatoes with green pepper. Toss gently.

3 Combine 6 to 8 tablespoons olive oil with onion and parsley and season with lemon juice, salt and cayenne to taste. Pour over salad.

CHOUCROUTE SALAD

1 **onion, finely chopped**
½ **cup olive oil**
2 **large (30 ounces) cans sauerkraut**
2 **cups chicken stock**
Dry white wine (optional)
Salt and coarsely ground black pepper
1 **to 2 cloves garlic, finely chopped**
2 **to 3 tablespoons vinegar**
2 **to 3 hard-boiled eggs, quartered**
1 **beet, cooked and sliced**

1 Sauté onion in 2 tablespoons of the olive oil until golden but not brown.

2 Place sauerkraut in a heavy saucepan with onion and pour in chicken stock. Simmer for 45 minutes, adding a little more stock or wine if necessary.

3 Cool sauerkraut; drain and season with salt and pepper, to taste, garlic, the remaining olive oil and vinegar.

4 Serve garnished with hard-boiled eggs and thin slices of beet.

RASPBERRY AND RED CURRANT TARTS

3 **to 4 pints raspberries**
1 **pint red currants**
5 **ounces sugar**
Lemon juice
6 **to 8 baked tart shells**
1 **to 2 tablespoons red currant jelly**
Kirsch (optional)

1 Combine raspberries, red currants and sugar in an enameled saucepan and cook over low heat, stirring gently, until the sugar melts. Add lemon juice to taste and drain fruit, reserving juices.

2 Fill tart shells with fruit and bake in a 350°F oven for 10 minutes.

3 Meanwhile add red currant jelly to juices and boil until syrup is thick, adding a little kirsch if desired. Cool tarts and strain syrup over fruit.

Let's Make It a Fondue Party

A good bet for informal entertaining for young parties is a Fondue Party, which comes to us from France and Switzerland. It is easy and fun. Fondues range from traditional Swiss fondue to fondue Bourguignonne, where each guest is given a small bowl of marinated steak cubes, a variety of sauces—béarnaise, mustard and herb, garlic mayonnaise and spicy tomato béarnaise—and a long-handled fork with which to cook his own meat piece by piece in a central pot of simmering butter and oil.

Guests spear cubes of beef with their fondue forks; hold each cube in the simmering butter and oil until done to their taste—a matter of seconds—and then dip it into one of the accompanying sauces. Serve fondue Bourguignonne with a good red Burgundy (Nuits-St.-Georges or Moulin à Vent) and French bread. Follow with a tossed green salad.

Swiss Fondue is an easily prepared communal dip-in that combines good Swiss cheese, fine wine and good cheer. The ideal setting is a roaring fire and a long table big enough to seat several people. Make sure all ingredients are at hand before starting as the actual cooking time is brief.

Equip each guest with a long fork, cubes of crusty French bread, a glass of dry white wine (I like a Sylvaner or a Niersteiner) and a napkin. Each person in turn spears a cube of bread from his plate, dips it in the creamy fondue mixture, and scoops out the bread, now coated with the creamy cheese mixture. Swiss tradition has it that if a man drops his bread into the pot he will have to pay for the meal; if a woman drops hers in she will have to kiss each man at the table.

So here I have given you two basic fondue recipes together with my suggestions for variations. First select your fondue, and then choose a first course and dessert to accompany it.

SWISS FONDUE

¾ pound Gruyère cheese, coarsely grated
¾ pound Emmenthal (Swiss) cheese, coarsely grated
1 teaspoon cornstarch
1 cut clove garlic
1½ to 2 cups dry white wine
2 to 4 tablespoons kirsch
Nutmeg, salt and pepper
French bread, cut into crusty squares

1 Toss grated cheese with cornstarch.
2 Rub inside of an earthenware casserole or fondue cooker with cut surface of garlic.
3 Pour in dry white wine and heat over very low heat until wine starts to bubble. Add

Fondue Bourguignonne with Sauces and Garnishes

cheese gradually, stirring continuously, until blended. When cheese and wine mixture is smooth and well blended, add kirsch and nutmeg, salt and pepper, to taste.

Note: Fondue should be kept warm, but not too hot. If fondue becomes too thick in cooking, add a little more dry white wine or kirsch.

4   At the table: each guest spears a cube of bread, dips it in the creamy fondue mixture, and scoops out the bread, now coated with the mixture. Serve with a **tossed green salad** (see page 146).

FONDUE BOURGUIGNONNE

- 2 **pounds top-quality beef fillet**
- ½ **pound butter**
- ⅔ **cup corn or peanut oil**

1   Dice meat into small bite-sized cubes, cutting off all bits of fat or gristle. Marinate for at least 2 hours before serving (see below).

2   Combine butter and oil in a fondue pot or chafing dish and keep it simmering gently in the middle of the table.

3   Garnish for each guest: individual bowls of 3 or more of the following: **mustard and herb sauce, garlic mayonnaise,** finely chopped garlic, finely chopped parsley and capers, **spicy tomato béarnaise, béarnaise sauce** (see page 142).

4   At the table: each guest spears a cube of beef with his fondue fork; holds it in the simmering butter and oil until done to his taste; and then dips it into one of 3 accompanying sauces or garnishes. Serve with a **tossed green salad.**

Marinade for Fondue Bourguignonne:

- 6 **tablespoons olive oil**
- 6 **tablespoons dry white wine**
- 2 **bay leaves, crumbled**
- 2 **tablespoons finely chopped parsley**
  Salt and freshly ground black pepper

Combine first 4 ingredients and pour into a flat serving bowl. Add cubed meat and toss well.

Season generously with salt and pepper, and toss again. Let meat marinate in the mixture for at least 2 hours before using.

Mustard and Herb Sauce:

- 2 **tablespoons wine vinegar**
- 1 **tablespoon Dijon mustard**
- ½ **cup olive oil**
- 1 **to 2 tablespoons finely chopped onion**
- 1 **tablespoon finely chopped parsley**
- 1 **tablespoon finely chopped chives**
  Salt and freshly ground black pepper

Combine vinegar and mustard in a small bowl and blend well. Whisk in olive oil gradually and then add onion, parsley, chives, and salt and pepper, to taste.

Garlic Mayonnaise:

- 4 **fat cloves of garlic per person**
  Salt
- 1 **egg yolk for each 2 persons**
  Olive oil
  Freshly ground black pepper
  Lemon juice

1   Crush garlic to a smooth paste with a little salt; blend in egg yolks until they form a smooth mixture.

2   Now take olive oil and proceed (drop by drop at first, a thin, fine trickle later) to whisk the mixture. The mayonnaise will thicken gradually until it reaches the proper stiff, firm consistency. The exact quantity of oil is, of course, determined by the number of egg yolks used.

3   Season to taste with additional salt, a little pepper and lemon juice. This sauce is served chilled in a bowl. Guests help themselves.

Spicy Tomato Béarnaise:

Make **béarnaise** (see page 142) and add ketchup, lemon juice and cayenne pepper, to taste. Sauce should be very spicy.

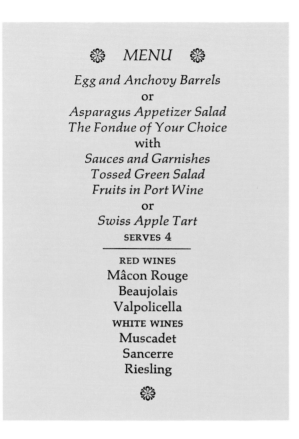

MENU ❀

Egg and Anchovy Barrels
or
Asparagus Appetizer Salad
The Fondue of Your Choice
with
Sauces and Garnishes
Tossed Green Salad
Fruits in Port Wine
or
Swiss Apple Tart
SERVES 4

RED WINES
Mâcon Rouge
Beaujolais
Valpolicella
WHITE WINES
Muscadet
Sancerre
Riesling

❀

EGG AND ANCHOVY BARRELS

    4 hard-boiled eggs
    8 anchovy fillets
    4 tablespoons mayonnaise (see page 141)
    ¼ teaspoon paprika
       Freshly ground black pepper
       Watercress
       Capers

1 Shell eggs and cut tops and bottoms off with a sharp knife dipped in cold water. Carefully remove yolks from broad end of eggs, being careful not to split whites.

2 Mash yolks to a smooth paste with 4 of the anchovies, mayonnaise and paprika. Season to taste with pepper and stuff eggs with this mixture. If mixture is too stiff, add more mayonnaise.

3 **To serve:** place eggs, broad end up, on a bed of watercress. Split remaining anchovy fillets and wrap around center of each egg. Top each barrel with capers.

ASPARAGUS APPETIZER SALAD

    1 bunch fresh asparagus, or 2 packages
         frozen asparagus
    1 head lettuce
    1 canned pimento, cut in strips
    2 hard-boiled eggs, sliced
       Paprika (optional)

Sour Cream Dressing:

    ⅔ cup sour cream
       Lemon juice
       Salt and freshly ground black pepper
    1 tablespoon each finely chopped fresh
         parsley, chives and tarragon
       Tabasco or paprika

1 **To prepare fresh asparagus:** wash stalks thoroughly and if sandy scrub them gently with a vegetable brush. Remove any isolated leaf points below the head. To remove the woody base, break the stalks rather than cut them. You will find that they snap off easily at the point where the tender part begins. Put the stalks in cold water as you clean and trim them.

2 Select a deep, narrow pan in which the asparagus stalks can stand upright and pour in boiling water to come halfway up the asparagus; in this way, the tough stalks will cook in water while the tender heads cook in steam. Simmer gently—for about 15 minutes from the time the water comes to the boil again is just about right. Remove asparagus from pan and drain.

Note: If you have no deep, narrow pan, stand the asparagus upright in the bottom of a double boiler. Add boiling water and cover asparagus with the inverted top of the double boiler. Or, crumple some aluminum foil into one side of a large, flat casserole with cover. Place asparagus in casserole, with heads supported on foil; add enough boiling water to cover stalks only. Cover casserole. Cook for about 15 minutes, as above.

3 Wash and dry the lettuce leaves and line a serving dish with them. Divide the cooked asparagus into 2 bunches and arrange them on the lettuce leaves. Garnish with strips of pimento and sliced hard-boiled eggs, reserving the end slices of each egg to chop for added garnish. Dust lightly with paprika if desired. Serve the dressing separately.

4 **To make sour cream dressing:** combine sour cream with lemon juice, salt and pepper, to taste. Stir in the herbs with a dash of Tabasco sauce or paprika.

TOSSED GREEN SALAD

(For the recipe, see **green salad and variations,** page 146)

FRUITS IN PORT WINE

> 2 **pounds ripe pears**
> **Juice and rind of ½ lemon**
> **Rind of 1 orange**
> 1 **cup port**
> 3½ **cups water**
> 1 **cup sugar**
> 1 **(8-ounce) jar brandied cherries**

1 Peel the pears and place them in a bowl of water to which you have added the lemon juice to keep them from discoloring. Reserve the lemon rind.

2 With a sharp knife remove the outer rind of the orange and half-lemon—just the rind, not the white pith. Cut the rinds into thin slivers.

3 Bring wine, water, sugar, lemon rind and the orange rind to the boil in an enameled saucepan. Simmer until the sugar has dissolved. Remove the pears from lemon water and add them to the syrup; simmer until tender. Add brandied cherries and chill. Serve fruits in syrup with a little slivered orange rind scattered over them.

SWISS APPLE FLAN

> 1 **baked pie shell**
> 1½ **pounds cooking apples**
> 2 **tablespoons butter**

Swiss Apple Sauce Filling:

MAKES ABOUT 2⅔ CUPS
> 2 **pounds cooking apples**
> 4 to 6 **tablespoons butter**
> 2 to 3 **lemon slices**
> 2 **tablespoons sugar**
> 1 **clove**
> 4 **tablespoons water**
> ½ **teaspoon vanilla**
> **Cinnamon**

1 **To make Swiss apple sauce filling:** wash, quarter and core 2 pounds apples.

2 Cut quartered apples into thick slices and put them in a large saucepan together with butter, lemon slices, sugar, clove and water. Bring gently to the boil; cover pan and simmer gently for about 10 minutes, stirring once or twice during cooking time to prevent sauce from scorching.

3 When sauce is thick and smooth, remove lemon slices and clove and puree sauce in a blender.

4 Flavor with vanilla and cinnamon, to taste, adding a little more sugar, if desired. Allow to cool before using. Half-fill baked pie shell with this mixture.

Apricot Glaze:

> 6 **tablespoons apricot jam**
> 3 **tablespoons water**
> 1 **tablespoon rum, brandy or kirsch**

5 **To prepare glaze:** heat apricot jam and water in small saucepan, stirring constantly, until mixture melts. Strain and if desired stir in rum, brandy or kirsch. Keep warm until ready for use.

6 **To prepare apples:** peel, core and slice apples as thinly as possible. Arrange in overlapping concentric circles on top of Swiss apple sauce filling. Dot with butter and bake under a preheated broiler for 3 to 5 minutes, or until apple slices are nicely browned. Coat with apricot glaze.

You Can Be a Pasta Master

It's a new Italian renaissance. Italian restaurants are booming. Italian specialty stores are springing up in towns and cities across the country. Italian products were featured on the shelves of every supermarket I visited this week.

The reason for this great new revival is simply **pasta.** Americans are crazy about pasta—so inexpensive, so easy to cook, so wonderfully easy to eat and enjoy, whether you serve it with a hamburger, make it the main dish of a company dinner, or serve it as a first course as the Italians do.

There are hundreds of types of pasta in Italy, and almost as many sauces. And each type of pasta—believe it or not—tastes quite different because of its shape, thickness or thinness and the way it takes up the sauce. Try it and see with one of the four most popular types below.

Tubular pasta: macaroni, spaghetti, vermicelli, etc.
Flat or ribbon pasta: noodles, fettuccine, tagliatelle, lasagne.
Envelope pasta: ravioli, manicotti, cannelloni—usually stuffed first, then cooked with a sauce.
Fancy-shaped pastina: innumerable types including bows, stars, shells, alphabet letters, etc. The very tiny ones—almost like confetti—are used only in soups.

To Cook Pasta Perfectly

All you need is a big pot, a *very* big pot.

You fill the pot with water, season generously with salt and bring the water to a fast boil. Then you put in the pasta. Don't break it, just push it in gently with your hand. For, as the pasta at the bottom of the pot softens in the hot water, it will gradually bend. Then stir the pasta so it will not stick to the bottom of the pot.

Now comes the all-important direction. No one can say exactly how long to cook pasta. The time varies with the type of pasta used. So it is useless to depend on the clock. You have to stand over the pot and taste.

To be perfect, pasta should be neither too hard nor too mushy, but at the beginning point of softness when it is just tender and a little resistant to the teeth. To test this, just fish out a piece of pasta with a fork and bite it, then decide on the perfect moment for yourself.

And take a tip from a pasta lover who knows: add plenty of butter before saucing. With a fork in each hand, lift the long strands a few times, almost tossing—spaghetti or noodles must be very hot so the butter will melt all through and separate the strands. Now on with the spicy sauce and a liberal helping of grated Parmesan cheese, freshly grated if you can get it—it tastes so much better—packaged, if you cannot.

For four persons, use a little less than 1 pound pasta if it is to be a first course. If it is the main dish of the meal, use more, depending on the appetites of your friends.

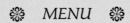

TOMATO ASPIC

5½ cups cooked or canned tomatoes
 1 celery stalk, chopped
 1 onion, chopped
 ½ lemon, chopped
 2 teaspoons sugar
 1 teaspoon salt
 2 bay leaves
 2 cloves
 1 clove garlic, chopped
 1 envelope gelatin
 ½ cup cider vinegar
   Worcestershire or Tabasco sauce

Garnish:

Small tomatoes
Cauliflowerets
Curly endive leaves
Radishes
Sliced green pepper
Sprig of parsley
Lemon slices

1 Combine the first 9 ingredients in a saucepan and simmer for 20 minutes. Strain the tomato mixture through a sieve, pressing the vegetables well to extract juices.

2 Soften the gelatin in the vinegar. Stir into the sieved tomato mixture until dissolved. Add Worcestershire sauce or Tabasco to taste.

3 Pour the mixture into a 6-cup mold. Refrigerate until firm.

4 **To serve:** unmold and garnish the aspic with small tomatoes, cauliflowerets, endive, radishes, green pepper and a sprig of parsley, and serve with lemon slices.

Note: The above recipe is quite delicious, too, if you fold diced green pepper, celery and baby shrimp into the "syrupy" aspic mixture before you refrigerate it. Garnish the mold as above.

CHEESE AND MACARONI LOAF

¾ pound macaroni
  Salt
  Butter
 2 tablespoons flour
   Freshly ground black pepper
 ½ teaspoon paprika
 2 cups milk
1½ cups grated cheese
 3 eggs

1 Cook macaroni in boiling, salted water until tender but not mushy.

2 Melt 2 tablespoons butter in the top of a double boiler; stir in flour and season generously with salt, pepper and paprika. Add milk and stir over low heat until sauce is smooth and thick. Add cheese and stir until cheese has melted. Stir in macaroni.

3 Separate eggs. Beat yolks until smooth and add to mixture. Heat through. Be careful not to let mixture boil at this stage, or your eggs will curdle.

4 Beat egg whites until stiff. Fold into mixture. Correct seasoning, adding a little more salt and pepper if necessary, and then turn mixture into a well-buttered loaf pan 9 × 3 × 5 inches and set in a roasting pan of hot water. Place pan over high heat until water starts to bubble, then place in a preheated 350°F oven for 50 minutes or until the loaf is firm. When ready to serve, turn out and serve hot.

Variations on a theme: Change this basic recipe by adding 2 tablespoons finely chopped cooked bacon, 2 tablespoons finely chopped fried onions, or 2 tablespoons finely chopped parsley and chives to the above. Or, wrap tomato wedges in a half slice of partially cooked bacon and bury in the cheese and macaroni loaf.

WATERCRESS AND SOY SALAD

    2 bunches watercress
    1 bunch radishes
    4 to 6 celery stalks

Soy Dressing:

    6 to 8 tablespoons olive oil
    1 teaspoon sugar
    1 tablespoon lemon juice
    1 teaspoon soy sauce
       Freshly ground black pepper
       Monosodium glutamate

1   Prepare watercress and chill in a damp towel. Trim and slice radishes; slice celery.

2   **To make dressing:** combine olive oil, sugar, lemon juice and soy sauce, seasoning to taste with pepper and monosodium glutamate.

3   **Just before serving:** place watercress in a salad bowl; arrange sliced radishes and celery in center. Add dressing and toss until every ingredient glistens.

PEACHES IN RED WINE

    2 to 2½ pounds small peaches
    ½ to ¾ cup sugar
    ¾ cup water
       Cinnamon
    ¾ cup red Burgundy
       Whipped cream

1   Peel peaches but do not remove the pits. Put peaches in a saucepan with the sugar and water and cinnamon to taste. Simmer them, covered, for about 15 minutes. Add wine and continue to cook, uncovered, over a low heat for 15 minutes.

2   Put peaches in a deep serving dish. Cook the liquid until reduced to the consistency of a light syrup. Pour syrup over the peaches and put in the refrigerator to chill. Serve very cold with whipped cream.

Tomato Aspic

❋ *MENU* ❋

Pasta Shells with Broccoli
Vitello al Herbe
Chocolate Refrigerator Cake
SERVES 4-6

WHITE WINES
Muscadet
Sancerre
Verdicchio

❋

PASTA SHELLS WITH BROCCOLI

  1 **pound fresh broccoli or 2 packages frozen**
     Salt
  ¾ **pound pasta shells**
  ¼ **large onion, finely chopped**
  2 **tablespoons finely chopped parsley**
  2 **to 4 anchovy fillets, finely chopped**
  2 **cloves garlic, finely chopped**
  2 **tablespoons olive oil**
  2 **tablespoons butter**
     Freshly ground black pepper
  2 **to 4 tablespoons freshly grated**
     Parmesan cheese

  1 Cook broccoli in boiling salted water until just tender. Drain well and chop coarsely.
  2 Cook pasta shells in boiling salted water until just tender. Drain.

Vitello al Herbe

  3 Sauté onion, parsley, anchovies and a little garlic in olive oil and butter until onion just begins to turn golden; add drained, chopped broccoli, season generously with salt and pepper, and continue cooking until broccoli begins to turn golden.
  4 Place hot pasta shells in a heated serving dish, add broccoli and toss until well mixed.
  5 Correct seasoning; sprinkle with a little freshly grated Parmesan cheese and serve immediately.

VITELLO AL HERBE

  1½ **pounds veal, cut into thin slices**
     Salt and freshly ground black pepper
  6 **tablespoons butter**
     Rosemary leaves
     Juice of 1 lemon
     Lemon slices

  1 Season veal to taste with salt and pepper.
  2 Melt butter in a thick-bottomed frying pan; add veal with rosemary leaves to taste and

Pasta Shells with Broccoli

sauté until golden. Add lemon juice and cook until tender (3 to 5 minutes longer). Serve garnished with lemon slices.

CHOCOLATE REFRIGERATOR CAKE

     8 egg yolks
     ½ cup sugar
     2 cups milk
     ½ to 1 teaspoon vanilla
     2 envelopes gelatin
     4 tablespoons cold water
  1½ ounces unsweetened chocolate, melted
     2 tablespoons melted butter
     4 tablespoons rum or kirsch
     2 cups heavy cream
        Ladyfingers
        Kirsch and water
        Whipped cream
        Walnuts

1   Combine egg yolks and sugar in the top of a double boiler and work the mixture with a wooden spoon until smooth. Bring the milk to a boil and add vanilla; then add milk gradually to the yolk mixture, stirring rapidly with a wire whisk. Cook over boiling water until the mixture becomes smooth and thick. Do not allow mixture to boil, or it will curdle.

2   Soften the gelatin in cold water and add it to the hot custard, stirring until it dissolves. Cool the custard.

3   Divide the custard into 2 portions and add melted chocolate, melted butter and rum or kirsch to one portion. Whip cream until stiff and fold half of it into each of the 2 mixtures.

4   Line the sides of a medium-sized springform pan with ladyfingers dipped in equal quantities of kirsch and water. Fill the pan with alternating layers of chocolate and vanilla cream, allowing each layer to set in refrigerator for about 30 minutes before adding the next. Set the cake (still in its pan) in the refrigerator to chill for at least 12 hours, or overnight.

5   When ready to serve, remove pan sides, leaving cake in the bottom of the pan. Top with whipped cream and walnuts.

❀ *MENU* ❀

Appetizer Salad
Spaghetti Bolognese
Italian Bean Salad
Cold Zabaglione
SERVES 4-6

WHITE WINES
Soave
Verdicchio
Lachryma Christi

❀

APPETIZER SALAD

     4 ripe tomatoes, peeled
     4 new potatoes, boiled
     1 avocado
        Juice of 1 lemon
     1 green pepper, seeded and boiled
     1 head lettuce
        French dressing (see below)
     1 small onion, cut into thin rings

1   Peel tomatoes in the following manner: place a tomato on the end of a kitchen fork and hold in boiling water for 1 or 2 minutes until skin begins to crack. Remove from water and with a sharp knife gently peel skin from tomato. Cut in thick wedges. Peel potatoes and slice thickly. Peel avocado, remove pit and cut crosswise in thick slices. Brush slices with lemon juice to prevent discoloration. Cut boiled pepper into thick strips.

2   Wash lettuce leaves well in a large quantity of water. They should be left whole, never cut. Drain well and dry thoroughly.

3   Make French dressing with 1 tablespoon wine vinegar and 3 tablespoons olive oil, generously seasoned with salt and freshly ground black pepper.

4   Line a salad bowl with lettuce leaves. Toss prepared vegetables lightly in French dressing and arrange in lettuce-lined bowl. Pour remaining dressing over salad and garnish with thinly sliced onion rings.

Italian Bean Salad

SPAGHETTI BOLOGNESE

    Butter, margarine or olive oil
¼ pound fat salt pork, finely chopped
1 large onion, finely chopped
4 carrots, finely chopped
1 celery stalk, finely chopped
½ pound lean ground beef
1 strip lemon peel
1 bay leaf
6 tablespoons tomato sauce
2 cups beef stock
    Salt and freshly ground black pepper
    Freshly grated nutmeg
1 pound spaghetti
    Freshly grated Parmesan cheese

1 Heat 4 tablespoons butter in a large thick-bottomed frying pan; add salt pork, onion, carrots and celery and sauté over moderate heat, stirring occasionally, until pork browns.

2 Add beef and brown evenly, stirring constantly. Add lemon peel, bay leaf, tomato sauce, beef stock, salt, pepper and nutmeg to taste. Cover pan and simmer very gently for 30 minutes, stirring occasionally.

3 Remove lemon peel and bay leaf and simmer, uncovered, for 30 minutes longer, or until sauce has slightly thickened.

4 Cook spaghetti in boiling salted water until tender. Drain. Dot with butter and serve with Bolognese sauce and Parmesan cheese.

5 Another version of this famous dish tosses cooked spaghetti with Bolognese sauce; spoons it into an ovenproof baking dish; sprinkles it with grated Parmesan cheese; dots it with butter and bakes it in a 375°F oven until golden.

ITALIAN BEAN SALAD

¾ pound fresh green beans
    Lettuce leaves
2 tablespoons chopped parsley

Garlic Dressing:

6 tablespoons olive oil
    Juice of 1 lemon
    Salt and freshly ground black pepper
1 to 3 large cloves garlic, chopped

1 **To make dressing:** combine oil and lemon juice, adding salt, pepper and garlic.

2 Cook the beans in boiling salted water until just tender. Drain and toss with garlic dressing while still warm.

3 Line a bowl with lettuce leaves and arrange the green beans in the center. Sprinkle with parsley and serve.

COLD ZABAGLIONE

6 egg yolks
¼ cup sugar
6 to 8 tablespoons Marsala or sherry
1 teaspoon gelatin
3 tablespoons brandy
¼ teaspoon vanilla
1 cup heavy cream, whipped
    Grated lemon rind

1 In the top of a double boiler combine egg yolks, sugar and Marsala. Whip the mixture over hot but not boiling water until it thickens.

2 Stir in gelatin, softened in 2 tablespoons cold water and dissolved over hot water.

3 Put the pan in a bowl of ice and stir the zabaglione well until it is thick. When it is almost cold, fold in brandy, vanilla and whipped cream, and pour into glasses. Chill. Decorate with grated lemon rind.

Three for the Pot

If you like long, slow, even cooking—the kind you don't have to watch—you will find that pot roasting is the easiest way to cook the Sunday roast that you've ever come across.

And it's economical, too. For by pot roasting your meat over the lowest of heats or in the lowest of ovens—up to 4 hours for a 5-pound roast—you can make the most inexpensive piece of meat so tender that you can cut it with a fork. And it's extra delicious if you add a few carrots, onions, turnips and just enough beef stock, water or wine to moisten the meat, not stew it.

Pot roasts are most successful in a heavy, tightly covered casserole, kettle or deep frying pan that is only slightly bigger than the cut of meat to be cooked. Inexpensive cuts of brisket, chuck, top round, and shin of beef respond well to this slow, moist method of cooking. Select cuts that are well marbled with fat or ask your butcher to lard some fat through the meat for you.

SLICED EGG APPETIZERS

Mayonnaise
Vinaigrette sauce (see below)
4 to 6 hard-boiled eggs
½ cucumber, seeded and diced
4 to 6 tomatoes, peeled, seeded and diced
1 to 2 tablespoons finely chopped parsley

1 Make mayonnaise, using quantities given on page 141.

2 Make a vinaigrette sauce, using 2 tablespoons wine vinegar, 6 to 8 tablespoons olive oil, coarse salt and freshly ground black pepper.

3 Shell eggs and cut into even slices. Place a bed of mayonnaise on a flat hors d'oeuvre dish. Cover with 2 rows of overlapping slices of egg.

Sliced Egg Appetizer

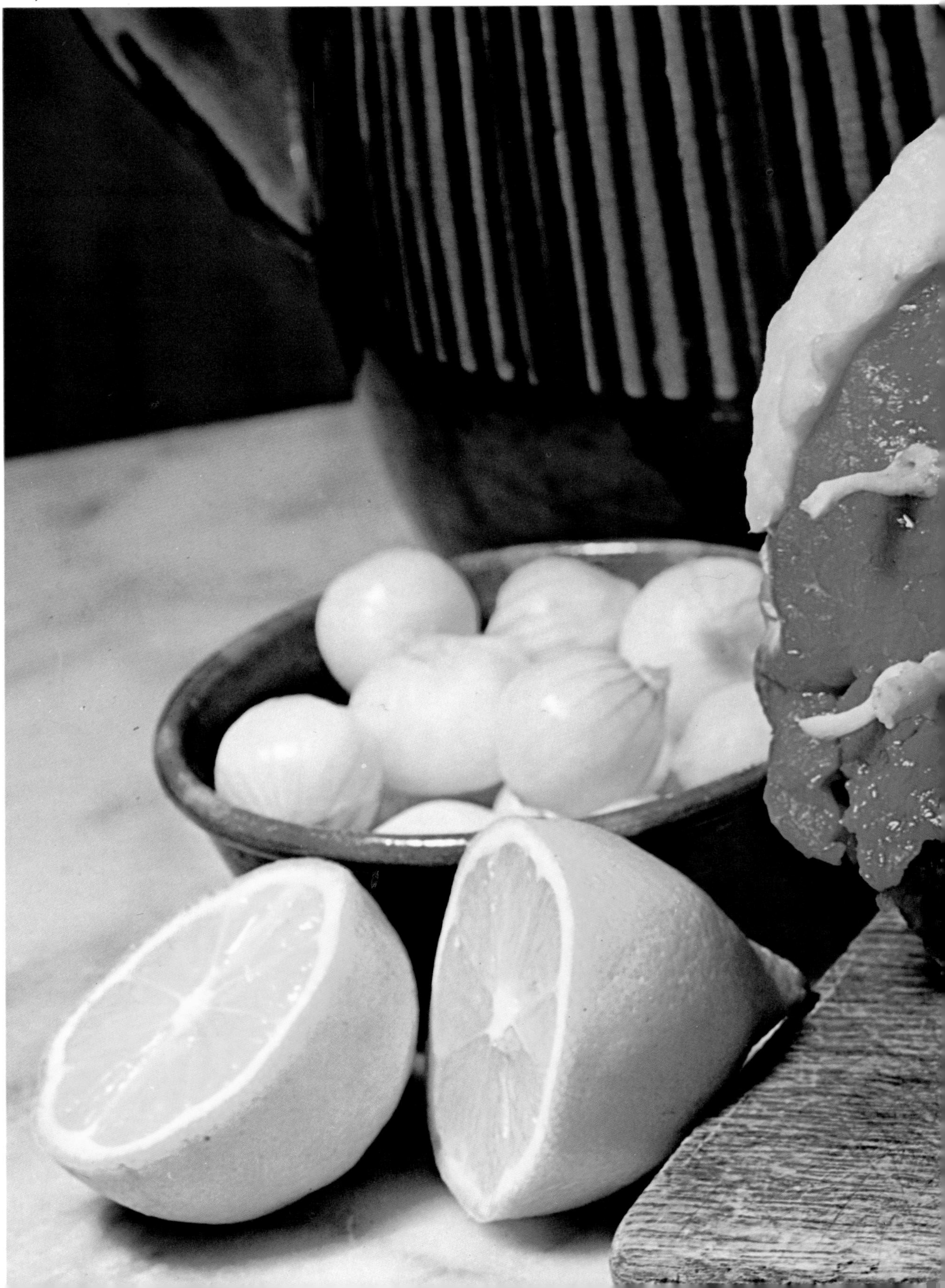

4 Garnish with a ring of cucumber and a ring of tomato. Sprinkle vegetables with a little parsley and vinaigrette sauce.

BEEF POT ROAST

4 to 6 pounds top round, or round steak
   (in one piece)
   Salt and freshly ground black pepper
½ teaspoon dried thyme
4 tablespoons bacon drippings or olive oil
1¼ cups rich beef stock
4 large carrots, cut into 1-inch lengths
2 onions, quartered
2 turnips, quartered
2 cloves garlic, crushed
8 peppercorns
4 whole cloves
2 whole allspice
2 bay leaves
1 tablespoon softened butter
1 tablespoon flour
   Finely chopped parsley

1 Rub meat with salt, pepper and thyme.
2 Melt bacon drippings or heat olive oil in a thick-bottomed, heavy iron ovenproof casserole. Add meat and brown well on all sides. Pour in half of the beef stock and bring to the boil; reduce heat until liquid barely simmers.
3 Add carrots, onions, turnips, garlic, peppercorns, cloves, allspice and bay leaves. Cover casserole and simmer for 3½ to 4 hours, or until meat is tender, turning roast once or twice during cooking time. Add remaining stock if necessary.
4 Remove roast to a heated serving platter and surround with vegetables. Keep warm.
5 Allow gravy to cool and skim off fat. Thicken by adding 1 tablespoon *each* softened butter and flour mashed to a smooth paste. Cook over high heat, stirring constantly, until sauce is smooth. Season to taste with salt and pepper.
6 Pour gravy over meat and vegetables, and sprinkle with parsley. Serve with **Greek lemon potatoes** and **haricots verts** (see below).

Soused Camembert

GREEK LEMON POTATOES

2 pounds potatoes
4 tablespoons butter
   Juice of ½ lemon
½ beef bouillon cube, crumbled
   Salt and freshly ground black pepper

1 Peel potatoes and cut in quarters lengthwise. Place in a shallow casserole with butter, half the lemon juice and the beef bouillon cube. Season to taste with salt and pepper.
2 Cook in a 400°F oven for 15 minutes. Turn potatoes over and return to oven for 15 minutes more.
3 Remove excess fat from dish; add remaining lemon juice and return to oven for 5 minutes more, or until tender.

HARICOTS VERTS

1 pound green beans
   Salt and freshly ground black pepper
2 tablespoons butter
1 tablespoon finely chopped parsley

1 Cook beans in boiling salted water until tender, about 20 minutes. Drain; place in a heated serving dish.
2 Season with salt and pepper; toss with butter and parsley.

SOUSED CAMEMBERT

- 2 ripe Camembert cheeses
- ⅔ cup dry white wine
- 8 tablespoons softened butter
  Salt
  Cayenne pepper
  Brandy
- 3 cups fresh white bread crumbs, toasted
- 6 tablespoons finely chopped parsley

1 Scrape crust from cheeses; cut them in quarters and soak overnight in white wine.

2 Remove cheeses from wine; dry gently and cream thoroughly with softened butter and a little of the marinating liquid, if desired. Add a little salt and cayenne if necessary, and flavor with a little brandy.

3 Press the cheese mixture into a 5-inch plain round flan ring on a foil-lined baking pan. Chill until firm.

4 Turn the cheese upside down on to very fine toasted bread crumbs and remove the flan ring and foil. Coat bottom with toasted bread crumbs and sides with finely chopped parsley. Serve with bread or crackers.

  MENU

French Onion Soup
Pot Roast of Pork with Grapes
with
Gratin Dauphinois
and
Crisp-Fried Zucchini
Floating Island
SERVES 4-6

RED WINES
Bordeaux Supérieur
Côtes-du-Rhône
Châteauneuf-du-Pape

FRENCH ONION SOUP

- 4 large onions
- 4 tablespoons butter
- 1 tablespoon sugar
- 6 cups beef stock or water
  Salt and freshly ground black pepper
  Toasted rounds of French bread
  Butter
  Freshly grated Gruyère cheese

1 Peel onions and slice thinly. Separate into rings. Heat butter in a large saucepan with sugar; add the onion rings and cook very, very gently over low heat, stirring constantly with a wooden spoon, until the rings are an even golden brown.

2 Add stock gradually, stirring constantly until the soup begins to boil. Then lower heat, cover pan and simmer gently for 30 minutes.

3 Just before serving, correct seasoning and serve in a heated soup tureen or in individual soup bowls, each one containing toasted buttered rounds of French bread heaped with grated Gruyère cheese.

4 French onion soup may also be served *gratinée*. When ready to serve, place thin rounds of toasted and buttered French bread in an ovenproof casserole; cover with Gruyère cheese and pour onion soup over toast. Sprinkle top

French Onion Soup

with more Gruyère and place casserole under the broiler or in a hot oven until cheese is browned and sizzling.

POT ROAST OF PORK WITH GRAPES

- 4 pounds lean loin of pork
  Salt and freshly ground black pepper
- 3 tablespoons gin
- ⅔ cup unsweetened grape juice
- ⅔ cup dry white wine
- 2 tablespoons butter
- 2 tablespoons flour

Marinade:

- 8 juniper berries, crushed
- 2 cloves, crushed
- 1 clove garlic, crushed
- 3 tablespoons olive oil
- 6 tablespoons dry white wine

Garnish:

- 2 tablespoons butter
- 1 pound seedless white grapes

1   Ask your butcher to skin, bone and roll a lean loin of pork. The rolled pork loin should weigh just under 4 pounds after being prepared.

Pot Roast of Pork with Grapes

2 Combine marinade ingredients. Pour over pork in a deep dish, cover and marinate at the bottom of the refrigerator for 24 hours. Turn pork several times to keep it thoroughly coated with marinade.

3 When ready to cook pork, preheat oven to 375°F.

4 Drain pork, reserving marinade, and put it in a roasting pan. Sprinkle with salt and pepper. Pour about ⅔ cup cold water around it and roast, basting occasionally, until cooked through but still moist. It will take about 1¾ hours, or 35 minutes per pound.

5 Ten minutes before taking pork out of the oven, **prepare garnish:** melt butter in a large, deep frying pan and sauté grapes for 4 to 5 minutes until golden brown. Reserve.

6 When pork is cooked, transfer to a deep, hot, flameproof serving dish. Pour 3 tablespoons gin over it, stand well back and set alight with a match. (Or, if you find it easier, pour gin into a heated metal ladle, set it alight and quickly pour all over the meat.)

7 Skim fat from juices left in roasting pan. Pour back into the pan any juices that have collected around the pork on the serving dish and return pork to the turned-off oven to keep hot while you finish sauce.

8 **To finish sauce:** add grape juice, wine and reserved marinade to the roasting pan and bring to the boil on top of the stove, scraping bottom and sides of pan with a wooden spoon to dislodge any crusty morsels stuck there. Allow to simmer for 2 to 3 minutes longer.

9 Meanwhile, blend butter and flour to a smooth paste in a small cup.

10 Strain sauce into the frying pan over sautéed grapes and, over low heat, stir in butter-flour mixture in small pieces. Continue to stir until sauce comes to the boil and simmer for 3 to 4 minutes longer to cook the flour. Season with salt and pepper.

11 **To serve:** spoon sauce and grapes over and around pork. Any extra sauce and grapes should be served with the meat in a heated gravy boat. Serve pork very hot, cut into thick slices with **gratin dauphinois** (see page 113) and **crisp-fried zucchini** (see below).

CRISP-FRIED ZUCCHINI

> **8 to 12** zucchini
> **2** tablespoons butter
> **2** tablespoons olive oil
> Salt and freshly ground black pepper

1 Slice zucchini thinly.

2 Melt butter and olive oil in a frying pan. Add zucchini and sauté over a medium heat until just tender, stirring from time to time to keep zucchini from browning. Season generously with salt and pepper.

FLOATING ISLAND

> **2** cups milk
> **2 to 4** tablespoons sugar
> 1-inch piece vanilla bean (or 1 scant teaspoon vanilla extract)
> **6** eggs, separated
> Salt
> **1** cup sugar
> Caramel garnish (see below)

1 **To make poached meringues:** combine the milk, sugar and vanilla bean in a shallow

Floating Islands

saucepan. (If vanilla extract is used, add it after milk has been scalded.) Bring to the boil, stirring well to dissolve sugar. Beat egg whites until stiff with a pinch of salt, gradually adding sugar and beating well after each addition. Test for stiffness by placing an egg on top of the beaten whites. If the egg doesn't sink, the whites are sufficiently beaten.

2 Shape the beaten egg whites with a tablespoon into small egg shapes and drop them into the scalded milk. After 1 or 2 minutes turn them carefully with a fork. Leave them in the hot milk for exactly 2 minutes more—no longer, or the meringues will collapse. Remove from the milk with a slotted spoon and drain on a dry dish cloth spread over a strainer.

3 To make sauce: strain the milk through a fine sieve into the top of a double boiler. Beat the egg yolks well and gradually add the warm milk to them. Return to heat and cook over water, stirring constantly, until the mixture just begins to thicken. Remove from heat and cool. Chill until ready to use.

4 To serve: pour the custard sauce into a bowl and float the meringues on it.

Caramel garnish: If desired, an attractive garnish can be made for the "floating island" by dissolving 1 cup sugar in 4 tablespoons water and boiling rapidly until the caramel is a rich golden brown. Pour immediately over the meringues.

Variations on a theme: Change this recipe by adding orange zest. Prepare sauce as above, and while still warm, add 2 thinly pared strips of orange rind and 4 teaspoons Grand Marnier.

🌸 MENU 🌸

Italian Pizza
with
Sautéed New Potatoes with Herbs
Orange and Onion Salad
Italian Cheeses
SERVES 4-6

RED WINES
Chianti Ruffino Red
Valpolicella

🌸

ITALIAN PIZZA

Pizza Dough:

- 2 cups flour
- ½ teaspoon salt
- 1 package active dry yeast
- ½ cup warm water
- Olive oil

Topping:

- 1 (35-ounce) can Italian peeled tomatoes, coarsely chopped
- Salt and freshly ground black pepper
- 3 ounces mozzarella cheese, thinly sliced
- 6 anchovy fillets, cut in pieces
- ¼ teaspoon oregano
- ¼ teaspoon basil
- Black olives for garnish

1 To make pizza dough: sift flour and salt into a warm mixing bowl. Put yeast into a small bowl. Add warm water and stir once. Set aside for 5 minutes and then stir with a wooden spoon until smooth. Pour into sifted flour with 1 tablespoon olive oil and work flour into yeast mixture with your hands to make a stiff dough. Knead with your hands, pressing the dough out and away from you with your palms. When it feels light and elastic, roll it into a ball and put it in an oiled bowl. Turn ball over to oil entire surface; cover with 2 thicknesses of clean dish towel and leave in a warm place until doubled in bulk (about 2 hours).

2   When ready to use, roll dough out on a floured board into a large circle about ¼ inch thick, or divide it into 2 or 6 pieces to make smaller pizzas. Brush with a little olive oil.

3   Finally, place circle of dough on an oiled cookie sheet large enough to let pizza expand in cooking. Spread dough with tomatoes; season with salt and pepper and arrange thin slices of mozzarella and cut anchovies over the surface. Sprinkle with oregano and basil; garnish with black olives and bake in a 450°F oven for about 25 minutes, or until pizza browns. Serve immediately.

ITALIAN POT ROAST

    4   to 6 pounds bottom round, in one piece
        Salt and freshly ground black pepper
    ½   teaspoon dried thyme
    4   tablespoons bacon drippings or olive oil
    1¼ cups rich beef stock
    4   large carrots, cut into 1-inch lengths
    2   onions, quartered
    2   turnips, quartered
    2   cloves garlic, crushed
    8   peppercorns
    4   whole cloves
    2   whole allspice
    2   bay leaves
    1   small can Italian peeled tomatoes
    ⅔   cup dry white wine
    2   tablespoons tomato paste
    1   teaspoon dried basil
    1   tablespoon softened butter (optional)
    1   tablespoon flour (optional)
        Finely chopped anchovies
        Finely chopped parsley

1   Rub meat with generous amounts of salt, pepper and thyme.

2   Melt bacon drippings or heat olive oil in a thick-bottomed, heavy ovenproof casserole. Add meat and brown well on all sides. Pour in half the beef stock and bring to the boil; reduce heat until liquid barely simmers.

3   Add carrots, onions, turnips, garlic, peppercorns, cloves, allspice, bay leaves, tomatoes, wine, tomato paste and basil. Cover casserole and simmer for 3½ to 4 hours, or until meat is tender, turning roast once or twice during cooking time. Add remaining stock if necessary.

4   Remove roast to a heated serving platter and surround with vegetables. Keep warm.

5   Allow gravy to cool for 5 minutes; then skim off fat. Thicken, if desired, blending the softened butter and flour to a smooth paste. Add to the gravy. Cook over high heat, stirring constantly, until gravy is smooth. Season to taste with salt and pepper.

6   Pour gravy over meat and vegetables. Sprinkle with equal amounts of chopped anchovies and parsley.

SAUTEED NEW POTATOES WITH HERBS

    2   pounds small new potatoes
    4   tablespoons olive oil
    1   tablespoon each finely chopped parsley,
        chervil and chives
    4   shallots, finely chopped
    1   clove garlic, finely chopped
        Salt and freshly ground black pepper
        Lemon juice

1   Peel potatoes and cook whole in a frying pan with olive oil and herbs, shallots and garlic.

2   Season potatoes to taste with salt, pepper and lemon juice and sauté until cooked through and golden. Serve immediately.

ORANGE AND ONION SALAD

    ¼   head curly endive
    1   head lettuce
    4   oranges
    1   large mild white onion

Dressing:

    4   tablespoons olive oil
    2   tablespoons vinegar
    1   clove garlic, crushed
    ¾   teaspoon salt
    ½   teaspoon dry mustard
    1   teaspoon sugar
        Freshly ground black pepper

Orange and Onion Salad

1 Wash endive and lettuce leaves carefully. Dry them and arrange in a salad bowl.

2 With a sharp knife, peel the oranges. Slice thinly. Peel the onion and slice it into thin rings. Arrange the orange and onion slices in the salad bowl.

3 Mix all the ingredients for the dressing; just before serving, pour it over the salad.

ITALIAN CHEESES

(See page 147.)

Cooking with Yogurt

If you want to live long, stay healthy and have a good digestion until the day you die—*eat yogurt*. That's the lesson I learned on a trip through the Middle East. Returning home after a three-week lecture tour in Australia, I stopped off on the way to enjoy the many varied flavors of the cities of Lebanon. There in the hill villages behind the major towns I was astounded to see men and women of 70 and 80 with all the vitality and mental agility of people half their age.

The answer, I was assured time and time again, was yogurt. Ever since the time of Abraham, the peoples of the eastern Mediterranean have relied on this lightly fermented and delicious natural food as a basic necessity for good health.

I first fell in love with yogurt—combined with diced cucumber, garlic, lemon juice and finely chopped fresh mint leaves—as a cooling summer appetizer in a small tiled restaurant in the old quarter of Beirut. I later found it equally delicious as a refreshing summer soup. In this case, the basic yogurt-garlic-lemon juice mixture is thinned down with chilled chicken stock, and the cucumber—peeled and seeded—is grated coarsely into it. A Balkan version of yogurt soup is served hot with diced cooked meats and a little cooked rice in it.

Today, I make homemade fresh yogurt often and use it in its natural state to add a tangy, fresh flavor to hot and cold soups and sauces. With a hint of vanilla and sugar added, it makes a fresh-tasting "carry all" for diced fresh fruits and berries.

Make Your Own Yogurt—It's Easy

To make your own yogurt: bring 2½ cups milk to the boil in a saucepan. Remove pan from heat and allow milk to cool until you can put your finger in it comfortably.

Place 1 heaping tablespoon of plain yogurt in a warm mixing bowl and beat until creamy. Beat in 1 tablespoon warm milk; then add 2 tablespoons warm milk and beat until well blended. Then add remaining warm milk gradually, beating continually until mixture is well blended. Cover bowl with a thick blanket and keep in a warm place—away from drafts—for 8 hours or until yogurt is as creamy as a custard. It will keep perfectly in the refrigerator for 4 days. Then you will be able to make a new batch of fresh homemade yogurt, using a tablespoon of your own mixture.

SAUCE FOR POACHED OR BROILED FISH

Blend equal parts of yogurt and homemade mayonnaise. Season with a dash of lemon juice and cayenne for a piquant sauce to serve with hot or cold cooked fish.

SUMMER SALAD DRESSING

Use yogurt as a dressing for a summer salad of diced cucumbers, sliced green onions and red and white radishes. Just add a little oil, lemon juice, salt and freshly ground black pepper and beat well before pouring over salad.

A LIGHT TASTING MAYONNAISE WITH YOGURT

Whisk equal parts yogurt and homemade mayonnaise (see page 141) until well blended. Stir in 1 teaspoon Dijon mustard, 1 tablespoon lemon juice and 2 tablespoons *each* finely chopped parsley, chives and fresh tarragon. Excellent for poached fish or chicken, hard-boiled eggs, tomato and cucumber salad, or coleslaw (shredded raw cabbage: dress with yogurt mayonnaise dressing and let stand several hours before serving).

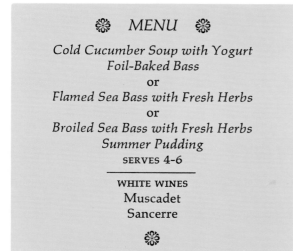

❀ *MENU* ❀

Cold Cucumber Soup with Yogurt
Foil-Baked Bass
or
Flamed Sea Bass with Fresh Herbs
or
Broiled Sea Bass with Fresh Herbs
Summer Pudding
SERVES 4-6

WHITE WINES
Muscadet
Sancerre

❀

COLD CUCUMBER SOUP WITH YOGURT

- ½ clove garlic
- 1 teaspoon salt
- 1 tablespoon olive oil
- 3 (8-ounce) containers plain yogurt
  Juice of ½ lemon
- 1¾ cups chicken stock
- 1 cucumber
  Chopped mint or chives

1 Mash garlic in the bottom of a large mixing bowl or soup tureen with salt. Add olive oil and continue to mash until garlic paste is completely smooth.

2 Add yogurt and lemon juice and beat until smooth.

3 Add cool chicken stock to yogurt mixture.

4 Peel cucumber; slice it in half lengthwise and remove seeds. Grate cucumber coarsely and stir into soup. Chill until ready to serve.

5 Just before serving sprinkle with mint or chives.

FOIL-BAKED BASS

- 1 (3-pound) sea bass
- 4 to 6 tablespoons softened butter
  Salt and freshly ground black pepper
  Lemon juice
- ½ teaspoon freshly grated nutmeg

Garnish:

- 2 tablespoons finely chopped parsley
  or onion tops
  Grilled tomatoes
  Sautéed new potatoes
  Lemon wedges

1 Clean the fish, removing the head, if desired, and place in the center of a piece of aluminum foil. Spread fish liberally with softened butter on both sides. Season with salt, pepper, lemon juice and nutmeg. Fold over foil to seal in fish. Broil for 15 to 20 minutes. Turn over and cook for 15 to 20 minutes longer. Turn back, open the foil and broil for 10 minutes longer.

2 Serve garnished with parsley or onion tops, grilled tomatoes, **sautéed new potatoes with herbs** (see page 188) and lemon wedges.

Foil-baked Bass with Sautéed New Potatoes with Herbs

FLAMED SEA BASS WITH FRESH HERBS

- **2 to 3** tablespoons flour
- **2** (3-pound) sea bass
- **2 to 3** tablespoons olive oil
  Salt and freshly ground black pepper
- **4 to 6** sprigs each rosemary, fennel and thyme
- **2 to 3** tablespoons hot cognac

1 Flour cleaned fish lightly; brush with olive oil, and season to taste with salt and pepper.

2 Broil for 3 to 5 minutes on each side, or until fish flakes easily when tested with a fork. Baste fish with olive oil from time to time.

3 Transfer fish to a heated serving dish which has been covered with dried sprigs of rosemary, fennel and thyme. Top the fish with additional herbs; pour hot cognac over them and ignite. The burning herbs give the fish a delightful flavor.

BROILED SEA BASS WITH FRESH HERBS

2 to 3 tablespoons flour
2 (3-pound) sea bass
2 to 3 tablespoons olive oil
Salt and freshly ground black pepper
2 to 3 sprigs each fennel, parsley and thyme

1 Flour cleaned fish lightly; brush with olive oil and season to taste with salt and pepper.
2 Stuff cavities of fish with herbs and broil for 3 to 5 minutes on each side, or until fish flakes easily when tested with a fork. Baste fish with olive oil from time to time.

SUMMER PUDDING

½ to ¾ pint red currants
¾ pound cherries
½ to ¾ pint raspberries
⅔ cup water
½ cup sugar
Thin slices white bread
Whipped cream

1 Strip all stalks from currants and pit cherries; combine with raspberries and wash if necessary. Place fruits with water and sugar in a saucepan and simmer until sugar melts.
2 Trim crusts from bread; cut each slice in half lengthwise and line sides of a bowl or soufflé dish. Cover bottom of dish with triangles of bread and trim off slices at rim of dish.
3 Fill dish with fruit mixture. Cut additional bread triangles to cover pudding. Place a flat plate on pudding; weight it and chill in refrigerator overnight.
4 When ready to serve, invert on to a serving dish and serve with whipped cream.

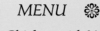

❀ *MENU* ❀

Paprika Chicken with Yogurt
with
Noodles with Grated Almonds
or
Plain Boiled Rice
Delmonico Salad
Cherries Jubilee
SERVES 4-6

WHITE WINES
Muscadet
Chablis
Vinho Verde

PAPRIKA CHICKEN WITH YOGURT

1 (3½-pound) roasting chicken, cut into
    8 serving pieces
    Salt and freshly ground black pepper
4 tablespoons butter
2 tablespoons olive oil
1 onion, chopped
1 green pepper, chopped
1 tablespoon paprika
1¼ cups chicken stock
2 tablespoons cornstarch
⅔ cup yogurt

1 Season chicken pieces well and cook in butter and olive oil until golden brown on all sides.
2 Remove from pan; add onion and green pepper and sauté until the vegetables just start to turn color. Stir in paprika, then add chicken stock.
3 Return chicken pieces to the pan; cover and simmer chicken and vegetables gently over very low heat for 45 minutes, or until chicken is tender.
4 Transfer chicken pieces to a heated serving dish. Add enough cold water to cornstarch to make a smooth paste; combine with juices in pan and bring to the boil, stirring until sauce is thick. Then add yogurt and stir over low heat until sauce is well blended.

5   Return chicken pieces to pan and warm through in hot, pungent sauce. Delicious served with **noodles sprinkled with almonds** (see below) or **plain boiled rice** (see page 89).

NOODLES WITH GRATED ALMONDS

> **Salt**
> **1 pound noodles**
> **8 tablespoons butter**
> **Freshly ground black pepper**
> **4 to 6 level tablespoons grated toasted almonds**

1   Bring 3 to 4 quarts of well-salted water to a boil in a large saucepan.

2   Add noodles and cook until *al dente*— tender but still firm "to the bite." Test by picking out a strand of noodle with a fork from time to time.

3   When noodles are tender, drain; add butter, salt and pepper. Mix well.

4   Sprinkle with almonds and serve immediately.

DELMONICO SALAD

> **2 heads lettuce**

Dressing:

> **6 to 8 tablespoons olive oil**
> **2 tablespoons wine vinegar**
> **2 tablespoons light cream**
> **2 tablespoons Roquefort cheese, crumbled**
> **Freshly ground black pepper**
> **Dash of Tabasco**
> **1 hard-boiled egg, finely chopped**
> **1 slice bacon, cooked and finely chopped**

1   Wash and prepare lettuce. Shake dry in a salad basket, or dry each leaf carefully with paper towels. Wrap in a dish towel and let crisp in refrigerator until ready to use.

2   **To make dressing:** combine olive oil, vinegar, cream and Roquefort in a small bowl, and whisk until smooth. Season to taste with pepper and Tabasco and stir in hard-boiled egg and bacon.

3   Arrange lettuce in salad bowl. Add dressing; toss and serve.

CHERRIES JUBILEE

> **1 large can pitted dark cherries**
> **2 tablespoons sugar**
> **1 cinnamon stick**
> **Juice and grated rind of ½ orange**
> **1 teaspoon cornstarch**
> **4 tablespoons cognac**
> **4 tablespoons cherry brandy**
> **Vanilla ice cream**

1   Drain cherries and measure out 1⅓ cups of the juice.

2   Combine sugar, cinnamon, orange juice and rind, cornstarch and cherry juice. Bring slowly to a boil in bottom of chafing dish. Allow to bubble for 5 minutes, stirring from time to time, until sauce is reduced to a syrup.

3   Add cherries and heat through.

4   Heat cognac and cherry brandy and pour over cherries, ignite, and when flames die down pour hot mixture over individual portions of vanilla ice cream.

Vegetables Without Water

Water is the enemy of the well-cooked vegetable. Remember this and you're well on the way to giving vegetables the importance they deserve in our daily diet. They're full of nutritive value and their vitamin content is high. But all too often they end up as a soggy, colorless, tasteless mess.

The secret of cooking vegetables is simply this—use no water! Any cooking water you throw away is waste water. So it follows that if you use less water, your food will have that much more flavor. This is the secret of Chinese cookery, with its delicious crisp and colorful vegetables. Little liquid is used. No liquid is thrown away. Therefore, no flavor is lost. Simple, isn't it?

In this way, you *add* flavor rather than subtract it. Even the firmest vegetables—like carrots and turnips—if cut in chunks and blanched before being simmered in a very little chicken stock and butter, are twice as flavorful as those boiled to death in the usual manner.

So whatever you do, don't drown your vegetables. My favorite method of cooking them is to use a little butter or olive oil, with just enough chicken stock (or water, white wine, or even steam) to bring out their delicate flavors and textures. And always serve vegetables slightly crisp.

I know what you are thinking. You're going to ask, "Won't the vegetables burn or dry up?"

No. And I'll tell you why.

By combining equal amounts of butter and chicken stock—4 tablespoons of each for an average serving of four—you will find that the chicken stock will reduce while the vegetables are cooking, leaving the cooked vegetables in a few tablespoons of beautifully flavored butter.

And, remember, it is better to undercook than to overcook. A fact which 999 people out of 1,000 forget.

Method

Melt 2 to 4 tablespoons butter in a saucepan; place washed fresh vegetables or frozen vegetables (prepared as below) in the pan; sprinkle with a little sugar to bring out their natural sweetness and add 2 to 4 tablespoons chicken stock (made with a bouillon cube) for extra flavor. Stir vegetables over high heat for a minute or two; *cover tightly* and simmer on the lowest possible heat for about 15 minutes, or until vegetables are fork tender. Taste vegetables, then add salt and freshly ground black pepper, as necessary, just before serving.

Green beans: whole, or cut into 2-inch pieces.

Zucchini: sliced, unpeeled.

Spinach: whole leaves, with stems removed.

Baby carrots: peeled or scraped, whole, sliced or cut into 1-inch pieces. Larger carrots must be blanched first.

New turnips: peeled, quartered, sliced or diced. Old turnips must be blanched first.

Small white onions: whole, but must be skinned and blanched first.

Peas: whole.

Asparagus: cut into ½-inch or 1-inch pieces. Use tender part only.

Celery: sliced or cut into ½-inch or 1-inch pieces but must be blanched first.

To Blanch Vegetables Before Cooking

Place prepared vegetables in a saucepan large enough to hold them comfortably; add cold water to cover vegetables; place saucepan over high heat and bring rapidly to the boil. Drain and use as directed.

GREAT CABBAGE

    1   small head cabbage
        Butter
    4   tablespoons chicken stock
    1   teaspoon sugar
        Grated nutmeg
        Freshly ground black pepper
    2   tablespoons finely chopped parsley
        Salt
        Lemon juice

1 Wash cabbage thoroughly and cut into wedges about 1 inch thick, removing all the core.

2 Combine 4 tablespoons butter and chicken stock in a large shallow saucepan (you will want all the cabbage wedges to spread out in the pan so that they can cook evenly and quickly); then add cabbage and sprinkle with sugar, a dash of grated nutmeg and pepper, to taste. Cover saucepan tightly and place over high heat until it starts to steam. Then reduce heat and simmer cabbage gently for about 15 minutes, or until cooked through.

3 Transfer to a heated serving bowl; sprinkle with parsley and serve with melted butter seasoned with salt, pepper and lemon juice, to taste.

GLAZED WHITE ONIONS

    1   pound small white onions
    4   tablespoons butter
    4   tablespoons chicken stock
    1   tablespoon sugar
        Salt

1 Peel onions and place them in a small saucepan; cover with cold water and cook over high heat until water boils. Remove from heat and drain.

2 Replace blanched onions in the saucepan; add butter and chicken stock; season with sugar and salt, to taste, and simmer over low heat until onions have absorbed the liquid without burning and are tender.

BUTTERED CARROTS

    1   pound small carrots
    4   tablespoons butter
    4   tablespoons chicken stock
    1   tablespoon sugar
        Salt

1 Peel carrots; slice thickly and place in a small saucepan; cover with cold water and blanch. Drain.

2 Simmer blanched carrots with butter, chicken stock, sugar and salt, to taste, until they have absorbed the liquid without burning and are tender.

GREEN BEANS—CHINESE STYLE

    1   pound green beans
    2   tablespoons peanut oil or lard
    ½   teaspoon salt
    ⅔   cup water
        Soy sauce or dry sherry

1 Wash and trim green beans; break or cut into 1-inch pieces.

2 Heat peanut oil in a thick-bottomed frying pan; add beans and cook over medium heat for 1 minute, stirring continually. Add salt and water; cover pan and cook beans for 3 minutes; remove cover and simmer, stirring from time to time, until all the water has evaporated (about 5 minutes). Add soy sauce to taste.

ZUCCHINI

    4   to 6 zucchini
    2   tablespoons peanut oil or lard
    ½   teaspoon salt
    ⅔   cup water
        Soy sauce or dry sherry

1 Wash zucchini; cut off ends and slice thinly.

2 Heat peanut oil in a thick-bottomed frying pan; add zucchini and salt and cook over medium heat for 3 minutes, stirring continually. Add water and continue to simmer, stirring, until the water has evaporated (about 5 minutes). Add soy sauce to taste.

FRENCH STYLE PEAS

1 **package frozen peas**
4 **tablespoons butter**
4 **tablespoons chicken stock**
1 **tablespoon sugar**
  Salt

1 Place peas in a small saucepan; cover with cold water and blanch. Drain.

2 Simmer blanched peas with butter, chicken stock, sugar and salt, to taste, until peas have absorbed the liquid and are tender.

SPINACH

2 **pounds fresh spinach leaves**
3 **tablespoons peanut oil or lard**
½ **teaspoon salt**
  Soy sauce or dry sherry

1 Wash spinach leaves in several changes of water; drain thoroughly.
2 Heat peanut oil in a thick-bottomed frying pan; add spinach and salt and cook over medium heat for 3 minutes, stirring continually. Add soy sauce to taste.

Christmas Entertaining

Informality is creeping more and more into the daily ritual of our meals. This very informality is a boon at Christmas, when entertaining is such an important part of our activities. From the traditional family Christmas dinner (roast turkey, game or goose with all the trimmings) to the more sophisticated approach of a midnight supper for lovers and friends (avocado and orange salad, timbale of duck and tulipes glacées à l'ananas), Christmas entertaining becomes a positive joy instead of a problem when close ones are carried gaily—drink in hand—into the preparations for the party. It's a great deal more fun to be brought right into the picture, to help serve the drinks, carve the bird or make the salad dressing.

That preparing the Christmas feast was already a family affair in Victorian England we know from the mouth-watering descriptions of the Cratchits' Christmas dinner as described by Charles Dickens. Mrs. Cratchit made the gravy "hissing hot"; Master Peter mashed the potatoes with all his force; Miss Belinda sweetened the apple sauce; and the young Cratchits, "mounting guard, crammed spoons into their mouths lest they should shriek for goose before their turn came to be helped."

After the whole family had been "steeped in sage and onion to their eyebrows" came the Christmas pudding. "Hallo! A great deal of steam! The pudding was out of the copper." And then Mrs. Cratchit entered, proudly bearing the great round pudding "like a speckled cannon ball blazing in a half a quartern of ignited brandy and bedight with Christmas holly stuck in the top."

Center your Christmas dinner around a golden turkey in the traditional manner; surround it with cranberry baked apples. Accompany it with mashed potatoes, green beans and a delicious winter salad of curly endive dressed with a mustard-flavored vinaigrette. The apples are placed in the roasting pan with the turkey 45 minutes before serving.

Precede the great golden bird with a chilled turbot salad with green olives, and end the meal with a traditional yule log cake, or, more simply, cheese and fresh fruits.

2 Remove skin and bones while fish is still warm. Dress immediately with olive oil, lemon juice and salt and freshly ground black pepper to taste. Add chopped parsley and onion; toss once and allow to cool.

3 Just before serving, correct seasoning, adding more olive oil and lemon juice if necessary. Spoon over mayonnaise and toss gently. Garnish with green olives.

 MENU

Christmas Turbot Salad with Green Olives
Roast Turkey with Sausage and
Chestnut Stuffing
with
Cranberry Baked Apples
and
Mashed Potato
and
Haricots Verts
Curly Endive Salad with Mustard Dressing
Christmas Yule Log Cake
SERVES 6-8

WHITE WINES
Pouilly Blanc Fumé
Riesling d'Alsace
Pouilly Fuissé

ROAST TURKEY WITH SAUSAGE AND CHESTNUT STUFFINGS

    1 medium-sized turkey, about 10 pounds
       dressed weight
       Salt and freshly ground black pepper

Sausage Meat Stuffing:

    6 to 8 bacon slices
    2 tablespoons butter
   10 to 12 slices stale trimmed white bread,
       cut into 1/3-inch cubes
 1 1/2 pound pork sausage meat
    1 onion, finely chopped
    2 tablespoons finely chopped parsley
  1/4 teaspoon dried thyme
  1/4 teaspoon dried marjoram
       Pinch of dried sage
    4 tablespoons turkey giblet or chicken stock
    1 egg, beaten
       Salt and freshly ground black pepper

Chestnut Stuffing:

    2 pounds chestnuts, peeled and skinned
       Turkey giblet or chicken stock (optional)
    1 to 2 tablespoons butter
       Salt and freshly ground black pepper

Basting Sauce:

  1/2 pound butter
 1 1/2 cups turkey giblet or chicken stock

CHRISTMAS TURBOT SALAD WITH GREEN OLIVES

    2 pound turbot
       Salt
    1 quart water
  2/3 cup milk
    5 tablespoons olive oil
       Juice of 1 lemon
       Freshly ground black pepper
    2 to 4 tablespoons chopped parsley
    2 to 4 level tablespoons chopped onion
  2/3 cup mayonnaise
   12 to 18 green olives

1 Cut turbot into slices about 3/4 inch thick and place in boiling salted water to which you have added milk to make fish white. Reduce heat so that water barely bubbles. It is important that the turbot cooks very slowly so that it does not lose its juices in the stock. When fish can be flaked with a fork, remove from heat and drain.

1 **To make sausage meat stuffing:** in a large frying pan, cook bacon until crisp. Remove from pan with a slotted spoon and crumble into a large bowl.

2 Add butter to fat remaining in pan. Heat until frothy. Then add bread cubes and toss over a moderate heat until they are crisp on the outside but still feel soft and spongy inside when pressed. Add to the bacon.

3 Add remaining ingredients. Mix by hand until thoroughly blended.

4 Having peeled and skinned chestnuts (see below), cook them in boiling stock, or simply in salted water, until they are quite tender, about 20 minutes.

5 Drain chestnuts thoroughly, reserving stock; return them to the hot, dry pan. Add butter; moisten with 1 or 2 tablespoons of the stock and swirl around until chestnuts are coated with buttery liquid. Season with salt and pepper.

6 Preheat oven to 425°F.

7 Wipe turkey both inside and out with a damp cloth.

8 Free the skin from the breast by working your hand down under the skin from the neck end. If skin refuses to come away at any point, do not force it or you may cause it to tear. Instead, separate the meat from the underside of skin with the tip of a small knife, or snip it free with a pair of scissors. Proceed carefully until you have loosened skin almost to the end of the breast and down each side to the legs.

9 Stuff breast with sausage meat mixture, pushing it right down and over sides of breast to keep the meat moist. Try not to pack it too tightly, however, as it does tend to swell. Draw the neck skin over the back, not too tightly, and either sew or fasten it in position with metal skewers or toothpicks.

10 Chestnuts should be stuffed loosely into the body cavity. (Any left over can be added to the pan juices to reheat about half an hour before bird is ready to come out of the oven; then strained out of the sauce with a slotted spoon just before serving.)

11 **To truss bird:** sew or skewer vent tightly to prevent juices escaping. Cut off ends of wings to use for the giblet stock. Tie legs together with string and fasten string around tail.

12 Place bird, breast side up, in a large roasting pan. Season generously with salt and pepper. With a sharp toothpick or skewer, prick the breast skin all over—this, too, helps to prevent it bursting should the stuffing swell.

13 Cover bird with butter-soaked cheesecloth and roast turkey on lowest shelf of oven for 15 minutes. Then reduce temperature to 350°F for the rest of the cooking time.

14 Using remainder of butter mixed with stock as your basting sauce, baste turkey at the end of the first 15 minutes, and every 15 minutes thereafter, making sure that the cheesecloth is completely remoistened with this liquid.

15 The total roasting time, including the first 15 minutes at the higher temperature, is calculated at between 12 and 15 minutes per pound, but this can only be a guide. The important thing to remember is that with a turkey you are dealing with two different kinds of meat, the delicate white meat of the breast, and the dark leg meat, which needs longer cooking. A balance must therefore be struck by roasting the bird just long enough to cook the legs through without drying out the breast. Test the leg by pushing a skewer into the thickest part close to the body—the juices should just run clear. If you then cut the string, the leg joint should wiggle loosely in its socket.

16 When turkey is cooked, discard cheesecloth, trussing threads and skewers, and transfer to a hot serving platter. Keep hot in the turned-off oven while you finish gravy.

17 Skim pan juices. You may find this easier to do if you pour them off into a bowl first. Leave gravy for a couple of minutes to allow all the fat to come to the surface so that you can skim it off.

18 Correct seasoning if necessary. Gravy may also be thickened with a teaspoon of cornstarch, worked to a smooth paste with cold water before it is stirred in and brought to a boil. Pour gravy into a hot gravy boat and serve.

19 Serve the turkey and trimmings surrounded by cranberry baked apples, and accompany them with **mashed potatoes** (see page 67), haricots verts (see page 103) and a **curly endive salad** dressed with **mustard-flavored vinaigrette** (see page 201).

To Peel Chestnuts:

1 With the tip of a small knife, cut a slit in the shell on the rounded side of each chestnut.

2 Heat 3 tablespoons cooking oil in a wide, heavy saucepan.

3 Add enough chestnuts to make more or less a single layer, and sauté over a high heat for about 5 minutes, shaking pan to keep chestnuts on the move and prevent them charring.

4 Transfer chestnuts to a colander with a slotted spoon. Rinse briefly so that they are cool enough to handle.

5 Shell chestnuts and peel away thin inner skins. They are now ready for cooking.

If you are preparing anything over 1 pound of chestnuts, you will probably have to fry them in batches. The oil in the pan will do for several batches.

Allowing for shells, skins and the odd bad or wormy nut, you can, on average, count on getting ½ pound from 1 pound chestnuts.

CRANBERRY BAKED APPLES

    1 can whole-berry cranberry sauce
    ¼ cup sugar
    6 large baking apples
    8 marshmallows, cut in eighths
    ½ cup finely chopped walnuts

1 Spread half the cranberry sauce in shallow baking pan. Add sugar and enough water to fill pan to a depth of about ½ inch.

2 Core apples, peel about ¼ inch down from stem end; place peeled side down on cranberry sauce in pan. Bake at 350°F for 30 minutes. Turn apples peeled side up.

3 Combine remaining cranberry sauce, marshmallows and chopped walnuts. Fill apples heaping full. Return to oven; bake 15 minutes longer or until apples are tender.

CURLY ENDIVE SALAD WITH MUSTARD DRESSING

    1 head curly endive
    6 mushroom caps
      Lemon juice
    6 walnut halves
    2 tablespoons chopped parsley

Mustard Vinaigrette:

    1 tablespoon lemon juice
    1 to 2 tablespoons wine vinegar
    ½ teaspoon dry mustard
    ½ clove garlic, finely chopped
    6 to 8 tablespoons olive oil
      Salt and freshly ground black pepper

1 Separate curly endive leaves from base of head. Wash well and discard any tough or damaged leaves. Shake dry and chill.

2 Wash mushrooms and trim stems; slice thinly and toss in lemon juice to prevent discoloration.

3 **To make the dressing:** combine lemon juice, vinegar and mustard. Add garlic, olive oil and salt and pepper, to taste.

4 **To serve:** pour mustard vinaigrette into salad bowl, arrange prepared curly endive leaves on top. Sprinkle with mushrooms, walnut halves and parsley. Toss well to ensure that every leaf is glistening with dressing. Check seasoning and serve.

CHRISTMAS YULE LOG CAKE

Elegant, exciting, and as festive as the season: Christmas yule log cake from France. The cake itself is a delicate sponge roll filled with vanilla butter frosting; the chocolate is shaped and surfaced like natural bark; and bright red glacé cherries and "leaves" of green angelica complete the traditional yule log look.

6 eggs, separated
1 cup sugar
2 tablespoons lemon juice
1 tablespoon water
Grated rind of ½ lemon
Salt
¾ cup sifted flour
¼ cup cornstarch
Butter

Vanilla Butter Frosting:

12 tablespoons softened butter, diced
¾ teaspoon vanilla
1½ tablespoons Grand Marnier
¾ pound confectioners' sugar
3 tablespoons hot water

Chocolate Butter Frosting:

4 to 5 squares (ounces) unsweetened chocolate
2 cups confectioners' sugar
6 tablespoons hot water
1 egg plus 1 egg yolk
12 tablespoons softened butter, diced

Garnish:

Apricot jam
Instant coffee or cocoa
Angelica
Glacé cherries

1   Preheat oven to 350°F.
2   Beat together egg yolks, sugar, lemon juice, water, lemon rind and a generous pinch of salt until light and fluffy (5 minutes at high mixer speed).
3   Sift ¾ cup flour and cornstarch and beat into egg yolk mixture a little at a time.
4   Beat egg whites until soft peaks form and fold gently into yolk mixture.
5   Butter and lightly flour a 9½ × 13½-inch jelly roll pan. Pour in cake mixture. Cut through mixture gently several times to break up any large air bubbles.
6   Bake cake for about 25 minutes, or until surface springs back when gently pressed with fingertip. Invert pan on a cake rack and let cool for 10 minutes. Remove cake from pan on to a sheet of waxed paper and cut off all the edges of the cake. Roll cake as for a jelly roll, without removing the paper. Cool and chill.

7   To make vanilla butter frosting: cream softened butter with vanilla and Grand Marnier in an electric mixer (medium speed). Gradually beat in sugar alternately with hot water until smooth.
8   To make chocolate butter frosting: melt chocolate in the top of a double boiler; combine chocolate, sugar and hot water in bowl of electric mixer. At high speed beat in egg and egg yolk. Add softened butter, a little at a time, beating until smooth. Continue to beat until thick enough to spread.
9   Unroll cake, remove waxed paper, brush with apricot jam and spread with vanilla butter icing. Roll as jelly roll, wrap in waxed paper and chill until icing becomes firm.
10   To decorate cake: when ready to decorate, remove waxed paper from cake; cut off a thin slice at one end diagonally; trim this slice to an approximate circle and place on top of cake to represent a sawn-off branch when frosted. Frost cake generously with chocolate butter icing, using a pastry bag with a flattened, notched tube, running strips of frosting along cake to look like bark. With vanilla butter frosting, cover 2 ends of the cake and top of sawn-off branch; smooth these with a spatula dipped in hot water and then decorate with thinly piped rings of chocolate. Sprinkle bark with a little instant coffee or cocoa and decorate with angelica leaves and glacé cherries. Store cake in a cool place until ready to serve.

Christmas Eve Menu

In France it is customary to celebrate Christmas Eve with a late-night supper. Menus range from oysters in the half shell and pâté de foie gras to superb casseroles or galantines of chicken and duck.

Our menu for Christmas Eve—or for any other festive evening during the holidays—is based on a spectacular timbale of duck, tender fillets of duckling with a highly seasoned forcemeat stuffing. This hot duck loaf, with its gay Christmas dressing of rounds of stuffed green olives is turned out on a platter just before serving and garnished with diced duck, stuffed green olives and a delicately flavored Madeira sauce.

MENU

Avocado and Orange Salad
Timbale of Duck
Tulipes Glacées à l' Ananas
SERVES 4

RED WINES
Moulin-à-Vent
St. Emilion
Pommard
or
CHAMPAGNE

AVOCADO AND ORANGE SALAD

2 ripe avocados
  Lemon juice
2 to 3 oranges
  Lettuce
  Vinaigrette sauce (see page 146)
  Finely chopped garlic
  Dry mustard

1 Cut avocados in half lengthwise. Remove pits and peel carefully with a knife. Cut avocados into ¼-inch slices crosswise and soak in lemon juice to prevent discoloration. Peel and segment oranges.

2 Arrange avocado slices and orange segments in nests of lettuce. Serve with **vinaigrette sauce** seasoned with garlic and dry mustard.

TIMBALE OF DUCK

1 (5-pound) duckling
  Softened butter
  Salt and freshly ground black pepper
  Dried thyme
4 carrots, sliced
2 onions, sliced
2 celery stalks with tops, sliced
1 clove garlic
1 bay leaf
8 peppercorns
1 pound stuffed olives, sliced

Marinade:

2 to 4 tablespoons Madeira
2 tablespoons cognac
1 clove garlic, finely chopped
2 tablespoons finely chopped parsley
  Salt and freshly ground black pepper

Forcemeat:

5 slices white bread
  Chicken stock, to moisten
2 cups ground veal
2 eggs
2 tablespoons finely chopped onion
2 tablespoons finely chopped parsley
4 tablespoons melted butter
4 tablespoons heavy cream
  Salt and freshly ground black pepper
  Nutmeg and cayenne pepper

Sauce:

2 tablespoons butter
2 tablespoons flour
  Pan juices from duckling (strained)
4 tablespoons Madeira
1¼ cups chicken stock
  Salt and freshly ground black pepper

1 **On the day before the party:** clean and singe duckling and rub inside and out with softened butter combined with salt, pepper and thyme.

2 Cover the bottom of an oval casserole with carrots, onions and celery. Add garlic, bay leaf, peppercorns and salt, to taste. Place duckling on this bed; cover casserole tightly and simmer duck and vegetables gently for 1 to 1¼ hours, or until tender. Remove duck and strain sauce into a bowl. Cool.

3 **On the day of the party:** skim fat from surface of stock. Discard skin of duck and cut meat from bones in long thin strips. Marinate strips for at least 2 hours in a little Madeira and cognac combined with garlic, parsley, salt and pepper, turning once or twice during this time to allow flavor to impregnate meat thoroughly.

4   To make forcemeat: trim crusts from bread and soak slices in a little chicken stock until well moistened. Place veal in a large mixing bowl; add eggs, onion, parsley, melted butter, cream and moist bread, which you have shredded. Mix well; add salt, pepper, nutmeg and cayenne, to taste, and work mixture into a smooth paste.

5   To make sauce: melt butter in the top of a double boiler; stir in flour and cook over water, stirring constantly, until roux is smooth. Add strained pan juices from duck, Madeira and chicken stock and stir until smooth. Season to taste with salt and pepper and a little more Madeira if desired. Allow sauce to simmer over hot water, stirring from time to time, until thick and smooth.

6   To assemble timbale: butter a loaf pan or oval terrine generously. Cut stuffed olives into thin slices. Line bottom and inside walls of loaf pan or terrine with olive slices so that bottom and sides are completely covered with olive rings. Carefully press a little of the forcemeat stuffing against olives, keeping your fingers wet so that stuffing does not adhere to them, continuing until mold is entirely lined with a layer of forcemeat. Then place a layer of duck strips in the terrine; cover with a layer of sliced olives; pour in 2 tablespoons of the sauce and top with remaining duck, finishing with 2 tablespoons of sauce. Close the mold with a layer of forcemeat; top with a piece of buttered aluminum foil and place the terrine in a large pan containing enough hot water to come halfway up the sides. Bring the water to a boil; cook terrine in a preheated 350°F oven for 1 to 1¼ hours.

7   Allow timbale to cool for 15 minutes; then unmold carefully on a large heated serving dish. Garnish with remaining duck strips, diced, remaining olives and sauce. Serve remaining sauce separately. This dish is equally good served cold.

TULIPES GLACEES A L'ANANAS

  1¼ **cups flour**
   1 **cup confectioners' sugar**
   2 **egg yolks**
   3 **egg whites**
   1 **large orange, greased, to form pastry shapes**
   1 **fresh pineapple, peeled and diced**
     Kirsch
     Vanilla ice cream
     Whipped cream

1   Sift flour and sugar into a bowl; add egg yolks and whites and mix well.

2   Grease a cold baking sheet and mark 4 circles on it with a saucer. Spread 1 tablespoon of mixture over each circle, using the back of a teaspoon. Bake in a 350°F oven for 5 to 6 minutes, or until edges just turn brown.

3   Remove each round from baking sheet; turn over and, working quickly, place each circle over top of a greased orange. Place dish towel over pastry to prevent burning hands, and mold pastry to fit orange. Remove and continue as above, baking 2 to 4 circles each time, and shaping them over the orange as you go. These will keep for several days in a cookie jar. This recipe makes 12 to 16 *tulipes*.

4   To serve: fill the 8 pastry tulipes with diced fresh pineapple which you have marinated in kirsch; add a scoop of vanilla ice cream and decorate with whipped cream.

A Gala Christmas Breakfast

To begin Christmas Day with an elaborate meal may seem like a lot of trouble. I admit that it is. But the British are famous for their breakfasts, so here is my menu for a memorable morning party.

MENU

Fresh Fruit Compote
or
Orange and Grapefruit Segments in Lemon Juice
Creamed Finnan Haddie
with
Cumberland Jelly
Hot Popovers
SERVES 6

CHAMPAGNE CUP,
TEA, CHOCOLATE OR
COFFEE

FRESH FRUIT COMPOTE

- 2 **oranges**
- 2 **pears**
- 2 to 3 **apples**
- 2 to 3 **plums**
- 1 **bunch grapes**
  Confectioners' sugar, to taste
- 2 **tablespoons brandy**
- 2 **tablespoons lemon juice**
- ¼ **bottle champagne**

1 Peel oranges and slice. Peel, core and slice pears and apples. Slice and pit plums, and halve grapes. Combine fruits in a bowl and sprinkle with sugar to taste; moisten with brandy and lemon juice; toss well and chill.

2 Just before serving, transfer to a serving bowl; pour chilled champagne over fruit and serve immediately.

ORANGE AND GRAPEFRUIT SEGMENTS IN LEMON JUICE

- 3 to 4 **large juicy oranges**
- 2 **large grapefruit**
  Lemon juice
  Sifted confectioners' sugar
- 6 **leaves fresh mint**

1 Prepare oranges and grapefruit as follows, working over a shallow dish so that no juice is lost: using a sharp knife, slice off top and bottom of each fruit, taking all the pith and outer membrane away with the peel.

2 Stand fruit on one cut end and, with sharp, straight, downward strokes, whittle off peel and membrane all around sides.

3 Turn fruit on its other end and again whittle off peel and membrane all around sides.

4 Finally, slice off ring of peel left around center. You should be left with a slightly angular-shaped fruit, completely free of pith as well as peel. With a little practice, and providing your cutting tool is really sharp, this method takes far less time than the more conventional one.

5 Now take fruit in one hand and slip your knife between each segment and the membrane holding it on either side. Cut segment out, keeping it whole if possible; remove any seeds and drop segment into the juice below. Proceed in this manner until all you have left is the central core and empty membranes, fanned out like the leaves of a book.

6 Squeeze out any remaining juice into the dish.

7 Toss orange and grapefruit segments with lemon juice and sweeten to taste with sugar. Chill.

8 Serve in individual glass dishes, decorated with a fresh mint leaf.

CREAMED FINNAN HADDIE

- 2 **pounds smoked haddock**
  Water and milk, to cover
- 3 **tablespoons butter**
- 3 **tablespoons flour**
- 2 **cups cream**
  Freshly ground black pepper and nutmeg
  Triangles of bread
  Butter

1 Soak haddock in water for 2 hours. Drain; place in a saucepan and cover with equal

amounts of water and milk and bring to a fast boil. Remove from heat and allow to stand for 15 minutes, then drain, reserving stock for use in step 2.

2   Melt butter in the top of a double boiler; stir in flour and cook over direct heat for 3 minutes, stirring continuously until smooth. Place top of double boiler over hot water, add cream and 2 cups haddock stock and continue to cook, stirring from time to time. Season to taste with freshly ground black pepper and a little grated nutmeg.

3   Remove skin and bones from haddock and break into pieces. Fold pieces into sauce and simmer gently until ready to serve. Serve in a shallow casserole with triangles of bread which you have sautéed in butter.

BAKED SMITHFIELD HAM

1   10 to 12 pound Smithfield ham
2   yellow onions, peeled
6   large carrots, scraped
2   stalks celery
2   cloves
2   bay leaves
6   peppercorns
     Toasted breadcrumbs (or cloves, brown sugar, dry mustard and cider or fruit)

1   Soak the ham in water for 24 to 48 hours to remove salt, changing water several times. Do not take off rind.

2   Place the ham in a deep roasting pan, cover with cold water and bring very slowly to boiling point to open pores gradually, extract salt and at the same time help increase the temperature of any cold core in the joint.

3   Change water; add onions, carrots and celery, cloves, bay leaves and peppercorns, and bring slowly to boiling point again; reduce heat as soon as boiling point is reached and allow temperature to drop to simmering point. Cover and simmer until tender—about 20 minutes per pound.

4   Allow the ham to cool in water in which it was cooked. Do not remove the rind until well set if you are going to serve it cold. (I leave mine overnight.) Then remove skin and sprinkle fat with toasted breadcrumbs; or if you prefer, score fat criss-cross, stud with cloves, sprinkle with brown sugar and dry mustard and brown in the oven for 20 to 30 minutes, basting from time to time with cider or fruit juice.

CUMBERLAND JELLY

     Rinds of 1 orange and 1 lemon
½   jar red currant jelly
     Juice of 2 oranges and 1 lemon
1   tablespoon dry mustard
1   envelope gelatin
⅔   cup port
2   tablespoons Cointreau

1   Pare rinds of orange and lemon as thinly as possible; cut into fine short strips and blanch for 5 minutes in boiling water.

2   Combine red currant jelly and strained orange and lemon juice in a saucepan and simmer until jelly is melted. Add a small quantity of this to the mustard, mix well and return to pan.

3   Soak gelatin in port and Cointreau for 5 minutes; then dissolve gently over heat and add to red currant mixture. Allow to cool a little before spooning into glass serving dish or crock. Just before setting, stir in blanched rind.

HOT POPOVERS

(For recipe, see Breakfast Bakery, page 103.)

Making the Most of Christmas Leftovers

If for Christmas this year you had a turkey—a fine, fat bird often seems the answer to a cook's holiday prayer—cheer up. There is no need to restrict your post-Christmas meals to cold sliced turkey and stuffing, or to turkey warmed up in gravy. Far better to whet family appetites this week with chilled turkey salad garnished with orange segments, black olives, almonds and seeded grapes; curried turkey and rice; turkey pie with a golden pastry crust; and last—but certainly not least—a delicious turkey soup.

TURKEY SOUP

MAKES ABOUT 5½ CUPS

    Carcass and bones (drumsticks, wing tips, etc.) of 1 roast turkey
7 **cups chicken stock**
4 **celery stalks with leaves, sliced**
2 **onions, sliced**
2 **bay leaves**
    Salt and freshly ground black pepper
    Sprigs of parsley
4 **to 6 level tablespoons rice**

1 Scrape stuffing from interior of turkey and discard.

2 Put carcass and bones in a large soup kettle. Add chicken stock, celery, onions, bay leaves, salt, pepper and parsley. Bring to the boil; skim froth from soup; lower heat and simmer gently for 2 hours. Strain. Remove any meat from bones and add to soup.

3 Fifteen minutes before serving, add rice; return to heat and cook until rice is tender. Correct seasoning and serve.

TURKEY PIE

4 **tablespoons butter**
4 **tablespoons flour**
2½ **cups rich chicken stock**
⅔ **cup milk**
1 **package frozen peas**
1 **pound cooked carrots, sliced**
1 **pound pearl onions, cooked and drained**
2 **cups cooked, cubed turkey**
    Salt and freshly ground black pepper
½ **pound flaky pastry**
1 **egg yolk mixed with 1 tablespoon water for glazing**

1 Melt butter in the top of a double boiler; add flour and stir until well blended. Add chicken stock and milk and stir until sauce is smooth.

2 Add peas, carrots, onions and turkey meat. Season with salt and pepper and pour into a large pie dish.

3 Top with flaky pastry; brush with egg yolk mixture and bake in a preheated 450°F oven for about 15 to 20 minutes, or until pastry is cooked and golden.

SUPER TURKEY HASH

½ **large onion, finely chopped**
½ **green pepper, finely chopped**
1 **clove garlic, finely chopped**
    Butter
3 **cups diced cooked turkey**
    Salt and freshly ground black pepper
1 **egg yolk, beaten**
2 **to 4 tablespoons whipped cream**
    Fresh bread crumbs

Sauce:

2 **tablespoons butter**
2 **tablespoons flour**
1½ **cups milk**
½ **cup heavy cream**
    Salt and freshly ground black pepper

1 Sauté onion, green pepper and garlic in 2 tablespoons butter until vegetables are soft. Add diced turkey and continue to cook, stirring constantly, until meat is heated through. Season with salt and pepper, to taste. Keep warm.

2 **To make sauce:** melt butter in a saucepan; add flour and cook until roux just starts to turn golden. Add milk and cook, stirring constantly, until sauce is reduced to about two-thirds the original quantity. Stir in cream. Season with salt and pepper, to taste.

3 **To assemble dish:** add 1½ cups sauce to the turkey mixture; season to taste with salt and pepper and pour into an ovenproof gratin dish. Combine remaining sauce with beaten egg yolk and fold in whipped cream. Spread over creamed turkey mixture. Sprinkle with fresh bread crumbs; dot with a little butter and brown in a 450°F oven or under the broiler.

TURKEY AND ORANGE SALAD

3 cups diced cooked turkey
4 shallots, finely chopped
2 celery stalks, sliced
4 small oranges, peeled and divided
    into sections
Lettuce leaves

Dressing:

Olive oil
Wine vinegar
Salt and freshly ground black pepper
Rosemary

Garnish:

8 to 10 black olives
Grapes, halved and seeded
Slivered toasted almonds

1   Combine turkey, shallots and celery with a dressing made with 3 parts olive oil to 1 part wine vinegar. Season with salt, pepper and rosemary. Toss well and marinate for at least 2 hours.
2   Just before serving, add orange sections; toss again, adding more dressing if required.

3   Line a glass salad bowl with lettuce leaves; fill with salad and garnish with black olives, grapes and toasted almonds.

CURRIED TURKEY

4 tablespoons butter
1 large onion, finely chopped
2 celery stalks, thinly sliced
1 apple, peeled, cored and diced
1 clove garlic, finely chopped
1 tablespoon curry powder
1 tablespoon flour
2 cups chicken stock
3 cups diced cooked turkey
2 tablespoons finely chopped parsley

1   Melt butter and sauté onion and celery until onion is transparent; add apple, garlic and curry powder mixed with flour; continue to cook, stirring constantly, until mixture begins to turn golden.
2   Add chicken stock and cook sauce, stirring, until it is smooth and thick.
3   Add turkey and parsley and simmer until heated through. Serve curried turkey in a ring of cooked rice.

Your Emergency Shelf

Every cook should have a selection of canned, packaged and dried foods on hand, ready for unexpected guests or an impromptu meal.

When shopping for emergency shelf items, remember that most can be kept for an almost unlimited time. So buy in quantity when they are on sale; you'll save both time and money.

I always have eggs, butter, milk, cream, Parmesan cheese and a small supply of sliced bacon, onions, carrots, garlic, tomatoes, lemons and lettuce on hand. In addition to these perishables I like to keep the following staples for emergency entertaining:

Canned Fruits

Pears
Pineapple
Peaches
Apricots
Cherries

Canned Vegetables

Mushrooms
Small White Onions
Italian Peeled Tomatoes
Tomato Sauce
Tomato Juice
Artichoke Hearts
Peas

Canned Meats

Ham
Liver Pâté
Luncheon Meat

Canned Fish

Lobster
Salmon
Tuna
Crabmeat
Sardines
Anchovies
Minced Clams

Canned Soups and Bouillon Cubes

Cream of Mushroom
Tomato
Green Pea
Clam Broth
Chicken Bouillon Cubes
Beef Bouillon Cubes

Dried Vegetables

Lentils
Haricots Blancs
Kidney Beans
Peas
Chick-Peas

Dried Fruits

Apricots
Prunes
Raisins
Currants

Pasta and Rice

Spaghetti
Noodles
Green Noodles
Long-Grain Rice
Risotto Rice

Miscellaneous

Olive Oil
Wine Vinegar
Canned Milk
Mayonnaise
Olives
Pickles
Relishes
Truffles
Pine Nuts
Pistachio Nuts
Almonds

Index